THE POLITICS OF RITUAL

The Politics of Ritual

MOLLY FARNETH

PRINCETON UNIVERSITY PRESS

PRINCETON & OXFORD

Published by Princeton University Press
41 William Street, Princeton, New Jersey 08540
99 Banbury Road, Oxford OX2 6JX

press.princeton.edu

All Rights Reserved
ISBN: 978-0-691-19891-0
ISBN: (pbk.) 978-0-691-19892-7
ISBN (e-book): 978-0-691-24892-9

British Library Cataloging-in-Publication Data is available

Editorial: Fred Appel and James Collier
Production Editorial: Jenny Wolkowicki
Cover design: Katie Osborne
Production: Lauren Reese
Publicity: Kate Hensley and Charlotte Coyne

Cover credit: Vigil candle by Nathan Dumlao; background by Mike Ralph / Unsplash

This book has been composed in Arno Pro

10 9 8 7 6 5 4 3 2 1

To Alda, Fannie, Steve, Josh, and Daniel,
friends I write with and for

CONTENTS

ILLUSTRATIONS

THE POLITICS OF RITUAL

Introduction

ON A STREET on the Upper West Side of Manhattan, a crowd of Jewish protestors gathered. Some wore kippot and tallit, head coverings and prayer shawls; others held signs with slogans such as "Equal Justice for All" or biblical verses and Talmudic phrases in Hebrew and English such as "Anyone who destroys one soul—it is like destroying an entire world." At the front of the crowd, a young woman spoke into a bullhorn. "We will sit a shiva in the street!" she cried, referring to the weeklong period following a Jewish funeral when relatives of the deceased stay home to mourn and receive visitors.

Earlier that day, it had been announced that the New York City police officer who had killed Eric Garner would not be indicted. These were the early days of the Black Lives Matter movement, and the killing of Garner, an unarmed Black man, on a sidewalk in Staten Island had been met with grief, anger, and mass protest. The Grand Jury's decision once again brought people to the streets throughout New York City and across the country. This particular protest, with the declaration that the protestors would sit shiva in the street, placed their actions in the context of Jewish practice and the rituals of mourning. It blurred the boundary between the home where shiva is ordinarily observed and the city street where the protestors had gathered, and between the supposedly private realm of religion and the public realm of politics.

In unison, the protestors recited the Mourner's Kaddish. "Yit-gadal v'yitkadash sh'meih raba, b'alma di v'ra chiruteih . . . ," their voices rising and falling together in an intonation familiar to any-one who grew up spending Saturday mornings in synagogue. This prayer is traditionally recited by Jews grieving the death of parents or other family members. The recitation of the Mourner's Kaddish is considered to be an obligation, reserved for the loss of one's closest kin, those to whom one owes one's very existence. The words of the prayer affirm God's goodness and Jewish continuity in the face of mortality, tragedy, and the absurd. Those words are spoken in Aramaic, an ancient language that few modern Jews are likely to understand, so the prayer is learned viscerally, its sound and rhythms taking shape in the mind and body as it is uttered day after day in mourning, week after week in worship, year after year in remembrance.

The gestures that accompany the prayer are learned, too, and dif-fer from one Jewish community to another. In some congregations, only mourners stand to recite the prayer, while others remain seated and add their voices to the recitation at moments of particular em-phasis. In other communities, mourners stand first and are then joined by the rest of the congregation who rise as they are able and recite the prayer with the mourners in an expression of solidarity.

At the protest, by reciting the Mourner's Kaddish together, the assembled joined their bodies and voices in an act of political mourning. A Kaddish for Eric Garner. Following their recitation of the prayer, the protestors spoke Garner's name and the names of more than twenty others who had recently been killed by New York City police. They uttered the words, "I am responsible."

The Mourner's Kaddish has since become a recurrent feature of progressive Jewish activism in the United States, but at that time, in December 2014, there had been few instances in which the prayer had been recited in protest.[1] I could not, and still cannot,

1. To my knowledge, the few times that U.S.-based activists had recited the Kad-dish in protest prior to the Mourner's Kaddish for Eric Garner were in response to

stop thinking about it. I thought about it when I returned to synagogue and listened to my fellow congregants recite Kaddish for their loved ones. And I thought about it a few years later when I heard about protestors gathering to recite Kaddish for migrant children who died in the custody of U.S. Immigration and Customs Enforcement, and about mourners assembling outside the Supreme Court to recite Kaddish for Supreme Court justice Ruth Bader Ginsberg. I wondered about the significance and effects of these recitations, what was happening when people gathered to recite that prayer, on the street or in shul or on the steps of the Supreme Court, in mourning for kin or for strangers. And so began the thinking that led to this book. How, and why, are rituals enacted toward political ends? How, and why, do rituals appear in protests and social movements that seek justice? And what do these seemingly extraordinary political enactments of rituals have in common with their more ordinary enactments?

The Politics of Ritual delves into these questions. It considers how rituals give rise to communities, by creating and transforming their boundaries and distributing goods within them, and it shows how rituals transform the people within those communities, by shaping their habits and dispositions. In particular, it considers when and how rituals are put to democratic and justice-seeking ends. When rituals are enacted in protests and social movements, they are often aimed at redrawing the boundaries of political communities and redistributing goods within them. Sometimes this means adapting, improvising on, or transforming existing rituals; other times it means creating and implementing new ones. When Jewish protestors recited the Mourner's Kaddish for Eric Garner, they drew on an existing ritual and adapted it to a new situation.

---

the deaths of Palestinians killed by Israeli soldiers. I wrote about the later recitation of the Mourner's Kaddish in progressive Jewish protests against U.S. Immigration and Customs Enforcement in summer 2019 in "For These Progressive Jews, Prayer Is Part of the Protest," *Religion & Politics*, September 10, 2019, https://religionand politics.org/2019/09/10/for-these-progressive-jews-prayer-is-part-of-the-protest/.

Their ritual innovation blurred the boundary between public and private, between politics and religion, between stranger and kin. Why they might have done so, and what their act *did*, for them and for others—those are among the questions that have haunted my thinking about that event and that I hope to answer in these pages.

———

This book begins precisely where my first book, *Hegel's Social Ethics*, ended. On the face of it, these two projects have little to do with one another. *Hegel's Social Ethics* offered an interpretation of nineteenth-century German philosopher G.W.F. Hegel's *Phenomenology of Spirit* that highlighted the ethical stakes of what Hegel calls reciprocal recognition—a relationship in which people treat one another as both authoritative and accountable agents. Hegel was interested in rituals, in their role in processes of conflict and reconciliation, and in how they could bring about this kind of reciprocal recognition, but his account of this is more implicit than explicit. I finished writing *Hegel's Social Ethics* shortly after the Kaddish for Eric Garner took place, and the final paragraph of that book turns to that event as a site of ritual innovation, political contestation, and expanded ethical obligation. The present book, *The Politics of Ritual*, is a result of my having been moved by that event and my seeking to better understand what was at stake in it. This book is not about Hegel, but I write it as someone committed to the ideas that norms are created and transformed through social practices, that power relations can be restructured from within, and that just and democratic authority is generated and sustained in relations of reciprocal recognition—commitments that I credit to having thought with Hegel for a while.

I wrote much of this book in a context both unsettlingly like and unlike the one in which I began to consider the relationship among ritual, politics, and protest, in the midst of a pandemic that seemed to change everything and the ceaseless repetition of anti-Black violence that seemed to insist that nothing would ever change. In summer 2020, after several months of social distancing, illness, and isolation, hundreds of thousands of Americans took to the streets to demand racial justice and political transformation. Protestors marked and mourned the murders of Breonna Taylor, George Floyd, and too many other Black and brown Americans killed by police. In the streets, at makeshift memorials, and in houses of worship, people protesting Taylor's death incanted, "Say her name!" Insisting on the importance of remembering and speaking Taylor's name, these protestors became, as Joseph Winters argues, participants "in a ritual of conjuring and mourning, . . . witness to the afterlife of black death."[2] Thousands showed up for the funeral and homegoing celebration for George Floyd. His homegoing took its place in a Black funeral tradition that resists the violence of living in a white supremacist society by insisting on the dignity of the deceased.[3] From die-ins to homegoings, protestors have been mourning and mourners have been protesting.

Rituals play a role in both protest and mourning, as well as in imagining and enacting a world that is better: more just, more democratic. Rituals can conjure not only a past but also a future, as Joshua Dubler suggested to me, "prefigur[ing] in the present the as-yet unrealized abolitionist future."[4]

———

Rituals involve sequences of bodily acts, shared by a group, and enacted in relation to a set of rules or norms for their performance.

2. Joseph R. Winters, "Nothing Matters: Black Death, Repetition, and an Ethics of Anguish," *American Religion* 2.1 (2020): 3.

3. On Black funeral traditions, see Nyle Fort, "Refusing to Give Death the Last Word," *Boston Globe*, June 4, 2020, https://www.bostonglobe.com/2020/06/04/opinion/refusing-give-death-last-word/; Karla F. C. Holloway, *Passed On: African American Mourning Stories* (Durham: Duke University Press, 2002). Holloway shows, in particular, the close connections between Black churches and funeral homes in the development and practice of mourning rituals.

4. Joshua Dubler, personal correspondence, March 25, 2021.

Rituals of mourning, for instance, are shared, norm-governed responses to the loss of someone who matters to members of the group. Because of this, rituals of mourning are value-laden. The question "Whom shall we mourn, and how?" is a normative, or evaluative, one. The answer is often taken for granted. But sometimes, people are jolted into asking and arguing about how they ought to answer. This may lead them to ask who the "we" are, how "we" are related to the person or people being mourned, what obligations people have to one another, and whether the usual ways of mourning are possible or even desirable under the present circumstances. It may lead them to ask whether they can and should enact the rituals that they have at hand, adapt them, or abandon them.

When Jewish protestors sat shiva in the street and recited Kaddish for Eric Garner, they took the received options for mourning in the Jewish tradition and adapted them to a new situation. Their answer to the question "Whom shall we mourn?" included Garner, a man who was neither Jewish nor protestors' kin but to whom the protestors took themselves to have an obligation nevertheless. Their enactment of the ritual moved it from its usual setting, the homes and synagogues of Jewish mourners, into a public space, a city street.

Likewise, during the Covid-19 pandemic, when people struggled to mourn the loss of the people who mattered to them, they considered the usual ways of burying and mourning their dead and asked whether they were possible under the current circumstances. In the early months of the pandemic, many traditional rituals of mourning were suspended or radically altered. There were no more large in-person funerals, no more condolence visits. I worried about how depoliticizing this might be. If people could not gather in ritual, what would the politics of the pandemic become? This worry may seem misplaced, a kind of non sequitur: *What do rituals have to do with politics, anyway?* But as elected officials ignored and downplayed the threat of the virus, my mind kept returning to the politics and protests of an earlier epidemic, the AIDS crisis, and the work of the activist organization ACT UP. As the death toll from AIDS rose and politicians ignored the virus and maligned its victims, members of ACT UP enacted political funerals that combined ritual and protest. Processing through city streets with caskets and urns that contained the remains of friends, lovers, and kin, these mourners-become-activists publicly grieved, demanded recognition for their losses, and sought to make politicians answerable for their callousness and cruelty.

In the midst of the Covid-19 pandemic's social distancing and physical isolation, what could make ordinary people's losses visible, known, public? How would people recognize one another in grief and solidarity, and hold one another responsible for sustaining the goods of the community they share?

As it turned out, rituals did not disappear during the pandemic, nor did the politics of ritual. Many people innovated and improvised on their existing rituals to mark and mourn loss, and to demand different policies, making the connections among grief, rituals, and politics explicit. Early in the pandemic, activists dropped mock body bags on a Trump property, protesting the Trump administration's indifference toward victims of the pandemic and demanding recognition for loss. In that act, the *absence* of ritual was the point; the unceremonious treatment of these unmarked body bags was intended to highlight the inhumanity of the administration's approach to the pandemic. The absence of ritual pointed to a failure of justice. Those who lost their lives weren't being recognized; they had been denied goods—not least, care and concern—that they were due. Then, in late spring 2020, as the death toll in the United States reached 100,000, a group of more than 100 Muslim, Christian, and Jewish clergy led a National Day of Mourning and Lament, marked by rituals of mourning and lamentation in mosques, churches, synagogues, and other houses of worship across the country, as well as interfaith vigils, prayers, and public ceremonies that honored the victims of the pandemic, recognized mourners' grief, and called for healing—both physical and political. Rev. Jim Wallis, president of the Christian social justice organization Sojourners and one of the organizers of the Day of Mourning and Lament, wrote that "our prayers for the healing of this nation must acknowledge the brokenness of our democracy and rededicate ourselves to repair the injustices this pandemic has revealed, even as we work for the healing of those who are afflicted with the virus."[5]

In this and other cases, people adapted existing rituals of mourning to mark their losses and protest the conditions of those losses. These acts alone may not have done much to change the outcome of the policies or the course of the pandemic. But, as I hope to show, that kind of political efficacy isn't the only mark of rituals' political power and significance. In each case, these adaptations and innovations had to make explicit the normative question—"Whom shall we mourn, and *how*?"—and to grapple with how to answer it. Who is the "we"? What do "we" owe to the dead, or to the grieving, or to the living?

The *Politics* of Rituals

Rituals are social practices. They are complex activities shared by a group and governed by the norms of that group. This way of describing rituals can help us see the work that rituals do in and for groups, and how they can change over time as people argue about the boundaries of the group and the norms that ought to be in force within it. It also highlights their political significance—and their democratic possibilities. That's because, as social practices, rituals distribute goods. They help determine who is included and excluded from a group, who occupies which roles and has what powers within it, which habits and virtues are cultivated, and which beliefs, passions, and stances are shared. They are *political* because they are among the practices by which people create and maintain communities. And they can be *democratic* when they involve collective action that aims to correct arbitrary exclusions and to redistribute goods to those to whom they are due in and around those communities.

Of course, there's nothing *necessarily* democratic about rituals. They can exclude as easily as they can include; they can preserve an unjust status quo and they can distribute power to the powerful. But neither is their political significance limited to the consolidation and maintenance of unjust power relations. I locate politics wherever people act in concert to create, sustain, and transform the relationships and structures of their communities. At times, my way of talking about the "politics" of ritual may strike some readers as overly expansive, too easily conflated with ethics or social life more broadly. Bonnie Honig has raised a similar concern about recent scholarship on the politics of lamentation. In her work on *Antigone*, Honig writes that "in the place of the currently seductive politics of *lamentation*, I find in the play [*Antigone*] . . . a more robust *politics* of lamentation, in which lamentation is not 'human', ethical, or material—tethered to the fact of finitude—but an essentially contested practice, part of an *agon* among fractious and divided systems of signification and power."[6] What makes lamentation political, Honig argues, is its role in contesting political structures and power relations. Heather Pool takes up Honig's concern in her work on political mourning, attending to the processes by which some deaths, and grief for those deaths, become a matter of democratic politics. Political mourning, Pool argues, differs from private (or even public, but non-political) mourning insofar as it aims to reconfigure the boundaries of the polis and to encourage people to take responsibility for the well-being of its inhabitants.[7] The charge, from both Honig and Pool, is to recognize

6. Bonnie Honig, *Antigone, Interrupted* (Cambridge: Cambridge University Press, 2013), 2.

7. Heather Pool, *Political Mourning: Identity and Responsibility in the Wake of Tragedy* (Philadelphia: Temple University Press, 2021), 12.

the distinctively *political* features of lamentation and mourning, respectively, and to distinguish those features from the merely social or ethical.

I take their charge seriously and have thought much about how this book addresses it.[8] As a scholar of theories of religion and religious ethics, I have devoted much of the book to developing a detailed account of the politics of *rituals* rather than the *politics* of rituals, to borrow Honig's formulation. But I insist on the politics, too, and so here, I want to be clear about what I mean by politics and why I think rituals are, or ought to be, an object of political analysis.

To begin with, let me say a word in defense of the broad sense of politics that I mentioned above: politics as involving concerted action to create, sustain, and transform the relationships and structures of communities. This way of thinking resists locating politics only in the actions of, and responses to, the nation-state, and it rejects any sharp distinction between communities that are properly public (and thus a site for politics) and those that are private. It casts a wide net.[9] This stems in part from my training in religious studies, which tends to the ongoing processes by which nation-states have attempted to wall religion off from the "political" proper. Such attempts cast religion as a matter of private conviction that appears in the public sphere of politics only as a tres-

---

8. I am grateful to the anonymous reader for Princeton University Press who challenged me to be more explicit about my account of politics, and to Joel Schlosser for pointing me toward Heather Pool's work on this point.

9. This sense of politics has affinities with what Luke Bretherton calls the "informal mode of politics," located in the relational practices of ordinary citizens as opposed to the "formal mode of politics" involved in law and statecraft. Bretherton thinks of this informal mode of politics not as activism, narrowly construed, but as "being neighbors," in the sense of working with and alongside those with whom one finds oneself to shape a shared community and to tend common goods. See Bretherton, *Christ and the Common Life: Political Theology and the Case for Democracy* (Grand Rapids, MI: Eerdmans, 2019); and "Politics in the Service of Society: My Response to My Interlocutors," *Studies in Christian Ethics* 33.2 (2020): 262–70.

passer. Religions, meanwhile, regularly transgress the boundaries drawn for them by nation-states as religious people and groups imagine and enact other ways of configuring such things as community, law and obligation, authority, and agency.[10] Religions stake claims about what people are like and how people thus constituted ought to live together. To locate politics in and around nation-states, without tending to the complications posed by religious people, practices, and life-worlds—whether those complications are posed at home, in places of worship, or in the streets—risks limiting our imagination for other ways of living with and alongside other human and more-than-human beings. When religious individuals and groups enact rituals, they often embody, if only fleetingly, these other ways of being and living.

Wini Breines coined the term "prefigurative politics" to characterize the political structures and activities of social movement groups of the 1960s New Left, groups such as Students for a Democratic Society.[11] These groups were committed to participatory democracy, a form of political engagement that was decentralized, non-hierarchical, and nominally leaderless. And while their radical vision was of a society governed by participatory democratic principles and practices, more immediately, they sought to implement this form of democratic life in their internal organizing and

10. These processes are the topic of secularism studies and of political theology, as the scholarly location of work that considers the relationship between religion and politics, the influence of (particularly Protestant) theology on the formation of the nation-state, and the tensions and ongoing negotiations between religious lifeworlds and contemporary political configurations. Apropos of this book's topic of the politics of ritual, the journal *Political Theology* recently published a roundtable discussion titled "Organizing, Protests, and Religious Practices," which considers how a variety of religious practices appear in, and *as*, forms of democratic action and protest. See Aaron Stauffer, ed., "Round Table Discussion: Organizing, Protests, and Religious Practices," *Political Theology*, March 18, 2021, https://doi.org/10.1080/1462317X.2021.1899701.

11. Wini Breines, *The Great Refusal: Community and Organization in the New Left, 1962–1968* (New York: Praeger, 1982).

decision-making processes.[12] This is what Breines refers to as pre-figuration, the flip side of the New Left's antipathy toward "strategic politics," the effort to build institutions and wield political power in ways legible to elected officials and governing institutions.[13]

Political analysts' distinction between prefigurative and strategic politics tends to cast the former as largely expressive and the latter as effective, in the sense of being concerned with bringing about a given end. As Francesca Polletta notes, for instance, in this literature "prefigurative goals risk sounding very much like expressive ones—defined only by their opposition to considerations of strategy."[14] But, Polletta argues, this misses much of what prefigurative politics does. Participatory democratic movements try to enact structures and practices that anticipate those of the society that they hope for; in doing so, they aren't merely expressing dissatisfaction with current political arrangements while pining ineffectually for something better. These movements, their structures and practices, also do the pressing work of forging solidarity and shaping citizens with democratic dispositions.

This distinction between prefigurative and strategic politics may sound familiar to readers who are acquainted with theories of ritual, for it echoes a similar distinction that is sometimes used to cordon ritual off from ordinary action. Ritual, on such accounts,

12. There are important criticisms of the particular form that the organizations of the New Left took, including the way that their apparent "leaderlessness" gave way to *unaccountable* leadership and decision making. See, for instance, Jo Freeman's classic essay, "The Tyranny of Structurelessness," which critically examines the organizational structure of early second-wave feminist groups (*Berkeley Journal of Sociology* 17 [1972–73]: 151–64). Francesca Polletta also considers the strengths and weaknesses of the structure of groups such as SNCC, SDS, and feminist consciousness-raising groups in the 1960s and 1970s in *Freedom Is an Endless Meeting: Democracy in American Social Movements* (Chicago: University of Chicago Press, 2002). I understand these authors' criticisms of the weaknesses of those movements' particular structures and practices to be distinct from a criticism of prefiguration as such.

13. Breines, *The Great Refusal*, 6.

14. Polletta, *Freedom Is an Endless Meeting*, 7.

is a kind of symbolic or expressive action, defined in contrast to more quotidian, strategic, or efficacious action. On this way of thinking, rituals symbolize or express things, whereas ordinary actions do things. But this distinction is just as unhelpful for understanding ritual as the prefigurative/strategic distinction is for understanding politics, and for similar reasons. Rituals unsettle any sharp distinction between expressive and effective action, not least because rituals, like all other human activities, *do* things. Rituals draw boundaries around groups; they distribute goods to members of those groups; they shape people's habits and dispositions; and they can, as Polletta writes of participatory democratic practices, "generate new bases for legitimate authority."[15] Rituals can prefigure other ways of being and living together, and any such prefigurations are rarely, if ever, *merely* symbolic or expressive.

When rituals are enacted in protests and social movements, they often anticipate a world that doesn't yet exist: a world in which nation-state borders are sites of hospitality and neighbor-love; a world in which human beings live in grateful relationship with the more-than-human inhabitants of the earth; a world in which the justice and peace for which people yearn have arrived. But even as rituals prefigure a world that is not-yet, they are *working* on the people and politics of the world that is: shaping them and making claims on them. As this book aims to show, rituals can be prefigurative at the same time that they are formative and performative—they enact an as-yet unrealized world, even as they transform the people who still reside in the world as it currently is. They can bring about social and political changes that nudge what currently is closer to what is not-yet.

The world anticipated by rituals may be more or less democratic than the one that practitioners inhabit. But rituals can anticipate and contribute to a democratic politics when they involve the concerted action of ordinary people to bring about a more just distribution of goods, including power and freedom. People act

15. Polletta, *Freedom Is an Endless Meeting*, 7–8.

not only politically but also *democratically* when they work to-gether to contest unjust power relations and social and political arrangements, acknowledge and distribute authority and account-ability, and encourage and cultivate habits of political participa-tion. Throughout the book are examples in which people enact rituals intended to do these very things.

The perspective on democratic politics taken here has affinities with agonistic democratic theories that emphasize the activities of ordinary citizens and the role of ongoing contestation in political life. But whereas many agonists locate democracy primarily in the disruption of the existing order and the arrival of the new, the view that I develop here explores how rituals, as political acts and as routinized and norm-governed activities, often move between reproduction and disruption or between tradition and critique. Because rituals often concern shared goods and sacred objects—because rituals relate to these goods and objects, tend them, regu-late access to them, and distribute them—it might seem like rituals are the sorts of activities that fall on the side of tradition, the status quo, the already-is. But they are far more dynamic than that. Rituals can be sites of tending *and* of transformation; understanding how they do these things can help us think about how people might go about caring for the communities in which they find themselves while enacting those that they hope to bring about.

The Book and Its Aims

The Politics of Ritual offers a social practical account of ritual, and it argues for rituals' political significance and power. In particular, it considers when and how rituals contribute to just and demo-cratic politics. It also reflects on how people adapt existing rituals or create new ones in order to redraw boundaries or redistribute goods, including power, around and within their communities. It argues, moreover, that these adaptations and innovations are part of a dialectic of continuity and change that is *always* part of people's ritual life, rather than an idiosyncratic feature of modern religion or politics.

The book focuses on justice-seeking rituals and democratic politics for two reasons. The first is that the impulse is often to view rituals as powerfully enforcing the status quo. This *can* be true, but it is not always. Rituals aren't static; they are dynamic social practices that involve change and contestation over time. The second reason is simply that rituals can and often *do* play an important role in the struggle for justice. I hope to convince readers, particularly those who want to envision and build a different kind of world together, of the need for rituals in which the communities people deserve can be enacted and embodied.

Nevertheless, the examples in this book are not confined to enactments of rituals in protests and social movements. Some of the examples involve activists enacting rituals in protests; others involve the denizens of a nation-state enacting civic rituals in everyday life.[16] Others still involve religious individuals or groups enacting the rituals of their tradition, but in ways that contest how those rituals configure community or distribute power. These contestations often take place in the midst of broader political contestation and change—as when, in the midst of second-wave feminist movements that demanded equal rights for women in political and economic life, Episcopal women enacted an ordination ceremony to demand inclusion in the (then) all-male priesthood. What holds these various examples together—what makes them worth thinking about under the banner of the "politics of ritual"— is that, in each case, they are enacted in ways that attend to the norms invoked and the communities created by them, and in ways attentive to the distribution of justice, power, and freedom. It is my assumption—typically implicit, although I'll make it explicit here—that distinctions between the religious and the secular (and

16. I typically use the term "civic ritual" to refer to rituals that have a political community or its associated symbols as their primary object. My reason for doing so is pragmatic; in religious studies, this is the term that's commonly used to refer to such rituals. However, in what follows (and particularly in chapter 4), I aim to show that there's a greater degree of disagreement and contestation over such rituals than might be assumed by the term and its association with scholarship on civil religion.

thus between, say, religious and so-called civic rituals) have little to do with the ways that people actually move among the spaces and communities they're in. The significance of religious ritual is never fully cordoned off from political concerns; the significance of civic ritual is best understood in light of theories and histories of religion.

To consider how and when rituals enact or bring about just or democratic ends we'll need to pay careful attention to what rituals are and what they do. I draw on ritual theory, social practice theory, and philosophy of language to attend to the latter. Like scholars in the field of "lived religion," such as David Hall, Robert Orsi, and R. Marie Griffith, I am interested in how people practice religion in their everyday lives, in how their religious practices emerge both within and outside of religions' institutional forms.[17] Like those influenced by theorists of practice such as Pierre Bourdieu and Catherine Bell, I am interested in how rituals, as bodily practices, can shape subjects and reproduce social, cultural, and political norms—but also in how they can transform them. My approach integrates the insights of these influential intellectual movements with renewed attention to belief and language, topics sometimes left by the wayside in the recent turn toward embodiment, practice, and power. The resulting account helps make sense of how, and why, rituals have political power and significance, and

17. See, for instance, Griffith, Hall, and Orsi's contributions in David A. Hall, ed., *Lived Religion in America: Toward a History of Practice* (Princeton: Princeton University Press, 1997). Robert Wuthnow's *What Happens When We Practice Religion?: Textures of Devotion in Everyday Life* (Princeton: Princeton University Press, 2020) offers a thematic survey of recent literature in and around religious studies that has taken this practical turn, including work influenced by lived religion, social practice theory, and ethnographic work outside of religious studies. Leigh Eric Schmidt's *Consumer Rites* and Kathryn Lofton's *Consuming Religion* are also relevant precursors to this project, particularly in the ways that they trouble the boundaries of the religious and the secular in their approaches to ritual. Schmidt, *Consumer Rites: The Buying and Selling of American Holidays* (Princeton: Princeton University Press, 1997); Lofton, *Consuming Religion* (Chicago: University of Chicago Press, 2017).

how, and why, people argue over existing rituals and, sometimes, create new ones.[18]

Readers eager to get to the politics may be tempted to skip the first chapter, which focuses on the term "ritual" and defines it for the purpose of this study. In doing so, however, they would miss the account of what rituals and social practices are and of how such practices change. This account is taken up and expanded upon in later chapters, each of which considers one or more of the things that rituals do, things that matter to our political lives. Each of the chapters should be intelligible on its own, although it is my intention that they build on one another to contribute to the broader framework and account of the politics of ritual.

18. This book is one of a growing number of recent works considering rituals and democratic practice. For instance, researchers associated with the project Reassembling Democracy: Ritual as Cultural Resource have published two volumes of essays that are interdisciplinary and international in scope, and constitute an archive of fieldwork-informed case studies on the use of ritual in democratic movements. While these volumes do not present a single analytical or theoretical framework, this book shares several of that project's assumptions: that there is no sharp distinction between religious and secular rituals, and that rituals can be deployed both to bolster and to transform existing political arrangements. Moreover, this book develops the theoretical claim, noted in the introduction to *Ritual and Democracy*, that "ritual acts and performances construct, reveal, and mobilise pervasive cultural and political resources," and, in doing so, they can shift and transform the "cultural and political processes that constitute society" (1). In what follows, I hope to develop this theoretical claim and offer a framework that can reflect back on the case studies and examples collected in that project and others like it. See Graham Harvey et al., eds., *Reassembling Democracy: Ritual as Cultural Resource* (London: Bloomsbury, 2021), and Sarah M. Pike, Jone Salomonsen, and Paul-François Tremlett, *Ritual and Democracy: Protests, Public and Performances* (Bristol, CT: Equinox, 2020). One of the lead coordinators of the Reassembling Democracy project, Sarah M. Pike, has also written an ethnography of eco-activists in organizations such as Earth First!, characterizing their protests and actions—including long-term tree-sits—as rituals and rites of passage. See Pike, *For the Wild: Ritual and Commitment in Radical Eco-Activism* (Oakland: University of California Press, 2017). See also, as mentioned above, Stauffer, "Round Table Discussion."

Chapter 1, "A Social Practical Account of Rituals," clarifies the terms and topic of my inquiry. It begins by discussing some "formal" characteristics of ritual: routine, repetition, and rules. I argue that, while these *are* typically features of rituals, focusing on these formal characteristics alone obscures how rituals work dynamically to shape—and change—people and societies. After all, if rituals are nothing more than routines, strictly governed by rules and repeatedly enacted, then how could they be anything but static and status quo supporting? By considering rituals as social practices that take place over time, we can begin to see how people improvise within these inherited frames, pull them into new contexts, and change the norms and routines themselves. Moreover, we can begin to see how rituals are bound up with concerns about power and justice.

Because rituals "belong" to groups—that is, because they are social practices—chapter 2, "Marking Boundaries, Distributing Goods," considers the relationship between rituals and the boundaries of groups. People engage rituals to create, maintain, and transform boundaries around and within their communities. In doing so, people both recognize the salience of certain roles and identities within their communities and allocate material and normative goods to the people who inhabit those roles and identities. This means that the presence, absence, and content of rituals can be matters of justice, whether a person or a group is recognized and given the goods that are their due. Disagreements and debates about rituals—whether they should be performed, who ought to be able to participate in them, what ought to be said or done in them, and what their consequences ought to be—are often disagreements about whether the structure and the distribution of goods and ills within a group are just or unjust. Rituals enacted at the U.S.-Mexico border highlight the contingency and injustice of nation-state borders by enacting other kinds of communities with other kinds of boundaries. Rituals do boundary work.

Chapter 3, "Performing and Recognizing Authority," builds on these claims about the goods and ills that rituals create and distribute, focusing on the relationship among rituals, power, authority, and recognition. Contrary to Bourdieu's claim that people's enactments of rituals involve the exercise of power that has been authorized in advance, I argue that people sometimes enact rituals in ways that exercise power that can only be authorized retrospectively. That is to say, sometimes people enact rituals that they aren't actually supposed to enact—and sometimes, their performances succeed nevertheless! I elaborate on the argument that rituals can be performative in the sense that they can "count as" something other than, or in addition to, the discrete bodily acts that constitute them. As performatives, rituals bring about changes in the social world. What makes an enactment of a ritual successful is not always fully spelled out beforehand; rather, the conditions for success are often recognized and negotiated after the fact. It is through novel enactments of a ritual that changes in what the ritual counts as, and who it counts for, can be brought about. Politically speaking, this matters because novel enactments of rituals can distribute power in new ways—including ways that challenge domination and unjust exclusion in religious and political relationships. As we'll see, Episcopal women, ordained to the priesthood in unsanctioned ceremonies in the midst of the women's movement, and Black Catholics, who innovated on Roman Catholic liturgy to enact new authority structures influenced by the Black Power movement, drew on existing ritual frames to claim authority. In this way, rituals can transform power relations.

Critical social theorists, including Bourdieu, often emphasize the role of rituals and other social practices in reproducing existing social structures and power relations. In chapters 2 and 3, I suggest how enactments of rituals *tend* to conform to the norms and standards of already-existing practices while regulating boundaries, sustaining social structures, and distributing power. But those chapters also include examples of people and groups who challenge and change those norms, standards, and practices in ways that encourage new structures and relationships. Chapter 4, "Habits, Virtues, and Freedom," takes on the apparent tension between these two things. In particular, it considers rituals aimed toward forming political subjects and constituting a people, and asks, "Which people? Constituted how? With what habits and virtues in mind?" Thinking through these questions alongside the work of scholars in ritual studies—including Bourdieu, Saba Mahmood, and Catherine Bell—I consider the constitution of habits and *habitus* that reproduce social norms and power relations, as well as the possibility that people engage in rituals in ways that self-consciously engage, and sometimes transform, those norms and relations. Rituals, I argue, can shape citizens with habits and dispositions that are just and democratic.

Many of the same scholars who emphasize rituals' role in discipline and habit formation resist the notion that rituals ought to be understood as expressing beliefs. In the examples that most interest such theorists, people's enactments of rituals are better understood as inculcating abilities and skills according to scripts, rules, and authorities than as expressing beliefs, attitudes, and intentions. But these two things—inculcation and expression—need not be treated as an either/or. Chapter 4 suggests a way of thinking about how people's repeated enactment of a ritual or set of rituals can inculcate habits and dispositions while also generating the reflective and expressive resources to challenge and change them; chapter 5 then shifts its focus to expression itself—to the idea that rituals express things, including political ideals and stances.

In chapter 5, "Expressing Beliefs, Passions, and Solidarity," I consider how rituals *express* things of political significance. Rituals can express commitments and ideals. They also express attitudes and emotions, including the passions of grief and anger and the stance of solidarity. I outline an account of expression in which the ritual expression of a belief or attitude creates and distributes obligations, entitlements, authority, and other statuses, rather than merely revealing otherwise private and inner mental states. I return to examples of rituals of mourning enacted in overtly political ways to mark untimely and unjust deaths, including the political funerals of the AIDS crisis and the die-ins of the Black Lives

Matter movement, and I consider the politics of expressing grief, anger, and solidarity in and through rituals. Finally, the conclusion, "The Rituals of Our Politics," returns to the relationship between rituals and democratic politics.

This book offers an approach to rituals that combines theoretical and philosophical considerations of rituals as social practices with context-specific analysis. The examples that appear throughout the book and in the conclusion are intended as contextual opportunities for thinking through the politics of ritual (and the rituals of our politics). There is a wide range of such examples. Many, although by no means all, are situated in relation to contemporary American politics; many, although by no means all, have Christian roots or resonance. Nevertheless, and as other examples in the book suggest, there is nothing uniquely modern, American, or Christian about the politics of ritual, nor about the ways that rituals can be contested or changed. Rituals create, sustain, and transform social and political worlds; the shape of the worlds we come to inhabit depends on the activities we undertake in common—crucially, on our rituals.

1

A Social Practical Account
of Rituals

A GROUP OF JEWISH activists recites the Mourner's Kaddish on the streets of New York City in the wake of another police shooting. Hundreds of East Jerusalem residents gather for iftar, the breaking of the Ramadan fast, in a neighborhood where Palestinian families face eviction from their homes. A Roman Catholic bishop passes the Eucharistic host between the slats in the fence at the U.S.-Mexico border, into the hands of the faithful standing on the other side. Eleven Episcopal women undertake ordination rites two years before the House of Bishops recognizes the legitimacy of women in the priesthood.

What *are* these acts?

We might identify each as an enactment of a *ritual*. The first enacts the Jewish rites of mourning; the second enacts the iftar meal; the third enacts the sacrament of communion; the fourth enacts the Episcopal ordination. But in each case, there's also something happening that seems distinctly different from what we might expect of a typical enactment of the ritual—something distinctly *political*. The location is unusual; the participants are unexpected. Each act appears to break with, or improvise on, the usual routine. The breaks and improvisations make the act's political stakes explicit.

But rituals *always* have such stakes, even when those stakes are implicit or taken for granted. Rituals help define the boundaries of communities, distribute goods to the members of those communities, shape people's habits and dispositions, and publicly express those people's beliefs, passions, and other attitudes. Getting clear on what rituals are—and how they can involve both routine and repetition, on the one hand, and contestation and innovation, on the other—will help us understand how they do all of these things. For that reason, this chapter is devoted to definitional and conceptual matters—specifying what's meant by "rituals," and moving outward from the formal features that are often taken to characterize them to the social, temporal, and power-laden contexts in which they are enacted and contested.

Rituals and Their Enactments

Rituals involve a series of acts that, when taken together, constitute a single unit or activity: a routine.[1] Some of the acts in the series might involve making sounds: speaking, singing, chanting, or ululating, for instance. Some of the acts might involve gestures, postures, or other movements: clasping one's hands, bending one's knees, bowing one's head, prostrating one's body, directing one's gaze. Sometimes, one or more of the acts involve interacting with other people or objects: anointing someone or something with oil, kissing a sacred object, ringing a bell, lighting a candle. Rituals are sequences of such bodily acts—acts involving sound, gesture, movement, and interaction—in a regular and prescribed order.

---

1. I work toward a definition of "ritual" in this chapter in order to fix the referent of the term for the purpose of this inquiry. Reference-fixing definitions of this sort are intended to delimit the topic, facilitating certain questions or lines of inquiry about that topic and foreclosing others. This book is concerned with the role of rituals in the political lives of human beings, in how they shape people and their communities, and in how they constrain, enable, and enact justice, power, and freedom. These concerns have shaped the way that I define the term. There are doubtless many other interesting and important things that an inquiry into ritual might consider, and such inquiries are likely to require a way of delimiting the topic that diverges from my way of doing so here.

This regularity is what makes the series of acts a routine. We can call it, following the work of Nicholas Wolterstorff, a *universal*.[2] Now, by this, I don't mean that the routine can be found in all times and places. It's not universal in *that* sense. Rather, I simply mean that it is repeatable, something that can be done over and over in more or less the same way. As Wolterstorff writes in his work on liturgy, "anything that can be repeatedly and multiply enacted is a universal. The Orthodox liturgy is a universal. More specifically, it's a type, a type whose enactments or instantiations consist of sequences of certain kinds."[3] The Orthodox liturgy—and here Wolterstorff is referring not only to the textual script of that liturgy but also to the implicit or unwritten script, which might include such things as intonation, timing, gesture, and so on—is a *universal* in this sense that it is a series of acts, or a routine. Or consider the Fajr or dawn prayer, the first of the five daily ritual prayers performed by Muslims. The Fajr prayer involves a sequence of verbal acts in which practitioners praise and petition

2. Wolterstorff's work on liturgy and on art as a social practice has been helpful to me in formulating these initial definitions and distinctions. In particular, his distinction between liturgies (as universals) and enactments of those liturgies (as particulars) informs how I think about rituals and their enactments. Ultimately, I depart from Wolterstorff's preferred language of "scripts" and "scripted activity" in order to emphasize the diachronic interplay of rituals and their enactments. See Nicholas Wolterstorff, *Acting Liturgically: Philosophical Reflections on Religious Practice* (Oxford: Oxford University Press, 2018); *Art Rethought: The Social Practices of Art* (Oxford: Oxford University Press, 2015); and *The God We Worship: An Exploration of Liturgical Theology* (Grand Rapids, MI: Eerdmans, 2015).

3. Wolterstorff, *The God We Worship*, 4–5. Wolterstorff distinguishes here and elsewhere in his work between act-types and act-tokens. On his account, a liturgy (as a universal) is a sequence of act-*types* whereas an enactment of a liturgy (as a particular) involves a sequence of act-*tokens*. We might think, for instance, of the difference between bowing as an act-type—a kind of thing that can be done—and bowing as an act-token, a particular *instance* in which someone does that kind of thing. I do not use this language of act-types and act-tokens here—for the simple reason of trying not to overburden the reader with distinctions—but it is operative in how I think about the difference between rituals and their enactments.

Allah, as well as movements and gestures in which practitioners stand, bow, prostrate, and kneel. The Fajr prayer involves, in other words, a *routine* that can be enacted on countless occasions by many different practitioners. And in this sense, it is a universal.

Specific performances, or enactments, of a ritual can be called *particulars*. When a practicing Muslim rises at dawn and performs *wudu* (ablutions) and *salat* (ritual prayer), they are enacting the Fajr prayer. In order for their activity to count as an enactment of the prayer, it has to follow the basic routine. On any given morning, there may be millions of enactments of the Fajr prayer undertaken by people around the world; they can all be said to be enactments of the same ritual insofar as they conform, more or less, to the routine.

We might be tempted to think about the relationship between rituals and their enactments—as universals and particulars, respectively—as unidirectional. That is to say, we might be tempted to think that people's everyday performances of rituals act out a script that is already written and can't be changed. After all, our account of ritual thus far suggests that someone can be said to *enact* a ritual insofar as they follow a routine—a sequence of acts in a regular order—that constitutes that ritual. But if that were the end of the story, it would be difficult to explain variations in rituals among different congregations or communities, or, more broadly, changes in rituals over time. And it would be impossible to explain the acts described at the beginning of this chapter *as* rituals—or, at least, as anything more than attempted-but-failed rituals, since each of those enactments departs from the usual order in one or more important ways.

As an empirical matter, we know that variations on rituals do exist and that changes to them do take place. During the Covid-19 pandemic, for example, mourners, along with funeral directors, clergy, burial societies, and others, tried to balance health concerns, laws and regulations, and the social and emotional needs of the moment. Roman Catholic priests administered last rites to dying patients over the telephone, Jewish burial society members symbolically cleaned and purified bodies over videoconference, mourners of all faiths and none gathered remotely for virtual memorial services and condolence calls. Activists enacted rituals of mourning to mark the loss of life and to protest the political failures that led to them. And beyond the rituals of mourning, people adopted new versions of long-standing practices: virtual iftars, spiritual communions, Zoom seders. To account for these variations and changes, we can't think of rituals as one-off events in which a person enacts an already-existing script. Instead, we need to think of rituals and their enactments as social and diachronic, that is, as taking place in social space and over time. People *enact* rituals, and their enactments can adapt and change the rituals themselves. The particular enactments are instantiations of the universal, but that universal can shift and change as a result of new enactments. To see how this happens, we need to think about how rituals function in, and as, social practices.

Rituals as Social Practices

Rituals aren't merely the idiosyncratic routines of isolated individuals; they are *social* practices, shared and tended by the members of a group.[4] As such, they involve multiple people who care about the

---

4. My way of characterizing social practices is informed by both Alasdair MacIntyre's influential account and Sally Haslanger's. Here's how each defines social practice: MacIntyre writes: "By a 'practice' I am going to mean any coherent and complex form of socially established cooperative human activity through which goods internal to that form of activity are realized in the course of trying to achieve those standards of excellence which are appropriate to, and partially definitive of, that form of activity, with the result that human powers to achieve excellence, and human conceptions of the ends and goods involved, are systematically extended" (*After Virtue*, 3rd ed. [Notre Dame: University of Notre Dame Press, 2007], 187). Haslanger, meanwhile, characterizes social practices as "patterns of learned behavior that enable us (in the primary instances) to coordinate as members of a group in creating, distributing, managing, maintaining, and eliminating a resource (or multiple resources), due to mutual responsiveness to each other's behavior and the resource(s) in question, as interpreted through shared meanings/cultural schemas"

practice and about the routines and rules that govern it. As Wolterstorff puts the point, a social practice is a focus of social interaction: "Typically [practitioners] watch how others perform the action in question, give advice to others, receive advice from others, get into discussions with others about better and worse ways of performing the action, perhaps try to imitate others, and so forth. Social interaction among practitioners takes place with the shared action as the topic of conversation and the object of observation."[5] As social practices, rituals belong to groups of people, all of whom have some stake in how they are enacted. Rituals' continuity over time depends on there being a group of people who care about tending the ritual, that is, getting it "right."

Understood in this way, rituals may be enacted privately or in solitude, but they remain in any case a matter of common interest and concern. For that reason, a person's individual routines are not rituals in the sense that I am using the term here. Let me clarify the difference. A person who enacts a ritual privately or in solitude is performing a routine that others also perform and care about,

---

("What Is a Social Practice?" *Royal Institute of Philosophy Supplement* 82 [July 2018]: 245). Both MacIntyre and Haslanger emphasize the social and cooperative nature of practices, as well as their role in the creation and/or realization of social goods. They share an understanding of practices as learned activities, transmitted from experienced practitioners to inexperienced practitioners through formal and informal education and habituation.

One significant difference between MacIntyre's and Haslanger's characterizations, however, concerns their account of what it is that is generated and distributed in and through social practices. MacIntyre focuses on the realization of social goods internal to the practice; Haslanger considers the movement or deployment of positive and negative resources that can be internal *or* external to the practice. On Haslanger's account, social practices can create, distribute, manage, maintain, and eliminate negative resources as well as positive ones. I follow Haslanger on this point, although I refer to that which is created, distributed, managed, etc., through social practices as goods and ills rather than "resources," in order to better capture the sense that they can be positive or negative, instrumentally or intrinsically valuable or harmful, and internal or external to the practice itself.

5. Wolterstorff, *Art Rethought*, 88.

as when a Muslim rises at dawn to perform the Fajr prayer. Millions of other Muslims also care about that practice—about what it is and how one ought to enact it. They may participate in it by praying, by learning from or teaching others about how to pray, by forming judgments about correct and incorrect ways of praying. The norms—that is, the implicit and explicit rules and evaluative standards—that govern the ritual are broadly shared among practicing Muslims, even when the ritual is enacted in solitude.

By contrast, if I have an unvarying routine for brushing my teeth—putting the toothpaste on the toothbrush in a specific pattern, brushing all of the left-side teeth first, then the right-side teeth, with ten little circles of the toothbrush on each—we might say that this is a series of acts, a routine, but that it is *not* a ritual in the relevant sense. It is individual, rather than social. Beyond the basic standards of dental hygiene, no one but me cares about whether I correctly enact my particular routine, nor is anyone but me committed to the rules and standards that govern it. Along the same lines, the quirky behavioral pattern of a tennis player between points in a tennis match is a routine comprising a regular sequence of bodily movements and gestures; this behavioral pattern may be recurrent and habitual, but because it is established, undertaken, and adjudicated by the tennis player alone, and according to rules and standards that only the player is concerned about, it is not shared in the relevant sense.[6] As social practices, rituals must be activities of shared interest and concern.

---

6. Many sports-related examples along these lines can actually become interesting in-between cases, since fans tend to identify with players or teams and may take themselves to have some stake in the players' performance of their idiosyncratic routines. For instance, fans might take it on themselves to judge a baseball pitcher who does not undertake his usual pre-pitch gestures, or who does them in the "wrong" way, and to blame the pitcher if the resulting game goes poorly. I have no particular stake here in including or excluding such cases from my account of ritual; the definition is not meant to identify what *really* counts as a ritual rather than some other kind of act but to delimit the object of this inquiry.

In order to participate in these activities, people have to learn the rules and standards that govern them. Knowledge of these rules and standards is often implicit rather than explicit—not a matter of reading a rule book or memorizing a script but rather of acquiring an embodied sense of what to do and how to do it. Many people acquire this embodied sense—what we might call practical knowledge—through a combination of imitation, modeling, discipline, and teaching by parents, teachers, elders, and role models. The practical knowledge required to participate in a social practice is handed down from experienced practitioners to inexperienced practitioners and initiates. Another word for the process by which practitioners acquire the practical knowledge that they need in order to participate in a ritual is *habituation*.[7]

Habituation into a practice involves the development of an embodied sense of how to participate in accordance with the norms that govern that practice. Some of these norms are made explicit in rules, laws, and textual scripts, but many of the norms are implicit in the conventions of the practice. The norms governing rituals concern such things as who is required or permitted to participate and in what capacities; when and where the ritual is to be enacted; and how the acts encompassed by the ritual are supposed to be done (for instance, for a verbal act, at what volume and with what intonation and emphasis). Norms vary with context. The norms governing the performance of *salat*, for instance, depend on such things as the branch of Islam, local or regional political and economic conditions, community and family observance, and so on.[8]

7. The outcome of this process of habituation—the acquisition of practical knowledge—is akin to what Catherine Bell calls "ritual mastery." She writes, "I use the term 'ritual mastery' to designate a practical mastery of the schemes of ritualization as an embodied knowing, as the sense of ritual seen in its exercise." See Bell, *Ritual Theory, Ritual Practice* (Oxford: Oxford University Press, 1992), 107. I engage with Bell's work and with other accounts of habituation at greater length in chapter 4.

8. For example, in her senior thesis, Julia Gan shows how Singaporean Malay-Muslims have adapted their ritual prayer practices in accordance with Singapore state guidelines and local work conditions. Gan, "The Study of Lived Religion through

Despite these variations and the social contexts in which rituals are enacted, we may still be inclined to think that rituals are relatively conservative. If rituals, as social practices, are handed down from one generation to another, and if initiation into them involves adherence and habituation to a set of rules and standards, then what room is there for contestation, innovation, or even rejection of existing rituals? Alasdair MacIntyre's influential account of social practices begs the question. MacIntyre writes that "to enter into a practice is to accept the authority of those standards and the inadequacy of my own performance as judged by them. It is to subject my own attitudes, choices, preferences and tastes to the standards which currently and partially define the practice. . . . The standards are not themselves immune from criticism, but nonetheless we cannot be initiated into a practice without accepting the authority of the best standards realized so far."[9] Initiation into a practice, MacIntyre suggests, involves accepting the rules and standards inherent to that already-existing practice and submitting one's performance or participation in the practice to judgments made on the basis of those rules and standards.

<hr />

Different Interpretations: An Ethnography on Perceptions of Singaporean Malay-Muslims' Islamic Prayer Ritual Practice" (Undergraduate thesis, Haverford College, 2020).

9. MacIntyre, *After Virtue*, 190. Although MacIntyre notes the possibility of criticism, it seems to me that he underemphasizes the reflective resources that people embedded in, and habituated into, social practices have for creatively innovating within and transforming their practices, norms, and standards. James Laidlaw includes a very good discussion of this issue in *The Subject of Virtue*, in which he distinguishes between MacIntyre's account of virtues, as involving "habituation through which one learns moral virtues in increasingly unthinking and unreflective terms," and Aristotle's account of virtues not as mechanical habit but as "reasoned practice." See Laidlaw, *The Subject of Virtue: Anthropology of Ethics and Freedom* (Cambridge: Cambridge University Press, 2014), 47–91. I discuss this Aristotelian account, and its implications for thinking about rituals, in chapter 4. Wolterstorff also presses against this point in MacIntyre's account of social practices, suggesting that MacIntyre "overstates the point a bit" (*Acting Liturgically*, 22).

And, of course, this *can* be how people experience initiation into a practice, as a matter of submission and habituation. But MacIntyre's characterization obscures the fact that the standards do not judge the performances for themselves; it is the people who are invested in the social practices who make these judgments from multiple points of view and with different interests in mind. Those people may be in agreement about some of the standards but in serious disagreement about others. Which standards are the relevant ones to turn to when making judgments about the correctness, or excellence, of a performance are often matters of debate. Initiation and habituation into a social practice can also involve initiation into those debates and mastery of the practical knowledge needed to make judgments about performances and about the standards available for use in judging them.[10]

We might think about the relationship between initiation into a practice, adherence to its rules and standards, and judgments about performances in light of Robert Brandom's common-law model of normativity—that is, his model of how norms develop their content and authority over time.[11] The English and American common law, as opposed to the statutory law, involves a body of legal concepts and principles that have developed through the application of precedents to novel cases. On this model, judges consider which previous cases bear enough similarity to the case under consideration to be relevant, and they identify the legal concepts and principles that guided reasoning in the previous case. Then, judges decide how those concepts and principles ought to guide the reasoning in the present case. The legal concepts and principles—the legal norms—do not float free from the actual cases in which they are

10. MacIntyre's characterization of traditions as "arguments extended through time" gets closer to the idea that I'm pursuing here, by highlighting the disagreements and contestations within them, although he still tends to treat traditions as more or less reified entities. I emphasize, by contrast, the permeability of boundaries around traditions and groups as well as their internal arguments.

11. See, for instance, Robert Brandom, *Reason in Philosophy: Animating Ideas* (Cambridge, MA: Harvard University Press, 2009), esp. 84–90.

applied. Past applications proffer the content, the meaning, of the legal norms. Judges determine which precedents are relevant to the case at hand and what those precedents have to teach about the relevant legal norms and their use. Through this process, the norms come to be useful and binding in determinations about the present case. When judges apply the norms embedded in precedents to new cases, those norms are developed in new directions. They gain content. In this process, the norms that are implicit in the precedents bear on novel cases, but their authority is not absolute or independent of their use; it can be overridden or annulled. The judge considers the precedents, decides which are relevant, applies them to the present case, and thereby creates a new precedent for future cases. Along the way, previously authoritative precedents can be left behind or overturned as the standards and norms are rearticulated and applied anew.

Thinking once again of rituals as social practices, we can begin to see how the norms that are taken up in enactments of rituals function in participants' sense of what constitutes a correct or excellent ritual performance. People may initially recognize the authority of existing norms, but they are also able to scrutinize them, change or delimit the sphere in which they hold sway, or overturn them. The authority of existing norms can be overridden. The common-law model helps us think about the authority of these norms and precedents. People improvise within inherited ritual forms, criticize them, overturn them, apply them in new contexts, or change the norms and routines themselves. Innovations in rituals happen, in part, when people enact routines in ways that adapt or overturn precedents and when these enactments are recognized and taken up by others as themselves authoritative precedents for future enactments. I enact a ritual in a new way—changing a word in a liturgical prayer, enacting a ritual in an unusual setting, or including participants who have been excluded in the past—and others who come later treat my enactment as a relevant precedent for their enactments going forward. They adopt the new wording of the prayer, or shift the setting for the ritual, or come to include those previously excluded participants as a matter of course. This means that the relationship between rituals (as universals) and their enactments (as particulars) is not as unidirectional as it may have initially appeared. Rituals do not simply appear before people as independently authoritative and fully articulated scripts. Instead, people establish, enact and perform, and judge rituals, often making determinations about these rituals' aims, the strengths and weaknesses of previous enactments, and the applicability of those previous enactments to present circumstances.

Rituals draw on the various precedents of a shared social practice to stake a claim about the people, goods, and values that the ritual *ought* to engage—and that the community in which the rituals are enacted *ought* to recognize. They do so, moreover, not only to express a commitment about how things ought to be (as though ritual and other bodily practices were merely acts of communication or deliberation by other means) but also to enact, and to bring about, new and different relationships and allocations of goods within that community. In this, they can change how the people participating in the ritual distribute goods to those within, and outside, their group—making rituals and their enactments matters of justice. It is to this feature of rituals that we now turn.

Rituals, Social Goods, and Justice

Rituals and their enactments can influence one another over time, with enactments of rituals taking up, or rejecting, the precedents set by earlier enactments as people go about making judgments about what counts—and what *ought* to count—as getting the ritual right. This process often takes place under shifting circumstances that change the available options or considerations for enacting rituals or judging them. Among the things that people have in mind when making these judgments are considerations about which people, goods, and values the ritual ought to involve. One of the most politically significant things that rituals do—or so I'll argue— is distribute goods among the members of a group according to the values of that group and the judgments that its members make about who ought to have access to which goods.

Sally Haslanger highlights this distributive aspect of social practices. Let's consider one of her examples. An academic lecture, Haslanger suggests, is a social practice that coordinates the members of a learning community around creating, distributing, and managing the good of knowledge (as "knowledge" is understood within twenty-first-century academic life). It does so through a complex, shared, and norm-governed sequence of acts in which people gather, sit in chairs to listen, stand at a podium to speak, exchange information and ideas through verbal acts of lecturing or answering questions, and so on.[12] Through repeated participation in the broader practice of twenty-first-century academic life, people who attend academic lectures become habituated into this practice, acquiring an embodied sense of the roles to be played and norms to be enacted as they sit and listen to, or stand and deliver, the lecture. These norms govern what each person is permitted and required to do in the context of that practice, according to the role that they are playing within it, whether as audience members or lecturers, faculty, students, staff, or members of the public. As a social practice, the academic lecture participates in the creation of what counts as knowledge; it also participates in the distribution of that knowledge according to the social structure and roles of the academy, from those designated as having knowledge to give to those designated as in need of knowledge. Every *particular* academic lecture is an enactment of the *universal* "academic lecture"; every academic lecture participates in this process of creating, distributing, managing, and transforming what counts as the social good of knowledge within the academy—even as some may apply, riff on, or overturn earlier precedents. (Some of the most memorable and exciting academic lectures I have attended have been clearly identifiable as enactments of that kind of activity, while also outright rejecting *some* of its norms.)

Notice that, understood in this way, social practices can be nested within other, larger-scale social practices. The academic

12. Haslanger, "What Is a Social Practice?" 245–46.

lecture participates in the larger-scale social practice of twenty-first-century academic life. That larger-scale social practice proffers at least some of the roles and norms that are enacted in *particular* academic lectures. At the same time, however, there are local and contextual variations in these roles and norms. One college may have somewhat different norms for academic lectures from another; certainly, disciplines such as philosophy, education, and biology have quite different norms for lectures, reflecting the different histories, values, and content of those academic disciplines.

In thinking about rituals, this means that we might consider *enactments* of rituals to participate in the social practices of those rituals, in general, and in the broader contexts of larger-scale social practices. The Eucharist is a social practice. A particular celebration of the Eucharist in a Catholic Mass *participates* in the social practice of the Eucharist, in the context of the larger-scale social practice of Roman Catholic liturgy and the social structure of the Roman Catholic Church. And all of this must bear in mind local variations in enactments.

Social practices regulate who within a group has access to which goods and ills: who occupies which roles; who exercises power and in which domains; who benefits from and who is burdened by what.[13] Rituals are among the social practices through which this distribution takes place, especially when the goods and ills in question are not, or not only, material but also normative and/or spiritual.[14] For example, according to the Roman Catholic Church, the Eucharist is one way in which God, and

13. Haslanger, "What Is a Social Practice?" 245.
14. Some of the goods and ills that are distributed through rituals are material; others are not, such as authority, entitlements, or obligations. Often, however, distributions of material goods and normative statuses are related. Authority and entitlement, for instance, often involve access to, and decision-making power over, material goods. A king in a feudal society has a set of normative social statuses (authority in making and enforcing the law, entitlement to deference, etc.) that correspond to and enable his access to material goods (wealth, natural resources, etc.).

God's grace, is manifest in the community. The Eucharist distributes spiritual goods; it also regulates access to those goods. Rules about who can take communion and under what circumstances, as well as rules about who can administer the sacrament, regulate the boundaries of the Eucharistic community and the distribution of goods within it.[15]

Vodou ceremonies, as described in Karen McCarthy Brown's ethnographic account of the Vodou priestess Mama Lola, also operate as economies of material, normative, and spiritual goods. These ceremonies distribute goods and ills to the human and spiritual beings who participate in them. Brown writes:

> Virtue for both the *Iwa* [Vodou spirits] and those who serve them is less an inherent character trait than a dynamic state of being that demands ongoing attention and care. Virtue is achieved by maintaining responsible relationships, relationships characterized by appropriate gifts of tangibles (food, shelter, money) and intangibles (respect, deference, love). When things go as they should, these gifts flow in continuous, interconnected circles among the living and between the living and the spirits or ancestors. In the ongoing cycle of prestation and counter-prestation, each gives and receives in ways appropriate to his or her place in the social hierarchy.[16]

---

15. Nancy Jay offers a critical, feminist perspective on the Eucharist that likewise emphasizes its role in the allocation of social goods. She argues that the Eucharist distributes spiritual and material goods in ways that maintain patriarchy. On her view, the Eucharist is a sacrificial rite, which, like other sacrificial rites, is "remedy for having been born of woman" (*Throughout Your Generations Forever: Sacrifice, Religion, and Paternity* [Chicago: University of Chicago Press, 1994], xxiii). Sacrifices function as rites of rebirth, which construct lines of (social) patrilineal descent while loosening (biological) matrilineal ties. In doing so, they distribute power, status, and wealth, placing these goods in the hands of men. The Eucharist, Jay argues, constructs a line of patrilineal descent through the all-male priesthood responsible for the administration of the Eucharist and thereby secures male power and status within the Church.

16. Karen McCarthy Brown, *Mama Lola: A Vodou Priestess in Brooklyn* (Berkeley: University of California Press, 2001), 6–7.

Attention to and care for the *Iwa* take place in the rituals of daily offerings and annual ceremonies. In these rituals and ceremonies, practitioners sing songs, enact gestures, prepare and present gifts of food, drink, and other offerings to the *Iwa*; a practitioner may be ridden or possessed by the *Iwa*, who arrives to engage with those who have gathered for the ceremony. In the complex performances of these ceremonies, practitioners act according to their roles, such as priestess or initiate, and goods (including spiritual goods, such as the protection and favor of the *Iwa*) are produced and distributed in relation to these roles.[17]

When people enact rituals, they engage in shared activities that create and distribute goods and ills around a community and at its boundaries. This means that rituals are wrapped up in concerns about *justice*. Justice requires that each person is given what is their due—that is, what they deserve. But who *deserves* the role, status, and goods of, say, adulthood? Answers to this question can be implicit in the rules or norms that govern a community's coming-of-age rituals. Those rules or norms may specify who is allowed or required to participate, and, therefore, who comes to be seen as an adult in the eyes of the community. Does the answer depend on age alone? Experience, skill, or training? What about gender? These are among the things that have determined, in different communities and at different times, whether and when someone may be eligible to participate in coming-of-age ceremonies and given the status and goods distributed therein. If a person deserves the role, status, and goods of adulthood but is excluded from the rituals that distribute those things, then we can say that they have been done an injustice. This would be both a *recognitive* injustice and a *distributive* injustice.[18] The person would not be recognized

---

17. Brown's description of Mama Lola's birthday party for the Vodou spirit Azaka offers a good example of this economy of material, normative, and spiritual goods. See Brown, *Mama Lola*, 36–78.

18. As I discuss in chapter 2, getting recognitive and distributive justice in the same frame is a key aspect of Nancy Fraser's work on justice, which has influenced my way of thinking and writing about rituals and justice in this project (see, for instance,

as having or holding the normative status that they deserve to have or hold, and they would be denied access to the material and immaterial goods that ought to come with that role or status. Similarly, people might ask who *deserves* the role, status, and goods of citizenship. This, too, is a normative question, debated among the people who live or work in, or who care about, the polis. Their answers to this question determine, in part, who has access to rituals such as naturalization ceremonies that regulate citizenship—once again, a matter of recognitive and distributive justice.

To summarize, rituals are social practices, in that they are complex, shared, and norm-governed activities that create and distribute goods and ills. They can be situated within larger-scale social practices. Relative to other social practices, rituals tend to be more routinized, to have more detailed and directive norms. These norms specify to a high degree what is to be done within the practice. For example, many groups have norms and expectations about when and how to eat meals: what people eat, how food is prepared (and by whom), who eats together, where and how they gather, and so forth. To eat a meal is to participate in a complex, shared, and norm-governed activity: a social practice. But there is also a great deal of flexibility and variation in an ordinary meal relative to a ritual meal. The Passover seder is an example of the latter. It is an annual occurrence in the Jewish liturgical calendar during which, through the recitation of prayers, telling of stories, singing of songs, and eating of symbolic foods, Jews remember God's deliverance of the Israelites from slavery in Egypt and praise God for God's covenant loyalty. The seder (which translates as "order") involves a series of acts. It is distinguished from an ordinary meal by this complex and detailed routine, which specifies to a high degree what the meal involves and how it is supposed to proceed.

Fraser, "From Redistribution to Recognition? Dilemmas of Justice in a 'Postsocialist' Age," *New Left Review* 212 [July/August 1995]: 68–93).

This example, the Passover seder, points to another feature that can be used to distinguish rituals from other social practices: namely, rituals' concern with people, events, and objects of heightened importance to a group. Rituals mark and enact the significance of the object of the ritual. They can be a way of valuing it. The Passover seder marks and enacts the significance of God's deliverance of the Israelites within the story of the Jewish people. Participation in the seder is a way of valuing that event and praising God ("Dayenu!"). For shorthand, I'll refer to this feature of rituals as "value-intensifying." Along with the degree to which the norms detail and delimit the possible moves within the practice, this value-intensification is part of what distinguishes a Passover seder from an ordinary weeknight dinner.[19]

Even with its complex and detailed routine and value-intensification, the Passover seder is subject to variation, adaptation, and innovation. It is not static. Because of its focus on freedom from domination and its insistence that participants imaginatively reexperience liberation from bondage, for instance, the seder has been adapted in light of modern liberatory politics. For example, the Freedom Seder crafted by Arthur Waskow in 1969 wove writing from Gandhi, Martin Luther King Jr., Nat Turner, and others into the traditional text and prayers of the seder. The Freedom Seder has been enacted thousands of times and has become the model for other variations on the seder that anticipate a future in which Black liberation, feminist liberation, and environmental liberation might be realized.

19. Of course, even with these distinctions in place, the boundaries around the category of "ritual" are a little bit fuzzy. Is a Sunday supper with the grandparents more like a Passover seder or an ordinary weekday lunch? Is it a ritual, or not? This is a good question, and I am happy to leave it as an open one. This book's account of rituals doesn't depend on a sharp boundary between rituals and other social practices. Some of the examples considered will be paradigmatic; others may be borderline cases. (A classic essay that takes up the differences among more and less formalized and scripted meals is Mary Douglas, "Deciphering a Meal," *Daedalus* 101.1 [Winter 1972]: 61–81.)

Rituals, Pragmatics, and Power

Rituals help create and distribute goods and ills, benefits and burdens, entitlements and obligations within a group or community. Consider an initiation ceremony that marks a person's entrance into a group. Through the initiation ceremony, the initiate gains access to resources that were previously unavailable to them, steps into roles or offices that were previously barred to them, and is recognized by others as having a status that they previously did not. Or, to be more specific, think again of a naturalization ceremony, in which a person passes from the status of non-citizen to citizen of a nation-state. The person's status changes. Along with that status change come various legal and political rights and responsibilities. These might include the right to vote, the right to due process, the responsibility to pay taxes, and so on. As I argue in more detail in the chapters ahead, in and through rituals, people distribute resources, assign social roles, bestow power and authority, and include people in (or exclude people from) their groups. In these and many other ways, rituals can function as *performatives*, actions that effect a change in the social world.

The category of "performatives" that I have in mind here has its roots in J. L. Austin's speech act theory. In *How to Do Things with Words*, Austin considers utterances that do more than merely describe or report on something in the world but that also bring about changes in the world.[20] He calls these utterances "speech acts." A promise is a classic example of a speech act. When a person says "I promise," that person undertakes the act of promising. The utterance is not a description or report of a promise that took place outside of the utterance itself. Rather, to say "I promise" just *is* to make a promise. When a speech act is successful (or what Austin calls "felicitous"), it *does* something, effecting a change in the social world. In the case of the utterance "I promise," the

---

20. J. L. Austin, *How to Do Things with Words*, 2nd ed. (Cambridge, MA: Harvard University Press, 1975).

speech act creates a new set of responsibilities and expectations, obligations and entitlements, that constitute the promise. These include a responsibility on the part of the one making the promise to do the thing they promised to do, as well as a reasonable expectation on the part of the one to whom the promise was made that the thing promised will be done.

One of the things that is required to make a speech act successful—that is, one of its "felicity conditions"—is that it follows certain conventions. These conventions can include linguistic formulae, as well as rules about who can perform the speech act and under what conditions. When a member of the clergy or a judge declares "I now pronounce you husband and wife" to a consenting couple, the speech act faithfully follows the conventions for enacting a heterosexual marriage. It enacts the ritual and it counts as marrying the couple. When a child declares the same thing to her playmates in a game of make-believe, it does not. As far as the adult world is concerned, the child's utterance is infelicitous; it doesn't enact a marriage.

There is a parallel here between rituals and speech acts. An enactment of a ritual and a speech act each brings about changes in the social world. The felicity, or success, of each in bringing about those changes can depend on whether and how the enactment follows the rules, norms, and conventions embedded in precedents. Enactments of rituals and speech acts alike can fail when witnesses or other interested parties don't think that they carry on the relevant precedents in the right ways. An initiation ceremony may fail to bring about a person's membership in a group if certain rules, norms, and conventions are not followed or recognized. The same is true of a promise or an enactment of a marriage. The children may follow the typical linguistic script for enacting the marriage, but they don't have the necessary standing to perform the speech act. Their act, therefore, won't be recognized by grownups *as* marriage.

Other philosophers of language and speech act theorists after Austin have explored how the success or felicity of a speech act is related to the social structures and power relations in which that act is undertaken. Who is *authorized* to perform a particular speech act, and who or what authorizes them? Which people need to *recognize* the speech act as having been performed in order for it to have its characteristic or intended force? How are these processes of authorization and recognition related to (and constitutive of) social structures and power relations? According to Quill Kukla (writing as Rebecca Kukla), for instance, speakers never have complete control over the felicity of their speech acts, and the members of some groups can be systematically disempowered in their ability to produce the speech acts that they intend (and are entitled) to produce, namely because others refuse to recognize their speech acts.[21] These are instances of discursive injustice.

Whether or not they involve language, rituals can function similarly to speech acts. When they do so, I refer to them as performatives.[22] They bring about changes in the social world, par-

---

21. Kukla argues, for instance, that women in male-dominated fields are often in a position in which their claims about their subject matter are not treated with the default weight ordinarily given to expert speech. Rather, women often find their speech treated as entreaty to enter the conversation or to be taken seriously in ways that refuse to recognize the speech act as expert speech at all. See Rebecca Kukla, "Performative Force, Convention, and Discursive Injustice," *Hypatia* 29.2 (2014): 440–57. Also see Miranda Fricker, *Epistemic Injustice: Power and the Ethics of Knowing* (Oxford: Oxford University Press, 2007).

22. Analytic philosophers distinguish between performatives and speech acts. My account of ritual draws on analytic philosophy of language and contemporary speech act theory, but I use the term "performative" somewhat differently from how it sometimes appears in that literature. I use the term "performatives" to describe rituals that enact a change in the social world, akin to what speech acts do through utterances. I use the term "performative" rather than "speech act" because not all rituals are verbal or linguistic; they can also enact such changes through gestures and other aspects of ceremony. As Wolterstorff suggests of liturgies, rituals often "count as" doing something else; for a ritual to function performatively is for the sequence of bodily acts to *count as* naming, blessing, petitioning, promising, confessing, authorizing, or accomplishing some other act. See Wolterstorff, *Art Rethought*, 68–69, 190–92.

ticularly by creating and distributing goods and ills, and by altering people's obligations toward one another, their entitlements to do certain things, and their authority in some particular domain. By participating in a ritual such as a marriage ceremony, for example, participants alter their normative statuses. They create new obligations and entitlements in their relationship, their families, and their communities. Like speech acts, ritual performatives are embedded in social structures and power relations. This means that there are implicit and explicit rules governing who can participate in them, what that participation ought to consist of, and what the people who see or hear about the performative have to do in order to "take up" or recognize the performance. But, as with speech acts, it turns out that this uptake is not a matter of merely acknowledging that criteria were met or a script was followed. Ritual performatives, and the uptake of the normative social statuses that they enact, can be creative acts in which new authority structures are recognized and brought into being. Although ritual performatives *tend* to depend on adherence to conventions and the default authority of certain precedents for their success, they sometimes break with convention and authoritative precedent and are recognized anyway—in spite of, or because of, that break. For this reason, ritual performatives don't merely reproduce existing social relations and structures. I'll say more about their novel effects in chapter 3.

From ancient Athenian rituals of supplication to Aztec rituals of sacrifice, early modern European coronations to contemporary presidential inaugurations, rituals are and have long been connected to power—projecting it, consolidating it, transferring it, contesting it.[23] This is equally true of the rituals of nation-states

23. See, for instance, David Carrasco, *City of Sacrifice: The Aztec Empire and the Role of Violence in Civilization* (Boston: Beacon Press, 1999); David Kertzer, *Ritual, Politics, and Power* (New Haven: Yale University Press, 1988); Edward Muir, *Ritual in Early Modern Europe*, 2nd ed. (Cambridge: Cambridge University Press, 2005); and F. S. Naiden, *Ancient Supplication* (Oxford: Oxford University Press, 2006).

(what are often called "civic rituals," such as inaugurations, naturalization ceremonies, flag ceremonies, military parades, and civic holidays) and the rituals of religious traditions. It is also equally true of the rituals implemented and regulated by civil or religious authorities who wish to *solidify* existing power relations, and the rituals enacted, adapted, and innovated by citizens, congregants, reformers, and radicals who wish to *disrupt or reshape* those power relations.[24] Rituals can serve the relatively powerful or the relatively powerless; they can support or sustain communities that are just or unjust. Contestation over rituals—that is, disagreement about which rituals ought to be performed, where, when, by whom, and with what effects—is often disagreement about what kinds of communities and relationships are worth having.

We can think of power, at the outset, as simply the capacity to bring about effects or, as Miranda Fricker puts it, "to influence how things go in the social world."[25] On this very general way of thinking about power, individuals, groups, institutions, and structures can all have and exert power. What Fricker calls *social power* encompasses both the power that is held and exercised by people (what she calls *agential power*) and the power exerted over people by structures (what she calls *structural relations of power*). "A socially situated account of a human practice," Fricker writes, "is an account such that the participants are conceived not in abstraction from relations of social power . . . but as operating as social types who stand in relations of power to one another."[26] An adequate account of people's social practices, in other words, needs to attend to the power that people exercise within the social structures that enable and constrain them—to both agential power and the structural relations of power.

---

24. Kertzer (*Ritual, Politics, and Power*) offers an account of the role of rituals in *symbolizing*, and thus deploying, power in politics.

25. Fricker, *Epistemic Injustice*, 9.

26. Fricker, *Epistemic Injustice*, 3.

Critical theorists often point to the extent to which the structural relations of power determine the identities, values, ideals, and relations available to and accepted by people in this or that particular place and time. Such power is everywhere, not least in the everyday practices that form and constrain subjects. Attention to this form of power is helpful for identifying the formative effects of rituals—the ways that rituals shape subjects with particular ways of being in the world—but it needs to be paired with attention to the capacities that subjects, thus formed, nevertheless have to adopt, adapt, endorse, reject, and transform their practices in order to bring about *other* effects. People can—and do—make choices about how to exercise their own capacities within, and sometimes against, these constraints. Becoming aware of their own formation, subjects can choose to endorse or reject the available social practices, to create or adopt new ones, and to accept, revise, or work to overturn the norms embedded within them. Subjects committed to a democratic politics do so in order to reject domination—a power relation in which one person or group has the capacity to exert its will over another, arbitrarily and with impunity—while building and exercising their capacity to bring about politically significant changes.[27]

The structural relations of power and agential power intersect in the politics of ritual. As routinized and norm-laden social practices, rituals can form subjects and reproduce situations and environments that support the status quo, shaping people's habits and constraining their creative and imaginative capacities. Much of this happens without the intention of the people participating in those rituals. At the same time, rituals are practices

27. Much of this work in critical theory follows from Michel Foucault's genealogical work on modern disciplinary regimes. By way of contrast, see Jeffrey Stout's account of the power of democratic agents in the footnotes of *Blessed Are the Organized: Grassroots Democracy in America* (Princeton: Princeton University Press, 2010), esp. 301–3n33, including the very helpful contrast between Stout's normative account of domination (which I basically share, and discuss in more detail in chapter 4) and Foucault's.

that are instituted, enacted, and argued over by agents; they can be self-consciously adopted and enacted for the purpose of shaping or reshaping one's habits, and they can be revised or rejected for the purpose of shaping or reshaping existing power relations. Rituals can themselves be sites of contestation and creativity, not least when agents seek to change themselves or their societies. In such cases, a number of questions come to the fore: Who has the power to institute, participate in, contest, or reject a ritual? And what power relations are modeled and reinforced in the ritual itself? Because rituals create and distribute goods and ills, answers to these questions about who has the power to institute rituals, or the authority created, enacted, and sanctioned in them, have ramifications for recognitive and distributive justice.

Rituals are social practices in which power is deployed and contested; they can also enact the power relations in a group. These power relations determine who has the authority to institute rituals or to change them, who is allowed to participate in them, what the rewards and punishments are for participating or refusing to participate in them, and even, in some cases, who, *as a result of participating in the ritual*, gains or loses power and authority. Think of an act of genuflection before a religious or political leader. That genuflection enacts the deference that the person undertaking the act is supposed to show toward the leader, reflecting and embodying the power differential between them. Or think of an ordination ceremony, in which a person is endowed with the right to hold and exercise power as a member of the clergy. As a result of having participated in the ordination ceremony, a person gains authority that they did not previously have.

Rituals can allocate power in ways that are just or unjust, and can often make unjust arrangements appear natural, traditional, or "just the way things are." When we think about the *politics* of ritual, we ought to notice how some enactments of rituals reveal the construction of these arrangements and enact a different way of distributing power and other goods. The rest of this book focuses on this process, both by thinking through what rituals do and by analyzing cases in which rituals challenge unjust and dominating power arrangements.

Conclusion

By moving outward from rituals' routines and rules to their status as social practices, enacted by people over time in accordance with partially shared but contestable norms, we can see how rituals can hold together continuity and change. Rituals involve sequences of bodily acts that are shared by the members of some group and engage the norms of that group—enacting, contesting, revising, or transforming them.

The next two chapters build on this account of ritual and develop, in more detail, an argument about how rituals can enact justice and injustice and support or transform existing power relations. Chapter 2 considers how rituals regulate the boundaries around groups, as well as the distinctions and divisions within them. In particular, it expands on the claim introduced in this chapter that, by regulating boundaries around groups and distributing goods and ills within them, rituals are part of the process of establishing just or unjust relations. Moreover, contestation over rituals—and the appearance of rituals in protests and social movements—is often about how goods and ills *ought* to be distributed. Chapter 3, then, turns to the distribution of power and authority. It argues that, through rituals, people can claim and enact authority that they didn't previously have. In the women's movement and Black freedom struggle, for instance, people who had been excluded from rituals—and from the roles regulated by those rituals—enacted those rituals in new ways in order to seize authority that they had previously been denied.

2

Marking Boundaries, Distributing Goods

FOR MORE than twenty-five years, people have gathered at the U.S.-Mexico border each December to enact the Posada sin Fronteras, or Inn without Borders. Traditionally, Las Posadas is an Advent custom that reenacts Mary and Joseph's search for a place to stay in Bethlehem. Las Posadas originated in colonial Mexico as Spanish colonizers and missionaries introduced participatory liturgies and rituals to evangelize and convert indigenous people to Roman Catholicism. Over time, it developed into a folk tradition that combined indigenous and Catholic elements and emphasized joyful communal celebration. Now, each year, throughout the Americas, and particularly in Mexico and the southwest United States, Catholics gather to reenact Mary and Joseph's search for hospitality. During Advent, people parade through their neighborhoods, knocking on doors, asking for lodging. Sometimes, participants are dressed as Mary and Joseph. They are rejected several times before they are finally met with hospitality and welcomed in. When this happens, they sing posada songs, read scripture, and offer prayers.

The Posada sin Fronteras enacts Las Posadas, drawing on precedents to perform the ritual. Many of the words, symbols, and gestures are traditional ones. Participants offer liturgical and spontaneous prayers, sing posada songs, carry crosses, light candles and luminarias. They proceed together, and they petition for hospitality. But their procession does not pass through neighborhoods, and the hospitality that participants seek is not at the homes of neighbors. Instead, participants gather in Border Field State Park/ Friendship Park and Playas de Tijuana, where the U.S.-Mexico border fence runs into the Pacific Ocean. They walk along the fence, stopping at points along the way where a migrant might attempt to cross the border. Those on the Mexican side of the fence petition those on the U.S. side of the fence for hospitality, but the American "innkeepers" keep turning them away.[1]

Unlike the traditional posadas, the Posada sin Fronteras does not end with unequivocally joyful celebration. As one of the organizers said in 2018, "in this case, we try from both sides of the border to complete the posada. We celebrate on both sides, we sing on both sides together. There's this great unity, and then at the end we try and sing the posada song, and we have to sing it divided, divided by the border. Hospitality in Christ is never supposed to be divided, and so it's an incomplete posada."[2] Because of the border fence, the Posada sin Fronteras is an incomplete posada. The participants can't achieve the unity that traditionally concludes the ritual. In keeping with this sense of an incomplete or interrupted posada, the Posada sin Fronteras includes acts of remembrance and mourning. Participants read the names of people who have died trying to cross the border. After each name is read, the assembled crowd chants, "presente," "here," indicating their remembrance of those who have died. They mourn the division represented by the border, as well as the lives lost as a result of that division. At dusk, they light luminarias, each of which bears the

1. See Pierrette Hondagneu-Sotelo et al., "'There's a Spirit That Transcends the Border': Faith, Ritual, and Postnational Protest at the U.S.-Mexico Border," *Sociological Perspectives* 47.2 (2004): 133–59.

2. Jamie Gates, quoted in Sojourners video, "The Inn without Borders/La Posada sin Fronteras," https://sojo.net/media/inn-without-borders-la-posada-sin-fronteras#.

name of someone who died crossing the border. Some simply say "no identificado" or "no olvidado"—not identified, not forgotten— for the unidentified dead.

The Posada sin Fronteras enacts Las Posadas in a way that highlights what the ritual has to do with borders and boundaries. Like traditional posadas, it begins with a community divided, with some seeking hospitality from others, who turn them away. Unlike traditional posadas, this division cannot be overcome. Implicit in both traditional posadas and the Posada sin Fronteras are answers to questions about who is or ought to be welcomed, what the boundaries of a community are or ought to be. The Posada sin Fronteras makes the political stakes of these questions and an- swers clear by enacting the ritual at the U.S.-Mexico border under the surveillance of border police. It demonstrates how the border and its policing undermine the unity that the ritual seeks. When people perform the posada at the U.S.-Mexico border fence, they mark the border's exclusions and injustices and call for some- thing else.

Rituals place people inside or outside of groups, as well as in roles within those groups. Rituals help define who is in and who is out, and on what terms. They help regulate who has access to what forms of power, social capital, and material goods within groups. The first section of this chapter considers how rituals regulate who is a member of a group and who has which roles and statuses within it. The second section argues that, in regulating membership, roles, and statuses, rituals also distribute goods. As mentioned in chapter 1, a ritual that marks the transition from childhood to adulthood— one of the many life-cycle rituals found in different forms in vari- ous traditions and sometimes referred to as "coming-of-age ceremonies"—distributes the obligations and entitlements that go along with the status of "adult." Someone who undergoes a coming-of-age ceremony enters the ritual with the obligations and entitlements of a child and exits the ritual with the obligations and entitlements of an adult, according to the norms of that com- munity. In the ceremony, the transition to adulthood is ritually marked, and the distinction between child and adult—as roles with different obligations and entitlements—is ritually enacted.

This distribution of goods can be unjust when people are denied access to social goods through an absence of ritual, exclusion from the existing rituals that regulate such access, or other people's refusal to recognize their participation in those rituals as legitimate. The final section of the chapter, therefore, considers how rituals are implicated in matters of distributive and recognitive justice. Who is recognized as belonging to a group, or as having a status within the group? Who has access to which goods within the group? Contestation over rituals—as well as the adaptation of existing rituals or innovation of new rituals—can be an attempt to achieve justice at the borders and boundaries of communities. Enactments of rituals, such as the Posada sin Fronteras, can try to do justice to those who are dominated or unjustly excluded, to properly recognize their role within a group or to give them the goods that they deserve.

Who's In and Who's Out

The central claim of this chapter is that rituals do boundary work—and that boundary work involves just and unjust ways of recognizing people's statuses and distributing social goods. This section sets up the argument by laying out the relationship among some related things: groups, boundaries, roles, and statuses.

All groups have boundaries. Boundaries mark the limits of inclusion in, and exclusion from, a group. They distinguish between those people who are a part of the group and those who are not. No boundaries, no group.[3] There isn't much of a boundary

3. A reader might object that there's a sense in which "humanity" or some similarly conceived universal might be a social group without boundaries of the sort I'm talking about here. I see problems with this objection on two fronts. First, it is not clear whether one learns anything about "humanity" by calling it a social group. Do its members have shared practices or norms? Does it, as a group, have a distinct social structure? Second, and to the extent that one *can* say anything determinate about

around a collection of people who, by chance, find themselves in the same place at the same time. Take, for instance, the people who happen to show up for the same movie, at the same theater, on a Friday night. To join this collection of Friday night movie-goers, someone simply has to show up, buy a ticket, and sit down in the theater. They don't need to do much to join, and they have only to follow the most basic rules of movie theater etiquette to stay for the duration. Once the movie is over, the collection of people disbands, and whatever collective experiences and shared practices they've undertaken are over. These Friday night movie-goers aren't likely to think of themselves or to be identified by others as a group, except in the weakest sense of the word.[4]

Contrast this collection of people with the members of the local Rotary club, who may meet weekly or monthly for a set of shared projects and practices held in common. To join *this* group, someone has to formally express their interest in becoming a member, wait to be contacted by the local chapter, attend a series of meetings and events, demonstrate their interest in and "fit" with

---

the group "humanity," it is not clear that that group really *does* lack boundaries. Who is included—all living human beings? What about the no-longer living, or the not-yet living? What about non-human creatures? What are the limitations on membership in a so-called universal such as "humanity"?

4. Here and in the following section, I have been influenced by Mary Douglas's account of social groups, which she analyzes in terms of what she calls "grid" and "group." On Douglas's account, "grid" refers to the degree of shared social structure (including differentiated social roles, differential distribution of power, shared symbol system, etc.); "group" refers to the degree of social pressure to conform to shared norms and, relatedly, the sense of the group as a unified and coordinated entity. Douglas suggests that, by graphing group members' experiences of these two coordinates on an XY graph, you can find characteristic "clusters" of social experience for different kinds of groups that are predictive of the sorts of social, religious, cultural, and symbolic activity that such groups are likely to engage in. I find the distinction between grid and group to be helpful; I am less convinced by the unidirectional predictive aspect of her account, which, it seems to me, reduces religious and cultural life to a *product* of social structure. See Douglas, *Natural Symbols: Explorations in Cosmology* (1970; London: Routledge, 1996), esp. 54–68.

the club, wait for a formal invitation, and then, finally, participate in an initiation ritual.[5] Whereas the Friday night movie crowd has a highly porous boundary, regulated primarily by the exchange of money at the box office, the local Rotary club has a distinct boundary that is highly regulated by rituals and other norm-governed social practices.

Groups often create and maintain their boundaries in part through rituals. Initiation rituals are common in civic organizations from the Rotary club to fraternities and sororities. Likewise, membership in many religious communities is regulated by rituals. People convert to Christianity by undertaking the sacrament of baptism; people become Jewish by immersing in a mikvah, or ritual bath, and reciting a set of blessings; people commit themselves to Buddhism by undertaking the vow known as "taking refuge." Each of these rituals moves people from one side of a boundary to another, changing their status—from non-member to member—while also affirming and enforcing the significance of the boundary.

In addition to external boundaries that mark and regulate who's in and who's out, most groups also have internal boundaries that mark and regulate who plays what role *within* the group. As with external boundaries, internal boundaries can be more or less permeable and the distinctions more or less socially significant. As Thomas Tweed writes in *Crossing and Dwelling*:

Religious homemaking not only maps the boundaries of the natal place . . . but also charts taxonomies of the people within and beyond its borders. In other words, it maps social space. It draws boundaries around *us* and *them*; it constructs collective identity and, concomitantly, imagines degrees of social distance. Social differentiation, which is complex in most modern nation-states but clearly present in the smallest itinerant band,

5. Rotary International, "Join Rotary," https://www.rotary.org/en/get-involved /join.

varies with the scale and form of the communal organization and the tropes and practices used to imagine social space. The classic example of social differentiation is the Indian caste and class systems, but most cultures have similar taxonomies, even if they are less elaborate and systematized.[6]

Social groups have external boundaries, often connected to territorial or geographical locations through what Tweed calls "spiritual cartographies of the homeland," but they also have distinct internal structures and differentiations among the people within the group. This differentiation includes a variety of roles, practices, and interactions between the two. Before turning to the relationship between rituals and these internal boundaries, it is worth saying a few words about social roles.

Social roles are the distinctive parts that people play within a group. Take as an example a Reform Jewish congregation. Within the congregation, there are a number of different roles that people play: the rabbi, the cantor, the Hebrew school teachers, the administrators, the adult congregants, the children. Each of these roles is governed by particular norms specific to that role. Role-specific norms can include expectations about the characteristics and abilities that make someone or something an excellent instance of their kind. So, for example, the rabbi's role is governed by role-specific norms that include expectations about wisdom, Jewish learnedness, and compassion. A rabbi who fulfills these expectations is conforming to the norms that govern their role and would be said to be a good or excellent rabbi. A rabbi who fails to live up to these expectations would likely be said to be a bad rabbi, according to the role-specific norms that govern the role of rabbi.

There are typically "right" and "wrong" ways to play a social role. And people meet with approval and disapproval, even reward and punishment, for playing their roles in the right or wrong way. As Stephen Bush notes: "A Muslim who performs *salat* (daily

6. Thomas A. Tweed, *Crossing and Dwelling: A Theory of Religion* (Cambridge, MA: Harvard University Press, 2006), 111.

prayer) without first achieving ritual purity by washing is violating a norm. An Orthodox Jew who performs manual labor on the Sabbath is violating a norm. In many churches, Protestant Christians who do not bow their heads and close their eyes while praying are violating a norm. Violations of religious norms will at the very least garner disapproval from one's coreligionists and in certain cases could lead to expulsion from the religious community or worse."[7] Conformity to social norms is met with approbation. Refusal or inability to conform to social norms is typically met with disapprobation. Approbation and disapprobation can be subtle or overt. A child who wriggles too much during Mass may get disapproving glances from his parents or priest; female clergy in a denomination that has traditionally or until recently not allowed women to serve in such roles may face harassment, marginalization, or censure by many of her coreligionists.

Just as the boundaries around groups may be more or less permeable, the internal distinctions among available social roles may be strong or weak. The Roman Catholic Church and the military are good examples of groups with strong internal boundaries and clear social roles. In both of these cases, there are distinctions among different roles—with particular norms governing each, and particular entitlements and obligations attaching to them. The pope, a priest, a woman religious (nun), and a layperson occupy four different roles within the Roman Catholic Church. While there are some norms that apply to all of them, regardless of the role that they occupy within the group, there are many norms that apply only to one or another of them. The norms that guide and constrain the pope in his actions are not the same as the norms that guide and constrain the layperson. Likewise, the entitlements and obligations attached to each role are different. What group members are allowed to do, and expected to do, depends on the role that they occupy within the group. The authority held by the pope within the Roman Catholic Church and the areas in which

7. Stephen S. Bush, *Visions of Religion: Experience, Meaning, and Power* (Oxford: Oxford University Press, 2015), 192.

he is entitled to exercise that authority far exceed the authority held by the lay Catholic. Likewise his obligations. What the pope is expected to do and the ways in which his actions are, in fact, *constrained* are quite different from the lay Catholic. It is also the case that there are clear norms governing who can occupy which of the available roles. These norms concern age, gender, and authorization. A child cannot be the pope. Nor can a woman, or a non-Catholic. Nor can any person who has not been authorized through the ritual process by which the cardinals of the Roman Catholic Church choose their pope.[8]

Social roles can have assumptions about age, gender, race, class, and other social categories built into them. For instance, some roles may be explicitly limited to people of a particular gender: according to canon law, Roman Catholic priests and bishops must be men. Often, however, social roles are *implicitly*, rather than explicitly, gendered and racialized. This is one of the challenges facing women, gender non-conforming people, and people of color when they aspire to or occupy roles traditionally occupied by white men. These roles still may be governed by and evaluated according to implicitly gendered and racialized norms, even when the formal and explicit rules about who can occupy the role have changed. For example, women, gender non-conforming people, and people of color who run for political office are often judged to be insufficiently authoritative in their performance of the social role—or, conversely, as *too* authoritative for someone of their gender or race—because they violate implicit gender- and racially coded norms governing the exercise of (in this case, political) authority.[9]

8. Sometimes, of course, norms change—even in the Roman Catholic Church. For an account of continuity and change in Catholic moral teaching and doctrine, see John T. Noonan Jr., *A Church That Can and Cannot Change: The Development of Catholic Moral Teaching* (South Bend, IN: University of Notre Dame Press, 2005).

9. Kate Manne writes about how women face sanctions for aspiring to or occupying male-coded roles and offices. Manne argues that these sanctions are, essentially, misogyny at work; she defines misogyny as the policing arm of the patriarchal soci-

The entitlements and obligations that come with social roles can be distributed through social practices, according to the norms that are circulated and enforced in those practices. By virtue of being a parent, for instance, I am entitled to exercise authority over the moral formation of my children. I share this authority with my partner and others in our community, and my exercise of this authority is constrained by both social and legal norms. But that authority goes with the role of parent, and its limits are set by the norms circulating in my family and community. There are also role-specific obligations. The obligations of parents and children are different from one another (and also vary, once again, according to the norms of any particular family and community).

The social roles available within any given group, along with the rules about who can occupy which roles and many of the norms that govern and constrain the occupants of particular roles, depend on the group in question. Because they can depend on local rules and norms, they are subject to both recognition and contestation. As I have suggested, some religious communities are highly structured internally, with distinct social roles available for clergy at different levels and laypeople, for men and for women, for children and adults, with people in each of these positions and offices having authority over different matters (or none), having access to different goods, and being evaluated as a good or bad occupant of that office according to criteria that are specific to it. In other religious communities, meanwhile, internal distinctions and divisions are relatively minimal, without dedicated clergy, sharp gender distinctions, or ways of marking the difference between children and adults. Think of the contrast between the characteristic social

---

ety. See Manne, *Down Girl: The Logic of Misogyny* (Oxford: Oxford University Press, 2018). One might see here how the norms governing evaluation of a social role and its associated practices can be implicitly gendered, such that the performance of a social role by a woman is evaluated according to male-coded norms that are wrapped up in what it is to be a "good" man. Changing the gender-coded norms related to a social role and its associated practices can be much more difficult than changing the formal rules about who is allowed to occupy that social role or office.

structures of a Roman Catholic parish and a Quaker (Society of Friends) meeting. The Catholic parish is clearly structured, with distinct social roles and a hierarchical distribution of power. The Quaker meeting has few internal distinctions and a relatively flat distribution of power; all of its members have more or less the same entitlements and obligations toward one another. There are no priests or clergy in the Society of Friends; decision making happens by consensus.[10] These differences are both aesthetic and structural; they are also normative, connected to the different commitments of the Roman Catholic Church and the Society of Friends concerning who or what is worthy of worship, what human beings are like, and what is good for human beings so conceived. The structures of these communities, with different available roles, offices, and attending statuses, obligations, and entitlements, are tied up with beliefs, practices, and norms about the divine, the human, and the good.

What does all of this have to do with rituals?

Just as the external boundaries of groups can be created, maintained, and transformed through rituals, so too the internal boundaries that distinguish roles and statuses within groups. Rituals can mark and enact the distinctions between roles, moving people across boundaries from one role to another. This is what happens in a coming-of-age ceremony that marks the distinction between youth and adulthood. The ritual moves people across the boundary, highlighting the significance of the distinction while allowing people to move from one role and status to another. Through the ritual, people gain the obligations and entitlements that go with their new social role. These routines, norm-laden and value-intensifying, affirm the group and its structure while distributing goods and statuses to the people who come to occupy the

10. Pink Dandelion's *The Liturgies of Quakerism* (New York: Routledge, 2005) responds to the assumption that the Quaker meeting lacks its own liturgies and rituals, arguing that even in a largely silent Quaker meeting, there is a unique liturgical structure.

various roles within it. They do so especially (although not exclusively) when these are not material goods but social statuses such as obligations, entitlements, and authority.[11]

The Distribution of Goods

Over the course of a lifetime, most people will enter groups and exit groups, and move from one status to another within them, traversing internal and external boundaries as they do. Rituals are implicated in these processes, regulating membership and distributing the goods that go along with membership.

As I have suggested, boundaries may be more or less permeable, more or less difficult to traverse, depending on the group. A perfectly permeable boundary, one that can be crossed by anyone or anything at any time without following any particular rules or standards for doing so, turns out to be no boundary at all. It fails to do what boundaries are supposed do: establish and maintain the limits of a group. Make the boundary perfectly permeable, and you have essentially eliminated the group. For that reason, existential anxieties about the permeability of borders and boundaries and the stability of groups are common. As Mary Douglas argues, people often perceive boundary crossings as dangerous, a threat to the integrity or existence of their group. The perceived danger is particularly acute when boundary crossers have not (or not yet) been properly integrated into the structure of their new group: "Danger lies in transitional states, simply because transition is neither one state nor the next, it is undefinable. The person who must pass from one to another is himself in danger and emanates danger to others. *The danger is controlled by ritual.*"[12] Rituals manage and mitigate the danger that people associate with these boundary crossings.

---

11. As discussed earlier, material goods and normative statuses are related. See chapter 1, footnote 14.

12. Mary Douglas, *Purity and Danger: An Analysis of Concept of Pollution and Taboo* (London: Routledge, 2002), 119 (emphasis added).

Some rituals are intended to solidify a boundary in danger of becoming too porous. Among the rituals of mourning revived by Cambodian Buddhists in the wake of the Khmer Rouge was the annual festival of the dead, *p'chum ben*. Because the people killed by the Khmer Rouge were often unceremoniously buried in mass graves, their bodies untended by the ordinary monastic rituals, many believe that the dead are hungry and restless. During the festival, people make offerings of food and enact rituals to transfer merit to the dead and to ritually re-create the boundary between them and the living.[13] On the final day of the two-week festival, people gather at the pagoda to distribute rice balls to their dead relatives by throwing them over the *sīmā*, or ritual boundary, that separates the gathering place of the living from that of the spirits. The festival ends when people return the spirits of the dead to the underworld, often by floating symbolic representations of them down a river, until the gates of the underworld close behind them. The revival of this ritual after the end of the war can be understood in part as a response to the anxiety about the *absence* of the ordinary burial rituals that would create and maintain the boundary between the living and the dead, and as an ameliorative effort to reinstate that boundary.[14] In the *p'chum ben*, the pagoda protects the living from "disturbance from restless souls"; the hungry spirits can come to the limits of the pagoda—its ritual boundary—but cannot cross over it.[15]

13. Inger Agger, "Calming the Mind: Healing after Mass Atrocity in Cambodia," *Intercultural Psychiatry* 52.4 (August 2015): 543–60.

14. Ian Harris argues, provocatively, that the revival of rituals marking this ritual boundary is connected to Cambodia's postwar "unique obsession with protecting the country's borders," thus linking, through a political theology, anxieties over the ritual boundary and the territorial nation-state border. See Harris, "Rethinking Cambodian Political Discourse on Territory: Genealogy of the Buddhist Ritual Boundary (*sīmā*)," *Journal of Southeast Asian Studies* 41.2 (June 2010): 215–39.

15. Alexandra Kent, "Peace, Power and Pagodas in Present-Day Cambodia," *Contemporary Buddhism* 9.1 (2008): 77–97.

Other rituals, like those referred to as "rites of passage," are intended to regulate how people cross boundaries. Such rituals, as Arnold van Gennep argued, move people across borders and boundaries, whether territorial or social.[16] In doing so, they mitigate the anxiety associated with boundary crossings, turning potential violations into licit crossings. Rites of passage, van Gennep claimed, typically share a common form and set of symbols. Their form is tripartite, involving a sequence of acts in three stages: rites of separation, rites of transition, and rites of incorporation. The first of these three stages marks the person's separation from their previous role, status, or group. The second stage marks their liminality, the condition of being "betwixt and between," no longer situated in their previous role or status but not yet rooted in a new one. As people move from one role or status to another within a group, or from a position outside of the group to a position within it, their position is liminal. It is this liminality—outside of the usual categories, roles, and statuses that structure the group—that people perceive as dangerous. By situating liminality, and the rites of transition, within a routine that orders and controls it, rites of passage control the danger and offset the anxiety associated with boundary crossings.[17] The third and final stage of a rite of passage marks the person's incorporation into a new role, status, or group. At each stage, a sequence of gestures, movements, and symbolic actions and objects enacts the transition. These can include physical separation or periods of isolation; nakedness, or stripping the participant of the signs and signals of belonging in the group; or passage

16. Arnold van Gennep, *Rites of Passage*, 7th ed. (Chicago: University of Chicago Press, 1975).

17. Victor Turner significantly developed van Gennep's discussion of liminality to include analysis of groups that attempted to create or sustain liminal states rather than to manage or overcome them through rites of passage. He notes, however, that such groups nearly always create a new kind of social structure. Groups cannot remain structureless forever but tend to move back and forth between moments or phases of structure and anti-structure (or liminality). See Turner, *The Ritual Process: Structure and Anti-Structure* (Ithaca: Cornell University Press, 1969).

through a tunnel or gauntlet, akin to a birth canal, or through a door or threshold. Not all rites of passage are so clearly demarcated as van Gennep suggests, but his framework remains relevant for thinking about the boundary work that rituals can do.

Consider a marriage ceremony, and much more specifically for the moment, the marriage ceremony of Kate Middleton and Prince William in 2011. This was a royal wedding, enacted within the Church of England according to the Anglican rite. There were several members of the clergy involved, but it was Archbishop of Canterbury Rowan Williams who conducted the marriage. The setting was Westminster Abbey. The beginning and end of the rite of passage were marked by Kate's entrance and later exit from the church down the aisle. In the pews on either side of the aisle sat family, friends, members of the British aristocracy, dignitaries, and political and economic elites from around the globe. At the beginning of the ceremony, Kate and her father walked down the aisle to the front of the church, where her fiancé and the Archbishop of Canterbury stood waiting. At the end of the ceremony, Kate and William exited, hand in hand, down the same aisle. The symbolism in this marriage ceremony, van Gennep would suggest, was standard stuff for a rite of passage. The initial walk down the aisle marked Kate's separation from her former role and status; the ceremony at the front of the church was a liminal moment; the recessional at the end of the ceremony marked Kate's (and William's) entrance into a new role and status. The ceremony invoked the symbolism of rebirth, with the walk down the aisle mimicking the passage through the long narrow corridor of a birth canal. Kate and William were reborn through their participation in the rite.

A pivotal moment of the ceremony took place a few minutes after Kate joined William at the front of the church. The Archbishop of Canterbury asked, "Who giveth this woman to be married to this man?" and her father, still standing at her side, picked up Kate's hand and reached forward with it to pass it to the Archbishop. The Archbishop took Kate's hand from her father and passed it to William. And then the vows began. According to the language and gestures of the ritual, Kate's father *gave her* to be wed into the hand of God (or, here, God's representative in the church), who delivered her to her husband. She was separated from her father, entered into the liminal or transitional moment between the role of daughter and wife (but under the protection of God in that anxiety-producing liminal moment), and then united with William. This was symbolized in the movement of Kate's hand, but it was not merely symbolic. The ritual enacted Kate's change in social role and status—as well as her political role and status, from commoner to member of the British monarchy—while also displaying and enacting her subordination to a series of male authority figures.

Weddings are an important rite of passage in many communities. But they're far from the only such rite. People mark and bring about a wide variety of important status changes with rites of passage. Conversion ceremonies, naturalization ceremonies, and other sorts of initiation rites regulate people's entrance into a group. Through these rituals, people who were not members of a group become members. They cross the group's external boundary and enter into it. Excommunication rites are among the rituals that mark people's *exit* from a group. Through these rituals, people who were members of a group become non-members; they traverse the group's boundary in order to leave it. Each of these rituals regulates movement across the external boundary that surrounds a social group. Meanwhile, weddings, along with coming-of-age ceremonies, graduations, ordinations, inaugurations, and coronations, are examples of rituals that regulate people's movement across internal boundaries. They facilitate and enact the movement from one role or status to another, a movement that typically carries with it new obligations, entitlements, social relations, and forms of power.

In early modern Europe, for instance, coronations functioned as complex rites of passage intended to alleviate the anxieties associated with political transition. The death of one king led to the liminal period of the interregnum when, as Edward Muir notes, questions about "*who* was in power and *when* did he or she take power came to the fore."[18] As a result, the interregnum was "fraught with dangers for the institution of the monarchy."[19] The funeral of one monarch and the coronation of the next were often tied together by a series of other rituals, each of which played a part in easing the transition and enacting the transfer of power. The coronation itself was the culminating event, not merely representing the ascension of the heir to the throne but also enacting it. Muir writes that "in many kingdoms, some combination of gestures and verbal statement was the necessary constitutive act of kingship."[20] In order to become a king, the heir to the throne had to undertake a complex ritual—or, indeed, series of rituals—that upheld the distinction between the king and those who were not (or not-yet) king, while managing people's anxieties about the transition. In and through the coronation itself, the heir to the throne *became* the king, stepping into a role that he did not previously occupy and taking on the obligations and entitlements associated with that role. Lest we assume that the inauguration ceremonies that characterize contemporary democratic political transitions merely *represent* rather than *enact* the political official's assumption of power, we might recall the first inauguration of President Barack Obama in January 2009, when Chief Justice of the U.S. Supreme Court John Roberts misspoke while administering the constitutionally specified oath of office. While reassuring the public that the oath was a mere formality, the administration made sure that Roberts readministered the oath the following day. This suggests that there is, at the least, some tension between the dueling conceptions of presidential inaugurations as *merely* formal and symbolic and as actually counting as the transition of power.[21]

18. Muir, *Ritual in Early Modern Europe*, 273.

19. Muir, *Ritual in Early Modern Europe*, 273.

20. Muir, *Ritual in Early Modern Europe*, 272.

21. Kathryn T. McClymond considers this example in *Rituals Gone Wrong: What We Can Learn from Ritual Disruption* (Oxford: Oxford University Press, 2016).

Rites of passage are successful when they manage the dangers associated with liminality, quell the anxieties of boundary violations, and result in the intended changes in a person's normative status. A person who successfully undergoes a rite of passage enters into a new role, acquires a different status, and gains or loses obligations, entitlements, and authority within a group. A non-Jew who undergoes the Jewish conversion rites becomes Jewish, thereby acquiring certain obligations (to perform the relevant *mitzvot*, or commandments) and entitlements (to count in a *minyan*, or quorum, for certain prayers, depending on the convert's gender and the Jewish community in question). Membership in the group—and, therefore, access to these rights and responsibilities—is ritually regulated. In referring to these effects as changes in a person's normative status, I want to draw attention once again to the norm-based or conventional nature of the group, its boundaries, and its structure. Boundaries around groups and distinctions within groups exist where and insofar as they are recognized and enforced by members of those groups. Rites of passage regulate movement across these boundaries, typically in ways that rely on a set of norms, conventions, and precedents concerning group membership and social structure.

Rites of passage that mark and enact internal boundary crossings depend on—and often strengthen—the differential distribution of power, status, and other goods within a group. They also produce and distribute goods within the group. To enter into a new role is to acquire new obligations and entitlements, including the ability to hold and exercise power in the ways that are normative for that role. For example, to undertake ordination rites, entering into the role of clergy, is (if successful) to be recognized as having the role-specific obligations and entitlements of a member of the clergy. In and through ordination rites, those obligations and entitlements are granted and recognized.

Rituals not only mark a role or status change for the person who undergoes them but also mark the difference between those people who are eligible to enter into certain roles and those who are not.

Many such distinctions are sexed or gendered, for example, with boys and men eligible for certain roles (as marked by their participation in the relevant rites of passage) and girls, women, and people who are gender non-conforming ineligible for those social roles. As Pierre Bourdieu suggests, communities in which circumcision is normative for males are marking not only the distinction between members of the community (who, if male, are circumcised) and non-members of the community (who, if male, may not be) but also, and perhaps more importantly, the significance of the distinction between people *within* the community who have penises and people who do not.[22] Gendered rites of passage, among other rituals, mark and enact not only a status change but also a system of gender differentiation and a differential distribution of power along lines of gender. Ordination and coming-of-age ceremonies are additional examples of these kinds of rituals, which not only enact a status change for the people who participate in them but also mark and police the distinction between those who can participate in them at *some* point and those who cannot. Ordination, as the next chapter shows, is a site of contestation in many religious communities and traditions, with some religious groups recognizing people of all genders as eligible to participate in the rite (and thus to become clergy or religious leaders) and others recognizing only men. Likewise, the creation of coming-of-age ceremonies for non-males in many religious and social groups is a corrective to practices that mark the transition from boy to man, but not the transition to adulthood of people of other genders, and that police the distinction between males and others, giving males exclusive access to certain goods. For this reason, it is not surprising that both ordination rites and coming-of-age ceremonies have been subject to feminist contestation and ritual innovation.[23]

22. Pierre Bourdieu, *Masculine Domination*, trans. Richard Nice (Stanford: Stanford University Press, 2001), 24–25.

23. For examples and analysis of feminist Jewish ritual innovations, see Vanessa L. Ochs, *Inventing Jewish Ritual* (Philadelphia: Jewish Publication Society, 2007).

Rituals in Search of Justice

A perfectly permeable boundary is, in the end, no boundary at all.[24] This is true of the external boundaries of communities and of the internal boundaries that differentiate among roles and statuses within communities. A boundary exists because and insofar as people recognize that boundary as separating two different roles or statuses, with distinct entitlements, obligations, and role-specific norms attending to each. If people believe those roles to be distinct and think that the distinction between them is worth preserving, then they are likely to have norms and practices in place for regulating movement across the boundary between them and for apportioning the entitlements, obligations, and other normative statuses that accompany one or the other role. People are likely to have rituals for creating, distributing, and managing the goods characteristic of the roles that they care about.

But who *should* be allowed to join a group, who ought to hold which roles and statuses within it, and who ought to have access to which goods? People argue about how they and others in their group ought to answer these questions, making judgments and claims about the justice and injustice of the prevailing or taken-for-granted answers to them.

Feminist and queer ritual innovations have often been motivated by the recognition that there are, in the lives of girls, women, trans people, queer people, and others who are nonbinary or gender non-conforming, boundary crossings that are unmarked and denied normative significance but that *ought* to be treated as significant. Hence the claim that there ought to be a ritual to celebrate menarche, for instance, or a ritual to mourn a miscarriage. These events ought to be marked, and the people experiencing

---

24. For the lovely phrase "rituals in search of justice," I am indebted to my late colleague Aryeh Kosman. After a talk I gave at Haverford, Aryeh suggested to me that this (rather than the title of my talk on that occasion, "Ritual Injustice") was the idea to which my work aspired. He was right.

them ought to be recognized and treated as moving through or across a socially significant boundary.

Let's turn our attention back to weddings. In most communities and traditions, weddings and marriage ceremonies are *social* events, attended not only by the people getting married but also by their families, friends, and other members of the community. They are also rites of passage. A marriage ceremony moves its central participants from one status (unmarried) to another (married). The ceremony also displays, enacts, and affirms socially significant roles and statuses within a particular community, not least how that community understands, produces, and enforces gender roles and norms. As David Craig writes, "While marriage rituals vary in detail, they typically reinforce gender roles through the spoken words, wedding attire, and visual display. As a result, these rites uphold more than the social border between heterosexual and homosexual; they are one of the primary public spaces in which the categories of male and female are performed."[25] Rooted in histories of economy and property transfer, the rituals and symbols associated with heterosexual weddings often enact female submission to male authority. This is evident in the highly ritualized wedding of Kate Middleton and Prince William. From Kate's long white gown, symbolizing her virginity, and William's military uniform, symbolizing his connection to the power of the state, to the passing of Kate's hand from father to priest to husband, the symbols, gestures, and even words of the liturgy express and enact a particular vision of men, women, and the power differential between them.

In the struggle for social, religious, and legal recognition of same-sex marriage, queer commitment ceremonies and weddings played an important role in enacting a new set of gender and sexual norms. Queer commitment ceremonies and weddings

---

25. David Craig, "Debating Desire: Civil Rights, Ritual Protest, and the Shifting Boundaries of Public Reason," *Journal of the Society of Christian Ethics* 27.1 (Spring/Summer 2007): 179.

challenge not only sexual norms but also the gender norms that are typically performed and enacted in most heterosexual marriage ceremonies. The more socially significant a community takes distinctions between men and women to be, the more resistant some members of that community are likely to be to changes in the rituals that so powerfully enact those distinctions and allocate goods to the people who participate in them. Same-sex marriage ceremonies and marriage ceremonies for partners who are nonbinary or gender non-conforming are creative acts that draw on existing routines for enacting marriage to challenge prevailing social boundaries, power relations, and social structures—and to enact new ones.

As social practices that create and distribute goods and ills within a community, rituals are bound up with matters of justice and injustice.[26] To create rituals where there are none, or to insist on performing a ritual that was not supposed to be "for" you, can be a call for recognition and for distributive justice. Ladelle Mc-Whorter describes planning and participating in a commitment ceremony with her partner Carole Anderson in 2002:

> Initially I had thought of the ceremony as something like a formal public announcement of a relationship that already existed, not really as what Arnold van Gennep called a "rite of passage." I wanted public recognition of a relationship that many people with whom I have daily contact refuse to respect. In other words, I wanted to change the behavior of some people around me. But I didn't anticipate changing my*self* in any deep way. As we and our friends planned and prepared, however, I began to realize that changes were occurring and that the ceremony might turn out to be a rite of passage in van Gennep's sense after all—*except*, not only the movement of passing through, but also the space to be passed into was evolving as we prepared.

---

26. Haslanger, "What Is a Social Practice?" 232.

We would be initiated not into a pre-fabricated institution of marriage but into something that had not existed before.[27]

McWhorter's commitment ceremony was not merely an announcement or symbolic affirmation of something that existed apart from, or prior to, the ceremony. It was a rite of passage. The ceremony—the preparation for it and the performance of it—created the union that McWhorter and Anderson entered into. It also aimed at reshaping the available roles, norms, and distribution of goods. On this view, McWhorter notes, "ritual can be a practice of freedom"[28]—and, I would add, a practice of justice. People who have demanded, created, and implemented rituals in their communities to mark socially significant moments and to enact transitions have demanded, in effect, recognition of roles or statuses that were not previously recognized, as well as access to the goods that accompany them.

In 2002, McWhorter and Anderson did not gain the legal entitlements associated with marriage. At that point, same-sex marriage still was not recognized in U.S. law. But McWhorter suggests that they did gain social entitlements (and, presumably, obligations too), a new set of social statuses and relations to one another and to their families and communities. This social recognition prefigured legal and political recognition; sometimes, as I argue in chapter 3, rituals claim and enact normative statuses that have not yet been recognized and, in so doing, help bring about the broader

27. Ladelle McWhorter, "Rites of Passing: Foucault, Power, and Same-Sex Commitment Ceremonies," in *Thinking through Rituals: Philosophical Perspectives*, ed. Kevin Schilbrack (New York: Routledge, 2004), 90. McWhorter analyzes ritual in terms of Foucauldian technology of the self, in which people undertake disciplinary practices to train their disposition or reshape their subjectivities, but I think that there are aspects of what she describes that exceed that framework. The social practice framework—in which rituals, like other social practices, are norm-governed activities that create and distribute goods in a group—helps account for the social and recognitive goods that McWhorter describes acquiring through the ceremony.

28. McWhorter, "Rites of Passing," 92.

social and legal recognition of those statuses. They can prefigure and enact a justice that is not-yet.

In some cases, it is the *absence* of ritual that constitutes the injustice. Douglas, for example, points to the often-permanent liminality that formerly incarcerated people experience when, after their release from prison or jail, they are not reincorporated into their communities. Recall the idea that rites of passage involve a central liminal stage, after a person has been separated from their former social role or status and before they have been incorporated into their new role or status. People can become stuck in that liminal phase, Douglas suggests, permanently outside the legible roles and statuses available within the community. Formerly incarcerated people often face social and legal barriers to reintegration into their communities; as Douglas writes, "a man who has spent any time 'inside' is put permanently 'outside' the ordinary social system. With no rite of aggregation which can definitively assign him to a new position he remains in the margins."[29] The U.S. legal system has complex legal rites in place to separate people convicted of a crime from their communities; those legal rites of separation are paired with people's physical separation from their community through incarceration. When a person is released from prison, however, the legal system has no rituals in place to incorporate them into a community—and indeed, countless legal and social barriers to reincorporation.[30] Many states deny formerly incarcerated people the services, and strip them of the rights, that are citizens' due. Likewise, many individuals and institutions stigmatize those who have been convicted of a crime or who have spent time in prison, discriminating against them in housing and employment and relegating them to the position of

---

29. Douglas, *Purity and Danger*, 121.

30. These laws are state specific. In many states, however, people who have completed a prison sentence remain under state surveillance in the form of parole; people convicted of felonies may be permanently barred from voting and denied access to public housing, food stamps, and other basic social goods.

outcast.[31] As Rima Vesely-Flad argues, incarceration and the failures of reentry are part of a broader cultural and political system
in which Black bodies are rendered as "impure," a perceived threat
to the social body.[32] Denied the status and goods that are their
due, formerly incarcerated people are done a recognitive and distributive injustice.

Social theorists who have noted the challenge of reentry have
suggested ritual frameworks for reincorporating formerly incarcerated people into the communities from which they were separated.[33] Rituals such as these—rites of reentry—enact a person's
return to their community. If these rituals were merely symbolic,
then we would not expect much to change with the introduction
of such rites of reentry. But if they were social practices in which
goods were created and distributed, then their presence would
be not only consequential but also a way of doing justice. More
profoundly, restorative and transformative justice practitioners
and those committed to the abolition of the prison industrial
complex often incorporate accountability circles and healing
rituals into their practices as part of the process of envisioning
and enacting justice while abandoning the harms and violence
of the carceral model altogether.[34] While such practices can involve the stages associated with rites of passage, they are *complete*

31. Douglas suggests that this sort of marginalization is a characteristic feature of
groups in which people experience the social structure as unstable, in which people
sense that shared symbols, traditional social roles and statuses, and ways of allocating
social goods are changing or under attack. Social instability—in the form of changing
statuses, roles, practices, and norms—can amplify the anxieties that Douglas identi-
fies, resulting in efforts to shore up the borders and boundaries of the group through
symbolic, legal, and social practices that project stability and order.

32. Rima L. Vesely-Flad, *Racial Purity and Dangerous Bodies: Moral Pollution, Black
Lives, and the Struggle for Justice* (Minneapolis: Fortress Press, 2017), esp. xix–xxi.

33. See Shadd Maruna, "Reentry as a Rite of Passage," *Punishment and Society* 13.1
(2011): 3–28.

34. See John Braithwaite, "Repentance Rituals and Restorative Justice," *Journal
of Political Philosophy* 8.1 (2000): 115–31.

rites that refuse to leave people behind in an unjust state of permanent liminality.

This way of thinking about rituals—as sites where people recognize others' social standing and distribute social goods—brings together two frameworks for thinking about justice: in terms of recognition and in terms of distribution. Recognitive justice concerns whether people are taken and treated as having the status or standing that they ought to have in some domain. A woman who has a PhD in physics and high-profile publications in her field but who is repeatedly ignored or undermined by her male colleagues is done a recognitive injustice by them. Distributive justice, meanwhile, concerns whether people are given the *goods* to which they have a claim. If the physicist is paid less than her male colleagues for doing the same job, she is done a distributive injustice. As Nancy Fraser notes, neither the cultural politics of recognition nor the socioeconomic politics of redistribution by itself gives us an adequate conception of justice, not least because many persistent injustices—racial injustice and gender injustice among them— involve failures of both recognition and distribution. Our conception of justice, therefore, must be "bivalent," encompassing both recognition and distribution.[35]

Because rituals regulate who is in and who is out—of groups, roles, and statuses—and distribute goods to the members of those groups and occupants of those roles, rituals are implicated in both recognitive and distributive justice. Who is recognized as having what role or status and who is apportioned which goods and ills are inseparable questions. Roles and statuses are packaged with goods and ills. Being recognized as having a status or occupying a

35. Fraser, "From Redistribution to Recognition?" A "bivalent" conception of justice is also one of the aims of Haslanger's work on social practice: a conception of justice in light of practices that distribute goods and ills, including material resources, at the same time that they produce and reproduce the roles and norms according to which those goods are distributed ("What Is a Social Practice?").

role entails having access to the goods that attend that status or role—the goods that are one's due.

Rituals create and maintain boundaries by organizing and distributing goods and ills—including positions within the structure of a group or community. When the absence of ritual, or exclusion from ritual, leaves someone marginalized, without role, status, power, or other goods within their community, that person is *wronged* in socially and materially significant ways. Other things being equal, a person who comes of age and is not ritually and performatively welcomed as an adult member of their group is done an injustice. A person who is released from prison and is not ritually and performatively welcomed into their community is done an injustice. *A demand for ritual can be a call for recognition and for distributive justice.* People who have pressed for, created, and implemented rituals in their communities to mark significant moments and transitions have demanded, in effect, recognition of a role or status that has not previously been recognized as significant, along with the goods that accompany that role or status.

Back to the Border

Rituals mark and enact boundaries. They draw on the norms of the group to include and exclude people and to move social goods and ills within and across their external and internal boundaries. The norms, roles, and practices involved may be unjust ones; they can fail to recognize people's status, or they can fail to distribute goods to those who are entitled to them. Rituals can dominate, exclude, and exploit. But they can also contest these things, by recognizing those who ought to be recognized and distributing goods to those who are entitled to them. These things—"who ought to be recognized" and "who is entitled to goods"—are taken up in political contestation. Returning to the U.S.-Mexico border, we can see the connection between rituals and political contestation in debates over borders and boundaries.

Boundaries, on my use of the term, mark the edges of a social body. They regulate inclusion in and exclusion from a community or group. Borders, meanwhile, mark the edges of a geographical body, regulating inclusion in and exclusion from a territory. Boundaries delimit social entities, while borders delimit geographical entities. Both boundaries and borders, however, are created, imposed, and enforced by people. And both are social constructs rather than natural facts about the world.

Although boundaries and borders are distinct phenomena, they often interact. A neighborhood, for example, is a geographical or territorial entity that is marked off by streets and landmarks. It has borders. The people who live within those borders count as residents of the neighborhood. Sometimes, the residents of the neighborhood come to have a sense of themselves as a social group. They have explicit rules and implicit norms; they have shared practices such as a Fourth of July parade or a Halloween costume party. They come to have a sense that there is a *socially significant* difference between being a resident of this neighborhood and being a resident of the next neighborhood over. "We" are the ones who live on these streets; "they" are the ones who do not. In this case, the residents of the neighborhood have a sense that the territorial border and the social boundary around the neighborhood are coterminous. This is how many people envision modern nation-states, too, as involving a people—a social group—that is perfectly or ideally coextensive with and sovereign over a land. On this view, the social boundary and the territorial border of the nation are imagined to be coterminous.[36]

36. See Didier Fassin, "Policing Borders, Producing Boundaries: The Governmentality of Immigration in Dark Times," *Annual Review of Anthropology* 40 (2011): 213–26. As Fassin notes, until recently, "borders were generally viewed as territorial limits defining political entities (states, in particular) and legal subjects (most notably, citizens), whereas boundaries were principally considered to be social constructs establishing symbolic differences (between class, gender, or race) and producing identities (national, ethnic, or cultural communities)." Social scientists pried these categories apart in order to correct classical anthropological studies that reified the

When territorial borders and social boundaries interact in these ways, people's anxieties about the boundaries of their social group can be reflected in their attempts to fortify their territorial borders. The white residents of a neighborhood may engage in discriminatory policies and practices to prevent people of color from moving into their neighborhood. Nation-states may build border walls and fences to keep immigrants and refugees from entering the country.[37] Many of the activities that take place at and along territorial

---

coincidence of territorial borders and social, cultural, or linguistic boundaries. According to Fassin, this reification should indeed be challenged, but not at the expense of analysis of the interaction of border and boundaries. The idea of the nation-state depends on the fiction of a people perfectly coterminous with and sovereign over a land. And because nation-states are imagined as territorially bounded social groups, the type of analysis on which Fassin insists is particularly important to understanding immigration, in which both territorial border and social boundary are traversed. Fassin writes, "In effect, immigrants embody the articulation of borders and boundaries, even beyond what is generally assumed by the studies of transnationalism (Kearney 1991). They cross borders to settle in a new society and discover boundaries through the differential treatment to which they are submitted" (215).

37. Such anxieties about border and boundary crossing are not hard to find in contemporary U.S. politics. We can identify the connection between border crossing and perceived threat in xenophobic immigration politics in the United States, in which immigration is characterized as a transgression of the border, and that transgression is characterized as a threat to the United States itself. Those who share this view describe immigrants, or those seeking refuge or asylum, as carriers of disease and agents of disorder. President Donald Trump played on this anxiety and perception of threat when he claimed that Democrats want to allow immigrants to "pour into and infect" the United States (Brooke Seipel, "Trump: Dems Want Illegal Immigrants to 'Infest Our Country,'" *The Hill*, June 19, 2018, https://thehill.com /homenews/administration/392977-trump-dems-want-illegal-immigrants-to -infest-our-country). Trump's statement gave voice to the very connection that Douglas names: the anxiety that the failure to prevent border violations will invite pollution and danger. Immigrants, this line of thought suggests, threaten the health of the country. Those who are convinced by this rallied around Trump's call for border walls and fences, physical barriers that do little to deter people trying to cross the border but that symbolize its inviolability. For one explanation of this phenomenon, see Wendy Brown, *Walled States, Waning Sovereignty* (New York: Zone Books, 2010). Brown argues that the urge to build border walls and fences is a psychological re-

borders are social practices. They are complex, shared, and norm-governed activities that create and distribute goods and ills. The U.S.-Mexico border is built, policed, crossed, protested, and imagined through social practices. The border fence and border wall, for instance, both symbolize and enact the edges of the territory and the group, regulating goods that include entry, access, membership, and rights. Fences, walls, checkpoints, and border policing are among the things that create and maintain the borders and boundaries of the nation-state; these things do not merely reflect the reality of those borders and boundaries as if they were separate from the practices that uphold them. Anxieties about border crossings are not only about territorial movement but also—and perhaps more importantly—about social boundaries.

It is not incidental, then, that nation-states have rituals in place for regulating their borders and boundaries. Naturalization ceremonies, for example, are formalized routines and rituals in which people take the oath that makes them citizens. This legal status—citizen—comes with social and political entitlements and obligations. Entrance into the group is regulated legally, to be sure, but also enacted in and through this rite of passage in which people become citizens. Likewise, in diasporic communities, where the community is connected to a spiritual or cultural homeland, even as its members no longer reside within the territorial borders of that homeland, rituals can affirm and enforce the *social* significance of a boundary that encloses a territorially dispersed people and binds them together. Rituals regulate access to or belonging in the diasporic religious community, creating what N. Fadeke Castor calls "spiritual citizenship." Among Ifá and Orisha practitioners in Trinidad and beyond, Castor argues, participation in initiation rituals as well as ongoing practices of prayer, offerings,

---

sponse to the anxiety of diminishing nation-state sovereignty. However, Brown's work, while compelling in many respects, does not account for the diverse responses that people have to these walls and fences. While some rally around the call for border walls, others enact posadas and border Eucharists to protest it.

ceremonies, and festivals create and distribute "the rights and responsibilities of belonging to community, informed by spiritual epistemologies."[38] Spiritual citizenship works alongside—and against—the categories of legal citizenship that mark inclusion and exclusion from a territorially bounded nation-state.[39]

That the borders and boundaries of nation-states and diasporic communities are both policed and contested through rituals should not come as a surprise. After all, rituals move people across boundaries and, as they do, they distribute the goods and ills that come with being a member of a community (or not). But these things are often contested—not least through the adaptation and innovation of rituals. The Posada sin Fronteras takes place at the U.S.-Mexico border fence, and it refuses the rituals and symbols associated with that fence. It aims to realize a different community, with different borders, and different ways of crossing them. The goods it seeks to distribute—neighbor-love, hospitality—are different from those that its participants see as characteristic of the militarized border and contemporary immigration politics. The Posada sin Fronteras does its own kind of boundary work at the nation-state border, even as its alternate vision of community remains incompletely realized. It is, as its participants note, an *incomplete* posada.

In the past decade, there has been a proliferation of what have been called "border Eucharists," enactments of the Eucharist or communion service at the U.S.-Mexico border. Mostly performed by Episcopal and Roman Catholic priests, they have taken place at various sites along the border fence, as well as in the middle of the Rio Grande River, in shallow crossings where the two countries meet. One such border Eucharist took place on April 1, 2014. A group of Roman Catholic bishops led by Cardinal Sean O'Malley gathered in Nogales, Arizona, to tour the U.S.-Mexico border area

38. N. Fadeke Castor, *Spiritual Citizenship: Transnational Pathways from Black Power to Ifá in Trinidad* (Durham: Duke University Press, 2017), 6.

39. Castor, *Spiritual Citizenship*, 6.

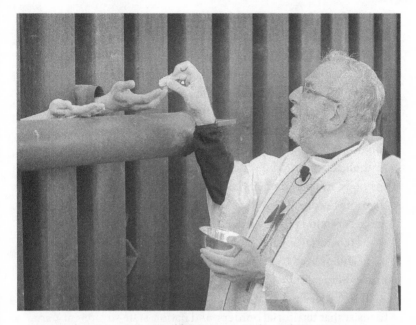

FIGURE 2.1. Most Rev. Gerald F. Kicanas, Bishop of Tucson, passes a communion wafer through the slats of the U.S.-Mexico border fence in Nogales, Arizona, to worshippers on the Mexican side, April 1, 2014. (AP Photo/Matt York)

and to celebrate Mass in remembrance of the thousands of migrants who have died while trying to cross the border. The bishops stood on the U.S. side of the border fence as Mexican and U.S. American lay Catholics gathered on either side. There was a reading of the parable of the Good Samaritan, and Cardinal O'Malley gave a homily that reflected on a Christian ethos of neighbor-love and hospitality that transcends territorial borders. O'Malley, along with the Most Reverend Gerald F. Kicanas, Bishop of Tucson, celebrated the Eucharist with all of those assembled, passing communion wafers between the slats of the border fence to those waiting, hands outstretched, on the other side.

In many respects, this border Eucharist was a typical celebration of the sacrament. The Mass followed the usual routine and order of the service. The Eucharist, as part of the Roman Catholic Mass, also followed the usual order. It was the setting that seemed dramatically different from the usual one and that highlighted its political significance. When the communion wafer and wine are distributed between the slats of a fence that physically divides the faithful, something that is *always* true of the Mass is made explicit: namely, that the sacrament enacts a community that transcends this-worldly borders and boundaries. According to the Roman Catholic tradition, the wafer and wine of the Eucharist become the body and blood of Christ. In and through the sacrament, participants become the Body of Christ, and God's grace is manifest in the community. The border Eucharist did not contest the reality of the territorial border, or of the social boundaries that are caught up in and policed by that border. But it did insist on the ultimacy of another reality.

The border Eucharist worked at and around the border fence to insist that territorial borders, and nation-state sovereignty, are penultimate. The sovereignty of God and the reality of God's grace, it suggested, not only transcend the nation-state border. They also transgress it, literally passing through the fence that aims to limit and separate. Hands reached through the border fence, demonstrating its porousness; the wafer and wine of the Eucharist, understood to be the body and blood of Christ, were carried from one side to another. In crossing the nation-state border, those hands and that Eucharistic offering were also enacting a community unbound by that particular border and fence. They enacted and embodied another kind of community, another set of social roles and obligations, and called for the justice of that other community to be realized at the border. The enactment of the ritual moved its participants and witnesses to imagine—and to enact—the U.S.-Mexico border crossing as community creation, as neighbor-love, hospitality, and calling.

Lest anyone imagine that the border Eucharist is a performance and celebration of open borders, let us remember that the ritual enacts its own set of boundaries. First, in the Roman Catholic Church, there are norms about who is allowed to participate in the

Eucharist and who is not. Those who have not been baptized, those who have been excommunicated, those who do not believe in the real presence of Christ in the bread and wine, and those who have not confessed and atoned for their sins according to the norms and practices of the Roman Catholic Church are among the people who are not invited to participate in the sacrament, whether in its traditional church setting or in its extraordinary border-crossing setting. Sometimes, rules about who is allowed to partake in the sacrament become explicitly entangled with nation-state governance and electoral politics, as with ongoing debates over whether politicians who support abortion rights ought to be denied communion.[40] These norms about who can and cannot participate regulate a boundary around the group—Roman Catholics—that is enacted and enforced in and through ritual action. They regulate *who* has *what* obligations and entitlements.

Second, the border Eucharist displays and performs some of the *internal* boundaries of the Roman Catholic Church. It is the all-male members of the priesthood who preach and who administer the sacrament to the laity. The distinctions here—between priests and laity, between men and women—are part of the internal social structure of the Church. The differential distribution of authority within the Church depends on these distinctions. This enactment of the Eucharist follows and reiterates those distinctions and internal boundaries.

Understanding the border Eucharist—as a sacrament, as a protest, and as a kind of boundary work—requires that we attend to the groups that are defined and contested by that ritual. What are their norms? How are they structured? And how are the people within those groups—the United States and the Roman Catholic Church, for instance—creating and contesting these borders and boundaries? Just as it is the case that not all U.S. Americans support

40. In June 2021, the U.S. Conference of Catholic Bishops took up this question once again and voted to draft a formal statement "on the meaning of the Eucharist in the life of the Church," intended, in part, to sanction President Joe Biden, who is Roman Catholic, for his position on abortion and reproductive rights.

the construction of the U.S.-Mexico border wall, not all Roman Catholics support the border Eucharist. Do enactments of the Eucharist at the border instrumentalize the sacrament to make a political point? And, to another side, are the boundaries created and maintained by border Eucharists, with their own inclusions, exclusions, and differential distributions of power, unjust in their own right? Should this act even *count* as an enactment of the ritual? Should it serve as precedent for future enactments?

Territorial borders and social boundaries are not fictions, but neither are they natural facts. Borders and boundaries are created and maintained in and through people's social practices. They are enacted when people name them, mark them, police them, and create, follow, and enforce rules for traversing them. At the territorial borders of nation-states, some of the most significant of these practices are legal and military. At other kinds of borders and boundaries—such as the invisible (but no less real) boundary around the members of a religious community—these practices also include rituals such as participation in rites of passage and recitation of liturgies. Like all social practices, those that create and maintain borders and boundaries are norm-governed. And like all norms, those that govern the creation and maintenance of borders and boundaries are contestable. We have in our midst multiple boundaries, norms, and practices, some of which reinforce one another and others of which call one another into question. The debates and disagreements within groups about what their boundaries ought to be and how they ought to be regulated are matched by the contestation among groups when borders and boundaries are drawn in intersecting, conflicting, and contrasting ways.

Rituals are among the social practices that create and maintain the borders and boundaries that delimit and structure communities. These borders and boundaries can be good or bad, just or unjust. It is up to the people who participate in rituals and other social practices to decide which enactments they will take up, and therefore which borders and boundaries they aim to make a reality.

3

Performing and Recognizing Authority

ON JULY 29, 1974, eleven women knelt at the altar of an Episcopal church in Philadelphia, Pennsylvania, waiting to receive the blessing and laying on of hands that would ordain them as priests in a denomination that did not recognize the legitimacy of that act.[1]

For many years, supporters of women's ordination had been working within the governing structures of the Episcopal Church to raise the issue of ordination and to move toward the inclusion of women in the priesthood. Those in power had sputtered and stalled. In December 1973—six months before the ordination service in Philadelphia—five women who were deacons in the Church decided to publicize their situation. They joined five men, who had become deacons at the same time as the women and were then eligible for the priesthood, in an ordination service at the Cathedral Church of St. John the Divine in New York City. In that soaring and dramatic setting, the women staged an act of protest and political theater by participating in the men's ordination service.

---

1. The following account of the ordination of the Philadelphia Eleven draws on Darlene O'Dell's *The Story of the Philadelphia Eleven* (New York: Seabury Books, 2014), and newspaper articles written at the time of the ordination in the *Philadelphia Inquirer, Philadelphia Tribune, New York Times,* and *Washington Post.*

The women, the male ordinands, and the ordaining bishop had devised a plan for the service. The women were to participate in the service up until, but not including, the final blessing and act of consecration known as the laying on of hands. They would begin with the Oath of Conformity, in which ordinands pledge their loyalty to the Church and their obedience to its canons and to the priests and bishops in positions of authority.[2] All of the deacons, both male and female, would take the oath, but while the men's voices would be amplified to the congregation over a loudspeaker, the women's voices would be intentionally silenced. The group would process together to the nave, where the men would be presented individually and the women as a group. When the ordaining bishop asked whether anyone knew of a reason why the ordination ought not to proceed, one of the women, Carter Heyward, would read a prepared statement calling for the ordination of women. Finally, when it came time for the blessing and consecration of the new priests, the women would step back while the men completed their ordination.

When the day came, the ordination service proceeded according to the agreed-upon plan until that final moment. But it was at that point that the women diverged from the plan. Rather than stepping back, they remained in place, kneeling and waiting for the bishop's blessing and his hand on their heads. Instead, he passed over them and said, "Go in peace." The women turned and, joined by many members of the congregation, walked out of the cathedral. They were not ordained that day, but in that theatrical ordination service they had laid bare the power relations between men and women in the Episcopal Church, making the disparity audible and visible to their audience.

Because women were ineligible for the priesthood—and thus could not become bishops either—they were dramatically underrepresented in the governing bodies of the Episcopal Church, the very bodies that had the power to officially recognize or reject

2. See *Book of Common Prayer* (New York: Oxford University Press, 1928).

women's ordination.[3] And because women could not serve in the role of priest or bishop, they were normally excluded from active and visible participation in ordination services, except as congregants and, occasionally, deacons. As a result, this dynamic, in which men held the power to make decisions that affected women without those women having concomitant authority or the power to hold the male decision makers accountable, was obscured in ordinary ordination services. The ordination service at St. John the Divine in December 1973 was intended to make that unjust exclusion visible by displaying how women were rendered silent and invisible in the Church hierarchy.

Less than a year later, eleven women, including some of those who had participated in the service at St. John the Divine, were once again kneeling before an altar rail in an ordination service. And this time, the ritual performance would not be merely theatrical; they *would* be ordained. The governing bodies of the Episcopal Church still did not recognize women's ordination as legitimate, and the bishops in the women's own dioceses were not willing to ordain them. Instead, the women planned an unauthorized ordination service at the Church of the Advocate in Philadelphia, a church whose rector, Paul Washington, was a powerful civil rights advocate, friend of the Black Power movement, and supporter

3. The two legislative bodies of the Episcopal Church are the House of Bishops and the House of Deputies. The House of Bishops consists of active and retired bishops. The House of Deputies consists of eight delegates from each of the dioceses, four of whom are lay leaders and four of whom are clergy. Before the ordination of women was recognized by the Episcopal Church, women could only serve as delegates to the House of Deputies; the House of Bishops was all male. The two houses must reach consensus for legislative changes to be made. Moreover, within the House of Deputies, changes to canon require a "vote by orders" in which the votes of the lay and clerical orders are counted separately. Each diocese can cast a single vote in each order and a majority of dioceses must vote in favor in *each* order for a motion to pass. Because women were structurally excluded from the House of Bishops and, largely, from the clerical order (some women did serve as deacons), they were dramatically underrepresented in the legislature.

of women's ordination. Three bishops who had also been vocal supporters of women's ordination agreed to participate as the ordaining bishops.

On the morning of July 29, 1974, the eleven women gathered at the Church of the Advocate for the service. They donned the white robes and colorful stoles of the clergy and, in the basement of the church, signed the Oath of Conformity. Upstairs in the main sanctuary, Rev. Washington spoke to the nearly two thousand people who had assembled for the service. When he finished speaking, the women entered the sanctuary and proceeded to the altar. Members of the church had decorated the altar with a frontal that featured a paraphrase of Galatians 3:28: "In Christ there is neither male nor female, bond nor free, Jew nor Gentile. We are one."[4] Dr. Charles Willie, vice president of the House of Deputies, professor of sociology, and a friend of Rev. Dr. Martin Luther King Jr., gave a sermon that drew a parallel between the civil rights movement and the women's movement. Echoing Dr. King's justification for civil disobedience in the "Letter from Birmingham Jail," Dr. Willie argued that "a law which demeans personhood is a law unworthy of obeying." His implication was that the exclusion of women from the Episcopal priesthood was just such a law and, therefore, that he and others were right to disobey it. Then, those who opposed the ordination had an opportunity to speak: "If there be any of you who knoweth any impediment, or notable crime [in the ordinands], let him come forth in the name of God and show what the crime or impediment is."[5] Several priests approached the chancel steps to argue against the ordination. One opposing priest, the Rev. George Rutler, compared the women's ordination to the work of the devil, saying, "God here now as father and judge sees you trying to make stones into bread. You can only offer up the sound and sight and smell of perversion."[6]

4. O'Dell, *Philadelphia Eleven*, 75.

5. *Book of Common Prayer*.

6. "Eleven Women Ordained Episcopal Priests," *Diocesan Press Service*, July 31, 1974. Also see Andrew Wallace, "11 Women Are Ordained," *Philadelphia Inquirer*,

After those opposing the ordination spoke, the officiating bishops responded that they were acting in obedience to the spirit of God. One of the bishops read the epistle, and the women stood to be charged. Finally, the women knelt in front of the altar rail to receive the laying on of hands. The Rt. Rev. Daniel Corrigan placed his hand on the forehead of the first ordinand, Jeannette Piccard. Nearly one hundred other bishops and priests (including some Roman Catholic priests) stood beside and around Bishop Corrigan, encircling Piccard and participating in the laying on of hands. Bishop Corrigan recited the liturgical blessing and greeted Piccard as a newly ordained priest in the Episcopal Church. As each of the women was ordained in turn, she joined the other priests and bishops in participating in the ordination of the remaining women. At the end of the service, the women—who came to be known as the "Philadelphia Eleven"—held the communion cup together for those who knelt at the altar rail, acting on the authority seized in the ordination by administering the Eucharist.

At the Church of the Advocate, the Philadelphia Eleven and their ordaining bishops enacted a ritual. They followed the sequence of acts constituting ordination, as written in the *Book of Common Prayer*. But that ritual, in and through which ordinands

---

July 30, 1974, 1-A. In a profile published a few days after the ordination, one of the ordinands, Suzanne Hiatt, attributed the resistance to women's ordination to the association of women with magic and witchcraft: "According to Ms. Hiatt, what differentiates a priest from a deacon is the performance of the magical duties of the church, the consecration of the sacrament and the giving of blessing and absolutions. 'This may sound ridiculous in today's enlightened society,' she says with a smile, 'but on the visceral level many people still fear that when you mix women and magic you get witchcraft.'" Hiatt's comment fascinates me, not least because of the care with which early anthropologists of religion sought to distinguish between ritual and magic, tacitly legitimating the former and disparaging the latter. To further connect this distinction to gender, and to see legitimate "ritual" as the realm of male ritual experts, adds another layer of complexity to the problems that have attended efforts to conceptualize "ritual" as a category distinct from magic. See Julia Cass, "Philadelphia's Woman Priest Talks about Her Defiance," *Philadelphia Inquirer*, August 4, 1974, 1-D.

FIGURE 3.1. Eleven women kneel at the altar of Church of the Advocate in Philadelphia during their ordination to the priesthood in the Episcopal Church, July 29, 1974. (Courtesy of The Archives of the Episcopal Church)

acquire the status and authority of priests, was not written for them. As women, the Philadelphia Eleven were not *supposed* to become priests; at the time, that role was still reserved for men. By enacting the ritual, however, the Philadelphia Eleven claimed a status and authority that had not been granted to them in advance of their act. Afterward, the House of Bishops declared the ordinations irregular and disciplined the participating bishops. It instructed the Philadelphia Eleven to refrain from acting as priests. For the most part, however, the women ignored the instruction. After their ordinations, the Philadelphia Eleven led services, gave blessings, and administered the sacrament.

How can a ritual—particularly a ritual that isn't supposed to be "for" the people who enact it—create new power relations and authority structures?

The struggle for women's ordination took place against the backdrop of social and political challenges to traditional gender norms, as second-wave feminists in the 1960s and 1970s demanded control of their own bodies, careers, and lives. These broader challenges set the stage for women's ordination in the Episcopal Church, and the reasons for that change—at *that* moment, in *that* religious tradition—are myriad. But my interest here is in the ordination service itself: how the Philadelphia Eleven claimed and enacted the authority of priests in and through the ritual, and how their priesthood depended on that act of claiming and enacting—and others' recognition of it.

One very important sort of authority, and the kind that I have in mind here, is the entitlement to hold and exercise power of one or another kind. "Authority," in this sense, is a normative term that not only describes a power relation but also expresses a judgment about it. To say that someone has authority in some domain is to say that they rightfully have power in that domain—a power that others ought to recognize and obey. Other things being equal, a parent or guardian has authority over matters pertaining to childrearing within a family. They have the legitimate power to make decisions and rules affecting their child's education and well-being. And, in most cases, others recognize them as having this authority. Not every competent adult has the legitimate power to make decisions and rules of that kind for a child; that authority is reserved for the people occupying the role of parent or guardian. The authority is role specific. But it is also contingent on the parent or guardian's use of that power in the service of the child's well-being. The exercise of power cannot be abusive or arbitrary or it is no longer recognized as legitimate.[7]

---

7. A subset of authority, thus understood, is *democratic* authority. By this I mean power legitimately held and exercised by citizens embedded in relationships of reciprocal recognition and engaged in shared activities to create and sustain a more just world. See also Molly Farneth, *Hegel's Social Ethics: Religion, Conflict, and Rituals of Reconciliation* (Princeton: Princeton University Press, 2017), 115–31.

In many religious communities, as in the Episcopal Church, a person becomes a member of the clergy through ordination, gaining the obligations and entitlements that attend that role. Among these entitlements is authority in certain matters of the church, including the administration of rituals and sacraments. Now, people sometimes assume that rituals mainly reinforce the status quo, conferring authority on the authorities, enacting power for the powerful. This can be true, but it is not always so. Sometimes, as in the ordination of the Philadelphia Eleven, an enactment of a ritual can confer authority in a way that was not determined or authorized in advance. Sometimes, rituals go rogue. As we'll see, the result can be a new configuration of power or authority.

The last chapter argued that rituals regulate membership in groups, roles, and statuses and distribute goods and ills to those members. This chapter focuses on one such good—authority— and its relationship to ritual, power, and recognition. The first section situates rituals as performatives, bodily practices that bring about a change in the social world. The second section argues that the "force of the performative," that is, the success of such an act in bringing about the relevant effects, is never determined in advance of the act. Rather, it depends on practices of recognition and uptake. I explore how these practices work in cases in which rituals hail, invite, or interpellate subjects, and how people's responses to those rituals can change in response to novel enactments. The third section, then, considers how rituals can enact an authority that was not previously recognized.

Because power is among the goods that can be enacted and conferred through ritual, religious or political elites sometimes institute rituals that are intended to preserve or augment their power. The people who participate in those rituals may or may not share the judgment that the power held by those elites is legitimate (that is, that they have *authority* proper). Contestation over such rituals—whether they should be enacted, how, by whom—often concerns whether the power that the elites have to institute those rituals or the power conferred by those rituals is legitimate or illegitimate. Because rituals also invite some people's participation, and not others, contestation over rituals also concerns who should be invited to participate in the rituals that enact and distribute power and authority. In other words, contestation over rituals often concerns who holds and exercises not mere power but legitimate power.

Rituals as Performatives

Rituals that move participants across boundaries, changing their roles or statuses, and distributing goods and ills to them and others, are *performative*. By that, I don't mean that they're merely theatrical. Much to the contrary. What I mean is that they bring about a real change in the social world. As a result of an initiation ritual, someone who was not a member of the group is now a member. Or, as a result of a coronation, someone who did not have the authority of a king now does.

In this way, as I briefly discussed in chapter 1, these rituals are similar to the speech acts that Austin calls "performatives." Performatives, in Austin's narrower linguistic sense, are utterances in and through which the speaker undertakes an action. When two betrothed people utter the words "I do" in the context of a marriage ceremony, they make a vow of marriage; when the officiant declares them to be wed, the deed is complete. Or, to take one of Austin's own examples, when a captain smashes a bottle of champagne against the side of his boat and utters the words "I name this ship the *Queen Elizabeth!*" he names the boat. In each of these examples, the speaker isn't just describing or reporting on an action that is otherwise being undertaken; the speaker is, in and through their utterance, undertaking an action.

Liturgical language is often performative, as when it hails its auditors and commands their attention or action. Here's an example: "Let us pray!" Uttered by the prayer leader in the context of a worship service, this simple phrase names a group (the "us") and issues an invitation to the members of that group: it invites them to pray together. That invitation seeks a response: namely, the members' participation in the prayer. Or to take another example, consider the Jewish prayer known as the *sh'ma*: "Sh'ma Yisrael! Adonai eloheinu, Adonai echad! / Hear O' Israel! The Lord our God, the Lord is One!" The opening words of the *sh'ma* are directed to the Jewish people—*O' Israel*—both those individuals who are uttering the words of the prayer and the broader religious community of which they are a part. It hails them, and it issues a directive or command: *hear!* By uttering these words, the speakers hail and call to attention those people to whom they direct their speech act, the Jewish people. As a result of the prayer leader's utterance ("Let us pray!"), an invitation has been issued. As a result of the recitation of the *sh'ma*, a people have been hailed and called to attention.

But what is it that makes these performatives "work"? How do they change the social world?

Perhaps performatives work when they follow an agreed-upon script. If that's right, then for a performative to be felicitous, to bring about a change in the social world, it would have to follow a sequence of acts and a set of rules for enacting that sequence. This ought to call to mind the initial—and relatively formal—account of rituals' rules and routines at the outset of chapter 1. For a ritual to "work" performatively, the circumstances would have to be right, with certain conditions met. As Austin writes, "speaking generally, it is always necessary that the circumstances in which the words are uttered should be in some way, or ways, appropriate, and it is very commonly necessary that either the speaker himself or other persons should *also* perform certain *other* actions, whether 'physical' or 'mental' actions or even acts of uttering further words."[8] The two betrothed people who utter the words "I do" must do so *in the right way* and *under the right conditions* for their words to constitute the undertaking of a vow of marriage. They would have to be consenting adults, in the presence of witnesses

8. Austin, *How to Do Things with Words*, 8.

and before an officiant who is authorized to lead and sanction the ceremony. Various legal and ritual conditions would have to be met. They would have to follow the script. Only then would their utterance be felicitous.[9]

A second, and related, thought is that perhaps performatives work when the script is followed *and* the participants have been authorized in advance to enact it. If so, then in order for the utterance "Let us pray!" to have force (that is, in order for others to recognize and treat it as an invitation to prayer), the speaker would have to have been granted authority as a prayer leader. Bourdieu holds something like this position, arguing that Austin fails to see the extent to which performatives' felicity really comes down to a matter of *authority*:

> By trying to understand the power of linguistic manifestations linguistically, by looking at language for the principle underlying the logic and effectiveness of the language of institutions, one forgets that authority comes to language from outside. . . . Language at most *represents* this authority, manifests and symbolizes it.[10]

Bourdieu argues that a performative has force not because of the faithful utterance of the words of the script. That utterance merely represents and transmits the speaker's authority. A performative's force, he writes, "is nothing other than the *delegated power* of the spokesperson, and his speech—that is, the substance of his discourse and, inseparably, his way of speaking—is no more than a testimony, and one among others, of the *guarantee of delegation* which is vested in him."[11] The performative's force, the felicity of the speech act, depends not on the linguistic formula uttered by

9. Kukla, "Performative Force."

10. Pierre Bourdieu, *Language and Symbolic Power*, ed. John B. Thompson, trans. Gino Raymond and Matthew Adamson (Cambridge, MA: Harvard University Press, 1991), 109.

11. Bourdieu, *Language and Symbolic Power*, 107.

the speaker but on the social power vested in the speaker in advance of the act as well as their ability to deploy that power in recognized ways.

Thus, on Bourdieu's view, the distinction between a felicitous and an infelicitous speech act is primarily a matter of the speaker's authority. He suggests that the performative will be felicitous if it is undertaken by a person vested with the authority to undertake such acts, and it will be infelicitous if it is undertaken by a person without such authority. Bourdieu's examples are mainly ritual ones, attributing what he refers to as a "crisis" in the Roman Catholic Church to a series of changes in the priesthood and liturgy that undermine the "social magic" of that liturgy. He writes that "what is at stake in the crisis of liturgy is the whole system of conditions which must be fulfilled in order for the institution to function, i.e. the institution which authorizes and regulates the use of the liturgy and which ensures its uniformity through time and space by ensuring the conformity of those who are delegated to carry it out."[12] Bourdieu contends that changes to the Roman Catholic Church, including changes to the priesthood as a result of the Second Vatican Council, call into question the authority of the priests to carry out a liturgy capable of achieving its characteristic force.

There's something to this view. Conventions matter, and so does already-recognized authority. But there's still something missing, for Bourdieu's view is too focused on what's *static* in rituals and other performatives and, concomitantly, too invested in the idea that authority is granted in advance of the act. As Judith Butler points out, "[Bourdieu's] judgment on what is a right and wrong ritual assumes that the legitimate forms of liturgical ritual have already been established and that new forms of legitimate invocation will not come to transform and supplant the old. In fact, *the ritual that performs an infringement of the liturgy may still be the liturgy, the*

12. Bourdieu, *Language and Symbolic Power*, 115.

liturgy in its futural form."[13] The problem with Bourdieu's account, as Butler insists, is in its suggestion that legitimacy (and, thus, authority) is already given, already determined. That idea is too static, too synchronic. As I argued in chapter 1, rituals *do* involve routines and rules, but as social practices, they're also enacted over time in ways that can change the routines, the application of the rules, and the rituals' characteristic force. As people make judgments about the "rightness" of particular enactments, they consider the relevance of past precedents in new contexts. Questions about legitimacy—what constitutes a legitimate form of the ritual, who has legitimate power to enact the ritual, and so on—are always being adjudicated and adjusted, according to changing norms, novel situations, and innovative performances. An enactment of a ritual can be prefigurative, calling forth new judgments about who or what ought to be recognized or taken up as a result.[14] Authority can be claimed, performed, and recognized in and through these novel liturgical and ritualized performances.

Who is authorized to utter the words, or to sanction their utterance? What legal regimes or ritual frames govern felicity or success, and who has the power to institute or change those things? In the case of the Philadelphia Eleven, these questions were asked and answered differently by ordinands, ordaining clergy, congregants and laypeople, members of the Episcopal governing bodies, and witnesses and interested parties outside of the Church. The people, acts, and conditions that are considered to be the "right" ones can

13. Judith Butler, *Excitable Speech: A Politics of the Performative* (New York: Routledge, 1997), 147 (emphasis added).

14. Connecting the work of Judith Butler and Jacques Derrida, Amy Hollywood shows how the repetition of ritual can give rise to new possibilities for subjects and societies, since every repetition introduces (to use Derrida's term) *différance* and possible infelicities ("Performativity, Citationality, Ritualization," *History of Religions* 42.2 [2002]: 93–115). My suggestion is that rituals can also introduce such possibilities not only in their *infelicities*, or misfirings, but also in unexpected felicity, creating new power structures and social arrangements when novel performances are recognized as having performative force.

change, sometimes abruptly. And so these initial suppositions—
that performatives are felicitous only when they follow an agreed-
upon script, or only when they are enacted by those who have been
authorized in advance to do so—fall short. Instead, we need to
know when and how people *recognize* the force of rituals and other
performatives during and after their enactment.

Authority and Recognition

For a ritual to work as a performative, the right people have to
enact the right sequence of acts under the right conditions. But
the "rightness" of these things—people, acts, conditions—is
judged by multiple people with different points of view. Participants, witnesses, and others who care about the ritual can all
make determinations about whether an enactment of the ritual
gets it "right" or not. In making these determinations, they're
likely to rely on a range of criteria: their knowledge of the ritual,
of past enactments (that is, of relevant precedents), of the relative
importance of different aspects of the ritual. When they determine that the ritual gets these things basically right, they *recognize*
it as an enactment of the ritual, and they *take up* the enactment
as having changed people's obligations, entitlements, or other
normative statuses.

These judgments typically happen *after the fact*, once the ritual
is enacted. Only then can the ritual be recognized (or not) and
taken up (or not) by other people. As performatives, rituals have
to be recognized and taken up in this way, taken and treated *by
others* as having worked. As Kukla argues, the people undertaking
or affected by a performative must be understood and treated by
others as having some new status as a result of its enactment. If no
one is disposed to act any differently as a result of the enactment—
treating the betrothed as having undertaken marriage vows, for
instance, or calling the ship by the name that the captain gave it—
the performative has been infelicitous. When my mother-in-law
allowed my partner to join me at my family's Thanksgiving dinner

shortly after we decided to get married, lifting the ban effected by her "no Thanksgiving without engagement" rule, she was, in effect, "taking up" our declaration of intent to get married.[15] Had she refused to lift the ban—and had everyone else similarly refused to treat us any differently as a result of our declaration—it could have been said that the performance (i.e., our engagement) was infelicitous or unsuccessful. This is because, as Kukla puts it, successful performatives usher in new normative statuses. They mark and effect changes in people's social roles, obligations, and entitlements. As a result of our engagement, my partner and I were treated differently, as people with a new relation to one another and new social roles in one another's families, entitled to attend gatherings reserved for family members (and, it turns out, obligated to do so too!). Normative statuses are "constituted by social rituals and conventions"—rituals and conventions concerning, in this instance, marriage and kinship structures, gender and sexuality, promise-keeping, holiday celebrations—while remaining dependent on people's ongoing recognition and endorsement of those rituals and conventions that are in force.[16]

People do not know in advance of an enactment of a ritual whether it is going to work—that is, whether it will have performative force—or not. Norms and conventions evolve; sometimes, they even change suddenly, in response to a particular enactment. Someone may invoke the standard script or follow the

15. My very lovely mother-in-law really did have this rule. Kukla offers a similar example in "Performative Force," 442.

16. Kukla, "Performative Force," 443. Kukla goes on to argue that the uptake—that is, the recognition of the performative's impact on normative statuses—"is not a separable event of passive recognition of something that already finished happening . . . ; instead it is *part of* the set of events setting the conventional context for the speech act. Neither the words nor intentions have *intrinsic* constitutive force; rather, force is constituted though the deployment of conventions and rituals that typically outlast the speech act itself" (444). In other words, in order to consider a speech act (or, more broadly, any performative act) in its entirety, one has to consider the utterance or act, its context, and its social repercussions as being all of a piece.

usual sequence of acts but find that others no longer recognize her performance as having the ritual's characteristic force. A ritual can fail. Alternatively, someone may change or challenge the script or sequence but find that others recognize the performative's force nevertheless. Two Jewish men stand under a chuppah and are married "according to the laws of Moses and Israel," as the traditional Jewish marriage ceremony states. At one point, their actions under the chuppah would not have been widely recognized, or taken up, as the undertaking of marriage vows; now, in many Jewish communities, they are. Eleven women receive the priestly blessing and the laying on of hands. At one point, those acts would not have been widely recognized as the consecration of new priests; now, in the Episcopal Church, they are. In both of these instances, the context in which the ritual took place was a changing one and the norms that governed that context (and, relatedly, that governed the ritual) were shifting. The enactment of the ritual, in a new context, with new norms at play, was recognized and taken up in novel ways. As a result, people who had not had access to certain obligations, entitlements, and authority claimed and enacted them. Gay men were married. Episcopal women became priests.

Debates about who is invited or authorized to perform or participate in rituals are rather common. As performatives, rituals' felicity depends on people's sense that the conditions for performance of the ritual have been satisfied, but judgments about *that* depend on norms and conventions that are often contestable and in flux. In performative acts of hailing, inviting, and interpellating, the role of judgment, recognition, and uptake is relatively clear, so let's take those as our examples for a moment. Each of these acts—hailing, inviting, and interpellating—involves people being called to participate in some norm-governed role or activity. And each of them can succeed or fail at (1) being judged and recognized as a call, and (2) being taken up in the way invited by the call. Let's see how.

In *'Yo!' and 'Lo!': The Pragmatic Topography of the Space of Reasons*, Kukla and Mark Lance draw out the pragmatic structure of a category of speech acts that call on others. They refer to these as "vocatives." Vocatives, Kukla and Lance write, "are hails. To utter a vocative is to *call* another person—in calling out 'Hello, Eli!,' I recognize the fact that that person there is Eli and I do so by calling upon him to recognize that he has been properly recognized."[17] A vocative, then, hails a person or a group. In doing so, it *recognizes* that person or group—recognizing Eli *as* Eli, for instance—and then calls him, inviting his response. Eli can *recognize* the call as directed to him, or not. As Kukla and Lance note, the invited response is the person's or group's acknowledgment that they have been properly recognized.

Vocatives shape the identities of the people to whom they are directed. When a person hails someone or something, they are not only recognizing the already-existing identity of that person or thing; they are also contributing to the creation or constitution of that identity within particular social structures. This is what Louis Althusser calls "interpellation." He writes:

> Ideology "acts" or "functions" in such a way that it "recruits" subjects among the individuals . . . or "transforms" the individuals into subjects . . . by that very precise operation which I have called *interpellation* or hailing, and which can be imagined along the lines of the most commonplace everyday police (or other) hailing, "Hey, you there!" Assuming that the theoretical scene I have imagined takes place in the street, the hailed individual will turn round. By this mere one-hundred-and-eighty-degree physical conversion, he becomes a *subject*. Why? Because he has recognized that the hail was "really" addressed to him, and that "he was *really him* who was hailed" (and not someone else).[18]

17. Rebecca Kukla and Mark Lance, *'Yo!' and 'Lo!': The Pragmatic Topography of the Space of Reasons* (Cambridge, MA: Harvard University Press, 2009), 138.

18. Louis Althusser, "Ideology and Ideological State Apparatuses: Notes towards an Investigation," in *Lenin and Philosophy and Other Essays*, trans. Ben Brewster (London: New Left Books, 1971), 174. This brings to mind comedian Demetri Martin's

Althusser argues that ideologies, through everyday rituals of inter-pellation such as greeting someone or shaking hands, constitute individuals as subjects. Gender ideologies—including roles and norms concerning what genders are and what people of different genders ought to do or be like—hail or interpellate us from birth. "It's a girl!" calls out the doctor, and the nurse swaddles the baby in the pink blanket.[19] "She's beautiful!" say the admiring visitors to the hospital room or birthing center. And on it goes.

Hailing, inviting, and interpellating are not only accomplished through speech acts. They can also be accomplished though bodily movements and gestures. At the end of my daughter's dental ap-pointment, her dental hygienist opens the drawer filled with tooth-brushes, spends a moment picking through them for all of the ones with princesses on them, and holds those out to my daughter to choose from. Nothing is said, except maybe "Have a toothbrush!" but the act both *expresses* a set of gender-related norms and expec-tations and *interpellates* my daughter as the kind of girl that the hygienist expects her to be. Speech, gestures, and rituals can all hail, invite, and interpellate in this way.

Liturgical language—"Let us pray!" or "Hear, O' Israel!"—can hail its auditors, calling to a person or group. In doing so, it also interpellates them, casting them as the people it calls on them to be and constituting them as subjects in a particular social struc-ture. Althusser would describe this as *ideology* constituting sub-jects through ritual. Those hails constitute individuals *as* Chris-

---

quip: "I was on the street. This guy waved to me, and he came up to me and said, 'I'm sorry, I thought you were someone else.' And I said, 'I am.'" Of course, Althusser's example is that of the police "hailing" a subject; the role of state power in processes of subjectification is crucial for him.

19. Judith Butler famously points to the doctor's pronouncement "It's a girl!" as a performative act constituting the baby as a (gendered) subject: "The doctor who receives the child and pronounces—'It's a girl'—begins that long string of interpel-lations by which the girl is transitively gendered: *gender is ritualistically repeated* whereby repetition occasions both the risk of failure and the congealed effect of sedimentation." *Excitable Speech*, 49 (emphasis added).

tians or *as* Jews of a certain sort, in accordance with a particular ideological formation and set of roles and norms. They also constitute the collection of people so hailed as a group. Althusser notes that this process involves both recognition and *mis*recognition: recognition of the fittingness of the hail, along with misrecognition of the broader ideological system that is constituted and maintained through these rituals.

But if we think of interpellation as performative, we might consider that it, like other performatives, may be felicitous or infelicitous, successful or unsuccessful. Althusser's account of interpellation does not leave very much room for the infelicitous act of interpellation. He insists that the hail provokes a response—that the "Hey, you there!" prompts the 180-degree turn. But is that always so? Could it be that the subject who is hailed plays a more active role in determining the felicity of the hailing than Althusser suggests? A hail calls for a response—namely, an acknowledgment of the fittingness of the hail. This response or acknowledgment is not a mere confirmation; as Kukla and Lance note, it is a "(more or less) explicit *taking on* of the normative status and responsibilities demanded of one by a given speech act."[20] If the congregants respond to the "Let us pray!" by joining in prayer, in addition to whatever else that act does, they are taking on the normative status and responsibilities of being included in the "us," and of being the invitee. "Because acknowledgement involves *recognizing* that a normative status has been imputed to me appropriately, along with expressing my acceptance of that status, the acknowledgement is itself another type of *recognitive* speech act. Here, though, what is recognized is not a fact or an object or a subject, but, in the first instance, the *force of a normative claim*."[21] My daughter might reply to the hygienist's "Have a toothbrush!" by looking past her into the drawer and responding, "Can I have the Batman one?" She would be rejecting the hygienist's interpellation of her as a

20. Kukla and Lance, *'Yo!' and 'Lo!'* 145.
21. Kukla and Lance, *'Yo!' and 'Lo!'* 148.

pink-loving, princess-admiring girl, refusing to take on the implied normative status.[22]

Kukla and Lance offer another example: the call-and-response structure of testifying, as when a preacher calls out "God is great!" and the congregants reply, "Amen!"[23] The preacher's normative claim "God is great!" carries with it an implicit invitation to respond in affirmation. The congregants' "Amen!" responds to the preacher's claim and its implied invitation with their endorsement. But, once again, there is nothing necessary about that endorsement. A preacher who isn't "in the spirit" might hear more silence than amens. The congregants can reject the preacher's performative act, declining its implied invitation and refusing to take up the force of the normative claim.

The congregants' "Amen!" is what Kukla and Lance call a recognitive speech act. It *acknowledges* the claim made by the original speaker (the preacher's "God is great!") and *recognizes* the performative force of that speech act. It takes up the original speech act, answering its call and responding in kind. Kukla and Lance write, "An acknowledgment in our sense never merely notes a change in normative status—it has to enact or express the uptake of the claim made by the speech act."[24] The original speech act is not only a declaration or report but also a call for recognition; the response enacts that recognition.

These acts—hailing, inviting, and interpellating—are closely connected and perhaps not entirely separable. To *hail* someone is to call to them and to invite them to respond as someone in particular, someone located in a particular social and historical

<hr>

22. James Martel explores the idea that people might show up when they are not the ones being interpellated. If my younger child walks over to the dental hygienist while she's holding out the princess toothbrushes, admiring them and grabbing one for himself, he is responding to a call that was not meant for him. Martel's point is that this kind of misinterpellation has radical anarchic potential. See Martel, *The Misinterpellated Subject* (Durham: Duke University Press, 2017).

23. Kukla and Lance, *'Yo!' and 'Lo!'* 145.

24. Kukla and Lance, *'Yo!' and 'Lo!'* 151.

context. That involves *recognizing* them as that particular someone in that particular context. To recognize someone, and to hail them as that someone, is also to *interpellate* them, to call on them to be the someone that one has recognized them as being. As people interpellated into ideological systems, we are often constituted in ways that constrain our imagination for other ways of being. Who and what we recognize are determined, *in part*, by commitments, assumptions, and ideologies that limit our ability to see, say, a woman as a duly authorized priest. But that's not to say that we're entirely bound by the roles into which we're interpellated. Interpellation can be ignored, corrected, refused, or resignified. This is as true in ritual as it is in ordinary speech. A prayer leader who says "Let us pray!" may have a particular "us" in mind, but the people who hear those words need not show up or respond as that "us." Sometimes unexpected people show up. Sometimes the expected people show up but respond in an unexpected way. And if the force of the performative depends on the context, the act itself, and the uptake of that act, then that force also depends on whether and how it is taken up *this* time, in *this* context, by *these* people. This is a dialectical and diachronic account of ritual. It suggests that the authority to perform a ritual, or to have one's role or status conferred or changed through such a ritual, depends on practices of recognition.

Enacting Authority, Provoking Recognition

"Authority," as I suggested earlier, refers not only to power but to *legitimate* power. When people make claims about who or what legitimately or rightfully holds and exercises power, they are making normative judgments. Judgments about whether someone or something has legitimate power in some area are subject to disagreement and contestation. Sometimes religious or political elites institute rituals that are intended to preserve or augment their own power. The people who participate in those rituals may or may not share the judgment that the power held by those elites is legitimate. Their willingness to engage in the ritual, or to recognize authority as having been conferred in and through the ritual, may depend on those judgments. Disputes over such rituals often have to do with whether the power that the elites have to institute those rituals and the power relations supported by those rituals are legitimate or illegitimate.

In other cases, a performance of a ritual might involve enacting authority that has previously been denied and calling on witnesses to recognize the legitimacy of that enactment. Something like this is what happened in the history of women's ordination in the Episcopal Church. The ordination ceremony at St. John the Divine—in which women participated but were *not* ordained— dramatized the power differential between men and women in the Episcopal Church and suggested that women's exclusion from governing bodies and positions of authority within the Church was unjust. The women's voices were silenced, symbolizing their exclusion from those decision-making bodies. The women were presented as a group, rather than as individuals, representing the Church's treatment of women as a group rather than as particular individuals with their own vocations and callings. And, perhaps most powerfully, the women knelt alongside their male colleagues in front of the male bishop who ordained the men and passed the women by.

The ordination of the Philadelphia Eleven a few months later not only displayed the existing relations of exclusion and marginalization but also enacted women's authority. In response to the recognitive and distributive injustices of their exclusion, the ordained women claimed a power not-yet-granted to them by the Church through acts that called for recognition and uptake. They claimed the power that was their due, a power that came to be recognized as legitimate in and through the performance itself. This enactment of authority could have failed if the power that was exercised was not recognized as legitimate. But it did not. Instead, it embodied a new model of authority within the Church, invited witnesses to take up the new normative statuses issued to the women, and began the long (and still ongoing) labor of realizing those power relations in the world.[25]

In this way, rituals can prefigure new social or political arrangements. Some theorists of ritual argue that rituals create a subjunctive or "as if" world, a kind of agreed-upon social world that is temporary and constructed.[26] Rituals can and do create such worlds, but novel performances of rituals can help actually *bring about* a world that is not-yet by calling on witnesses to recognize and take up new entitlements, obligations, statuses, and relations—to be surprised or moved or provoked into recognizing something new.

We can see this dynamic in the ritual innovations and experimentations among Black Catholics in the United States in the late 1960s and 1970s. In the wake of the Second Vatican Council and alongside the civil rights and Black Power movements, some Black Catholics began to integrate elements of African and African American religious practices into traditional Catholic worship, creating new and contested liturgies.[27] One service, known as the Black Unity Mass, took place at St. Dorothy Church in Chicago in

25. Cameron Partridge argues that the ordination ceremony was an enactment of "gender irregularity" that destabilized the gender binary by claiming for women power traditionally reserved for men. This connects to the discussion in chapter 2 of same-sex marriage ceremonies as disrupting not only (hetero)sexual norms but also gender norms by displaying and enacting a different set of symbols and relations. See Partridge, "Toward an 'Irregular' Embrace: The Philadelphia Ordinations and Transforming Ideas of the Human," in *Looking Forward, Looking Backward: Forty Years of Women's Ordination*, ed. Fredrica Harris Thompsett (New York: Morehouse Publishing, 2014), 131–41.

26. See, for instance, Adam B. Seligman et al., *Ritual and Its Consequences: An Essay on the Limits of Sincerity* (Oxford: Oxford University Press, 2008).

27. Matthew J. Cressler offers an excellent account of these liturgical innovations, especially in the context of the Black Power movement in Chicago. See Cressler, "Vatican II, Black Power, and the Emergence of Black Catholic Liturgies," *U.S. Catholic Historian* 32.4 (Fall 2014): 99–119, and *Authentically Black and Truly Catholic: The Rise of Black Catholicism in the Great Migration* (New York: New York University Press, 2017), esp. 135–50.

1969. Incorporating African American spirituals, drums and dancing, African fabrics and vestments, the Mass enacted a particularism that belied the supposed universalism of traditional Catholic Mass and structure. At the time, a coalition of Black Catholic Chicagoans, white Catholic allies, and secular Black Power organizations were demanding that the cardinal appoint Black priests to positions of power in the archdiocese. The Black Unity Mass emerged from members of that coalition and their demands, a protest of the power structures of the Roman Catholic Church in Chicago and beyond.

The participants in the Black Unity Mass and other similar rituals produced a Black Catholic liturgy that they had not been "authorized" by the Catholic hierarchy to produce. Black Catholic liturgist Father Clarence Rivers describes how these liturgies claimed and enacted Black Catholics' authority, despite their limited representation in positions of power within the Church. As Matthew J. Cressler writes:

> In his 1974 book *Soulfull Worship*, Father Rivers recalled that "unauthorized" black liturgies began to appear following the inaugural publication of *Freeing the Spirit* [a periodical focused on Black Catholic liturgy] and how "this upset some of the bishops." Rivers' response was telling. "Of course, if we were going to do anything about black Liturgy in the Roman Catholic Church in the United States it had to be *'unauthorized' presently*," he pointed out, "since nobody in authority was black." Rivers elaborated on this point later in an answer to his rhetorical question "Where, indeed, does true authority lie in the matter of authentic Afro-American Catholic worship?" While acknowledging that the first authority in matters of worship lies with the bishops, Rivers repeated the blunt fact that "no *present* group of bishops with ordinary authority in the United States are competent judges of what is authentically Afro-American." Rivers hoped that when bishops realized "that blacks themselves must ultimately decide on their own authen-

ticity as blacks, the bishops must find a way of sharing their Catholic authority with blacks."[28]

Father Rivers initially describes Black liturgy as "unauthorized presently," in the sense that the white Catholics who occupied positions of power had neither authored nor authorized them in advance of their enactment by Black Catholic Chicagoans. Like the Philadelphia Eleven, who began their ordination by signing the Oath of Conformity and affirming the authority of Episcopal bishops, Rivers affirms the authority of the Catholic hierarchy *even as he insists* that its authority is incomplete or, he implies, not entirely legitimate without the meaningful inclusion and participation of Black Americans in the governing structure of the Church.

In the Black Unity Mass, as in the ordination of the Philadelphia Eleven, people performed a ritual in and through which they claimed and enacted authority that had not yet been granted but was nevertheless their due. Rivers's insistence that "no present group of bishops" was in a position to judge the authority of Black rituals is an insistence that the Black Unity Mass is prefigurative, enacting authority in ritual as a way of claiming it and calling it into being. It is, as Butler might put it, ritual in its "futural form."

Conclusion

The histories of women's ordination in the Episcopal Church and of Black Catholic liturgical innovation provide two extraordinary examples of how rituals engage the politics of authority.[29] In both cases, people drew on existing rituals to display unequal and unjust

28. Cressler, "Vatican II, Black Power, and the Emergence of Black Catholic Liturgies," 117–18 (emphasis added).

29. One might also consider early same-sex marriage ceremonies, in which couples and officiants claimed an authority to perform that rite of passage that was rarely granted in advance by religious or legal authorities. The authority that was claimed and enacted in those ceremonies gradually came to wider and fuller—though still by no means universal—recognition.

power relations within their religious communities and to perform new power relations. The ordination of the Philadelphia Eleven defied the power structure of the Episcopal Church. The Black Unity Mass overrode the power of the diocese. Despite the important differences in the way that the governing bodies of the Roman Catholic Church and the Episcopal Church conceive and structure authority, both of these ritual performances involved participants enacting and claiming a kind of authority that was not granted in advance by those governing bodies. While these two cases are exemplary, similar sorts of things happen all the time in more mundane and less dramatic enactments of rituals.

I have focused on rituals that function as performatives, bringing about some change in the normative status of a person or group. Rites of passage tend to function in this way, enacting a change in the social role, status, obligations, or entitlements of the people or groups who pass through such rites. To be successful as performatives—that is, to bring about the intended change in normative status—participants typically enact a sequence of acts in accordance with a set of norms and conventions, including conventions about who is authorized to initiate them, participate in them, and carry them out. But as we have seen, judgments about these things happen after the fact, by diverse people with different concerns and precedents in mind. Those judgments can and do change, sometimes in response to innovations, experimentations, and transformations of existing rituals.

The authority to perform rituals is a matter of ongoing practices of recognition rather than prior authorization. Likewise, the authority conferred in and through rituals depends more on recognition than on authorization. We don't always know ahead of time whether someone will gain the authority they seek through the ritual. Often, of course, those who are recognized as having the authority to perform or participate in rituals will be those who have a particular social role or status that is recognized in advance of a particular enactment of a ritual. But not always—even when legal and governing bodies are invested in the status quo. Sometimes people are moved to recognize the authority of the virtuoso in the excellence of her performance, even to their own surprise.

The ordination at the Church of the Advocate shows something new performed into being. An ordination service is a rite of passage, which marks and effects the ordinand's change in status from deacon to priest. The ordination is performative, marking and effecting that change in status though a set of linguistic and bodily acts. As a performative, it is conventional; that is, certain conventions and norms must be met in order for the performative to have force. The social role into which the person enters— "priest"—is a normative status. To be a priest, a person must be recognized *as* a priest by others and endowed with the relevant entitlements and obligations. A person who undertakes the ordination rites but is not recognized by others as a priest is *not* a priest in the relevant sense. In the Episcopal Church, this typically means undertaking the ordination rites as they appear in the *Book of Common Prayer* and receiving the blessing and laying on of hands of a bishop, one whose authority has likewise been conferred through a set of liturgical acts authorized and is recognized by the Church and its members.

The bishops who ordained the Philadelphia Eleven *had* been authorized by the Episcopal Church to perform ordinations—of men. And so the ordination of eleven women set off a firestorm of controversy in the Episcopal Church. As the *Philadelphia Inquirer* reported the day after the ceremony: "There has been a great deal of speculation about just what authority the women would have. The presiding bishop of the church, John M. Allin, and Bishop Ogilby both have said that the ordinations would be 'irregular but valid.' However, most bishops have said that if the women were made priests, they would not allow the women to practice."[30] Indeed, the House of Bishops, one of the two legislative bodies of the Episcopal Church, did declare the ordinations *irregular*. It also

30. Wallace, "11 Women Are Ordained."

disciplined the bishops who had participated in the ordinations and instructed the women to refrain from performing clerical duties, including the administration of the Eucharist. By and large, however, the women did not comply with these instructions. Their ordination rites may have been irregular but, it seemed, they were not infelicitous, at least according to the thousands of laypeople who would receive blessings and sacraments from these women. The ordination rites had their performative force. The women were priests, even if neither they nor the bishops who ordained them had received *prior* authorization to make them priests. Two years later, women's ordination would be recognized by the House of Bishops.

By that point, however, the House of Bishops was recognizing something that was *already happening.* Their official authorization of women's ordination was a belated one. The women, and the bishops who ordained them, had already claimed that authority, and the thousands of laypeople who attended the ordination and who received blessings and sacraments from the women in the subsequent years had already recognized it. In this, we see that, contra Bourdieu, the force of the performative need not depend on *prior* authorization. It is sometimes an assertion of an authority that has not *yet* been granted or acknowledged but that comes to be recognized in a performative act.

Indeed, it was the women's assertion of their authority that was at the root of many responses to the ordination service. Those who balked at the service were appalled at women's assertion of an authority that was not supposed to be theirs to assert. As Pamela Darling writes:

> Most shocking of all was the fact that—unlike the campaign to seat women in the House of Deputies—women had taken it upon themselves to act within the church without permission. The ordinations had to be performed by male bishops, but it was women who had laid the groundwork, raised the money, gathered the support, and persuaded them to participate. Although

the official reaction focused on punishing the ordaining bishops and male priests who invited women to celebrate the Eucharist, its intensity was rooted in outrage over the fact that women had seized the initiative, claiming and exercising power to bring about change on their own timetable.[31]

The hate mail and threats that the women received in the wake of their ordination were the outpouring of misogyny, defined by Kate Manne not as the hatred of women but as the policing function of a patriarchal society.[32] On this view, acts of misogyny are defensive moves against women, gender non-conforming, queer, and nonbinary people who claim an authority not granted to them by a patriarchal and heteronormative gender system. Stepping into roles usually occupied by cisgender men, claiming and enacting power typically reserved for those men, and/or refusing to acknowledge the legitimacy of male power over others, non-cis-male people are policed and punished through acts of misogyny. The Philadelphia Eleven stepped into roles not appointed for them; they claimed authority and entitlements that, according to their opponents, were not theirs to claim, and they were therefore to be disciplined, punished, put back into their place.

At the same time, there were responses of surprised *recognition* of the authority claimed and conferred in and through the act.[33] Pauli Murray, a Black, nonbinary civil rights activist who was ordained in the Episcopal Church a few years later, attended the ordination with some trepidation about the norm that was being

31. Quoted in O'Dell, *Philadelphia Eleven*, 80–81.

32. Manne, *Down Girl*.

33. As Partridge writes, "I was particularly intrigued by the 'irregularity' of the event, a reference to its lack of authorization either by the bishops or the standing committees of the women's own diocese. To many of its critics, this 'irregularity' signaled its 'invalidity.' To its participants and proponents, its 'irregularity' signaled its Spirit-driven, transformative character" ("Toward an 'Irregular' Embrace," 132).

violated.[34] Murray later wrote, however, that "the joyous spirit that enveloped the congregation swept away all my doubts as to the rightness of the action taken that day."[35] Murray recalled kneeling before one of the newly ordained priests and receiving a blessing from her. The joyous spirit in the room was confirmation of the ceremony's legitimacy, confirmation that the authority claimed was also authority recognized. As far as Murray and many others were concerned, the women would be, had already become, priests.

34. Important recent scholarship on Pauli Murray includes Troy R. Saxby, *Pauli Murray: A Personal and Political Life* (Chapel Hill: University of North Carolina Press, 2020); and the documentary film *My Name Is Pauli Murray*, dir. Betsy West and Julie Cohen (Amazon Studios, 2021).

35. Quoted in O'Dell, *Philadelphia Eleven*, 79.

4

Habits, Virtues, and Freedom

EVERY MORNING, in public school classrooms across the United States, children recite the Pledge of Allegiance. They stand up, face the U.S. flag, place a hand over their hearts, and say the words: "I pledge allegiance to the flag, of the United States of America, and to the republic for which it stands: one nation, under God, indivisible, with liberty and justice for all."

To recite the Pledge of Allegiance is to participate in a ritual. The pledge involves a sequence of verbal and gestural acts, a routine shared by a group and governed by the norms of that group. It is scripted. The words, bodily acts, and expected decorum are highly prescribed. The pledge is also value-intensifying in a way that other homeroom activities, such as taking attendance and making announcements, are not. It is a way of valuing and tending a shared ideal. Like many—but not all—rituals, it is also not only repeat*able* but also repeat*ed* by the same participants, many of whom recite it day after day. For those participants, the recitation of the pledge becomes a matter of habit.

When schoolchildren first learn the pledge, often in kindergarten or first grade, they learn to produce the sounds and gestures without thinking or knowing much about their meaning. Francis Bellamy, the Baptist minister who wrote the pledge in 1892, later noted that "when you analyze it, you find a mouthful of orotund words; most of them abstract terms—a bunch of ideas rather than concrete names. . . . In that latter characteristic of national doctrine and aspiration, this pledge would seem far better adapted to educated adults than to children."[1] But Bellamy's aim in writing the pledge was not to give voice to something that young schoolchildren already understood and endorsed. Rather, it was to shape their habits and dispositions so that they would *become* the sorts of citizens who understood and endorsed those ideas.[2]

Bellamy had been asked by the popular magazine *The Youth's Companion* to write the pledge as part of a patriotic program for public schools in commemoration of the 400th anniversary of Christopher Columbus's journey to the Americas.[3] Bellamy believed that this flag-based ritual could endow children—particularly immigrant children—with a set of patriotic ideals and values. In a speech to the National Education Association, Bellamy reported

1. Francis Bellamy, "The Story of the Pledge of Allegiance to the Flag," *University of Rochester Library Bulletin* 8.2 (Winter 1953), https://rbscp.lib.rochester.edu/3418.

2. In this respect, the pledge differs from the oath of allegiance that is read during the naturalization ceremony, in which the oath expresses new citizens' loyalty and responsibilities to their adopted nation: "I hereby declare, on oath, that I absolutely and entirely renounce and abjure all allegiance and fidelity to any foreign prince, potentate, state or sovereignty, of whom or which I have heretofore been a subject or citizen; that I will support and defend the Constitution and laws of the United States of America against all enemies, foreign and domestic; that I will bear true faith and allegiance to the same; that I will bear arms on behalf of the United States when required by law; that I will perform noncombatant service in the Armed Forces of the United States when required by the law; that I will perform work of national importance under civilian direction when required by the law; and that I take this obligation freely, without any mental reservation or purpose of evasion; so help me God." The naturalization ceremony ends with the new citizens' recitation, in unison, of the pledge. While both the naturalization oath and the Pledge of Allegiance are ritualized acts, only the latter is *repeated* by the practitioner. The repetition of the performance is important to the pedagogical and habituating aims of those who institute it. See U.S. Citizenship and Immigration Services, "Naturalization Oath of Allegiance to the United States of America," https://www.uscis.gov/us-citizenship/naturalization-test/naturalization-oath-allegiance-united-states-america.

3. This program was also part of a marketing strategy for *The Youth's Companion*, which profited from the sale of U.S. flags to schools in connection with the Schoolhouse Flag Movement.

that, in his view, the recitation of the pledge had had a positive influence "on children of foreign parentage; to them it is a daily object lesson in patriotism for the land of their adoption."[4] Bellamy thought of the pledge as a routine—a daily ritual—that could produce patriots.

Others agreed. By the end of the nineteenth century, the pledge had been instituted in schools across the country, including in New York where, in 1898, the legislature passed a law making its recitation compulsory in public schools. Bellamy later wrote that "this little formula has been pounding away on the impressionable minds of children for a generation, awakening a daily enthusiasm for the flag, driving in the idea of loyalty, giving them a notion of the great republic, reminding them of a liberty and justice for all,—*thinking those thoughts for them*."[5]

Bellamy's "lesson in patriotism" was instituted in the midst of a rapid growth in immigration and, in response, anti-immigrant sentiment, as well as the failure of Reconstruction and birth of Jim Crow. Bellamy, along with those who tasked him with writing the pledge and those who would adopt and implement it in schools, believed that children who recited the pledge would develop the habits and dispositions of good citizens. Understood in the context of late nineteenth-century immigration policies, nativism, and xenophobia, Bellamy's understanding of what it was to be a "good citizen" had both racial and religious connotations, marked by his emphasis on assimilation into a normatively white and Protestant citizenry.[6] Bellamy's text draws on Daniel Webster's January 30, 1830, speech against the prospect of Southern succession. Webster's speech urged unity between Southern and

4. Quoted in Richard J. Ellis, *To the Flag: The Unlikely History of the Pledge of Allegiance* (Lawrence: University Press of Kansas, 2005), 31.

5. Quoted in Ellis, *To the Flag*, 69 (emphasis added).

6. Ellis argues that "five anxieties loom particularly large in the creation, propagation, and amending of the Pledge of Allegiance. First, and most important, is the anxiety about immigrants" (*To the Flag*, xi). The other anxieties concern materialism, freedom and individualism, radicalism, and communism.

Northern white Americans; it attempted, as Danielle Allen notes, "to draw rebellious Southern whites into accord with their white brethren up north . . . celebrat[ing] 'Union, now and forever, one and inseparable.'" Allen continues, "under Bellamy's pen, the national ideal became 'one nation indivisible.'"[7] This ideal of unity was both represented in the words of the pledge and enacted in the postures and gestures assumed in its recitation: standing together, facing the flag, speaking in unison, embodying the "oneness" proclaimed therein.[8]

Thinking of the pledge today, we might consider it (with greater or lesser degrees of enthusiasm) as one of the rituals of America's civil religion. In his 1967 essay "Civil Religion in America," Robert Bellah argued that there is, in America, something

7. Danielle S. Allen, *Talking to Strangers: Anxieties of Citizenship since Brown v. Board of Education* (Chicago: University of Chicago Press, 2004), 14.

8. Allen, *Talking to Strangers*, 193–94nn6–7. Allen argues that this particular conception of unity or oneness (as opposed to what she calls "wholeness") codifies domination. Subsequent changes to the pledge—its words and gestures—reveal the changing political context and evolving anxieties about immigration, fascism, and communism, as well as debates about what habits and dispositions U.S. citizens ought to have. During the National Flag Conference in 1923, for example, members of the American Legion and the Daughters of the American Revolution agreed to change the phrase "my flag" to "the Flag of the United States" in order to clarify that immigrant children who recited the pledge were directing their loyalty to the United States rather than to their native countries. The following year, the Flag Conference further clarified this point, adding the words, "of America." In 1942, the adoption of the Flag Code, a federal law that established advisory rules for the treatment of the U.S. flag, offered another opportunity to refine and codify the Pledge of Allegiance. Motivated by concerns about similarities between the extended arm salute that originally accompanied the recitation of the pledge and the Nazi salute, Congress stated in the Flag Code that the Pledge of Allegiance "should be rendered by standing at attention facing the flag with the right hand over the heart." Finally, in 1954, with encouragement from President Dwight Eisenhower and leadership from the pious Rep. Louis Rabaut, Congress passed an amendment to the Flag Code adding the words "under God." This addition, Eisenhower had insisted, would "reaffirm the transcendence of religious faith in America's heritage and future," a reaffirmation that took place against the backdrop of worries about the creep of godless communism.

like a shared religion—a set of beliefs and practices relative to sacred things—that binds people together.[9] But, he insists, this religion is not, in any straightforward way, Christian. Rather, he argues that it is a *civil* religion, which draws on the ideas and symbols of Christianity to craft a national narrative and to forge solidarity that transcends religious difference and sectarianism. America has its own sacred texts, prophets and martyrs, and ideas about sin and redemption.

Bellah's characterization of civil religion is almost perfectly Durkheimian. On Durkheim's classic definition, a religion is "a unified set of beliefs and practices relative to sacred things, that is to say, things set apart and surrounded by prohibitions—beliefs and practices that unite its adherents into a moral community called a church. . . . Religion must be something eminently collective."[10] By bringing individuals together in collective action, Durkheim claimed, rituals have the power to create social cohesion. Religion's primary effect—and for Durkheim, its function— is to unite a people. Rituals, in particular, are powerful engines of social cohesion, bringing individuals together in collective action. Compare Durkheim's definition of religion to Bellah's characterization of American civil religion. Bellah writes, "What we have, then, from the earliest years of the republic is a collection of beliefs, symbols, and rituals with respect to sacred things and institutionalized in a collectivity."[11] They both define religion by common beliefs and practices that unite people around a shared

---

9. There is much to say about civil religion, and about the scholarly debates about it, particularly in the sociological literature of the past few decades, but it is beyond the scope of my argument to engage them here. I have learned a great deal from Philip Gorski's recent work on this topic, particularly *American Covenant: A History of Civil Religion from the Puritans to the Present* (Princeton: Princeton University Press, 2017).

10. Émile Durkheim, *The Elementary Forms of Religious Life*, trans. Carol Cosman, ed. Mark Cladis (Oxford: Oxford University Press, 2001), 46.

11. Robert N. Bellah, "Civil Religion in America," in *Beyond Belief: Essays on Religion in a Post-Traditional World* (New York: Harper & Row, 1970), 175.

conception of the sacred. And like Durkheim, Bellah suggests that the purpose and effect of civil religion, and of its rituals, are to turn disparate individuals into a people, a nation.

But people argue about civic rituals all the time—about their meaning and effects, about whether children ought to learn them or be required to perform them, about their place in other state-sanctioned events, and on other grounds. People protest them, refuse them, and create alternatives to them. Rituals such as the Pledge of Allegiance are often intended to enact and cultivate virtues such as *piety*, the virtue associated with the proper treatment of those to whom one owes one's being. Because piety is typically unidirectional, indicating a power or status difference between the person exhibiting piety and the person to whom their piety is directed, it can raise questions about these power or status differences. Are they just, or are they relations of subordination and domination? Moreover, are political configurations such as nation-states appropriate objects of piety? And, even if they are, how should that piety be enacted? Should the habits associated with piety be habits of submission? Of gratitude and reciprocity? Of vigorous engagement and critique? And what other virtues ought to be cultivated alongside such piety? How about the virtue of justice, which, in many cases, involves standing *against* existing social structures and power relations? Or of practical wisdom, which involves discernment about what to do, when? Are these virtues of democratic citizens too?

A monk who kneels in prayer expresses humility before God and cultivates the habits of a humble and pious servant. A subject who bows before a king expresses deference to the king and cultivates the habits of the humble and pious servant. But what of the children who stand and face the flag to recite the pledge? Readers may recoil at Bellamy's suggestion that the pledge has been "pounding away" at children's impressionable minds, inculcating in them an unthinking patriotism. The recoil, I suspect, comes from a sense that the inculcation of such habits and dispositions leaves children unfree in some important way—that it leaves them thinking these thoughts and having these dispositions, uncritically or unreflectively. If that's right, one worry may be that people won't be able to criticize the pledge or the nation, because of their habituation. It may be tempting to think that the attitude-inculcating, habit-forming, and disposition-shaping tendencies of repeated rituals are inherently at odds with freedom—as if we are all becoming the king's deferential subjects. Habit formation, on this line of thought, tends to diminish a subject's capacity to act freely or to take responsibility for their actions. But that doesn't seem quite right, given the evidence. In fact, some rituals appear to be aimed at cultivating habits and desires that make possible forms of action that otherwise wouldn't be possible. And other rituals, including some civic rituals, seem to be aimed at cultivating the habits of free and reflective citizens.

There is excellent work on habits, habituation, and ethical formation that can help us think about rituals in relation to these things. But much of this work doesn't connect the dots among all of them. We desire habits that we don't have, and we have habits that we'd like to get rid of. We reflect on our desires and our habits, and we do so in contexts that shape and constrain the options for those desires and habits. We are habituated into the practices of unjust societies, and we innovate within that habituation or work to cultivate other ways of being. My task in this chapter is to draw out these connections to show how rituals and the habits they cultivate can be amenable to reflection and critique and thus appropriate for a diverse, engaged, and democratic-minded citizenry.

Habits and Virtues

Imagine that you are driving home from your first day at a new job. As you head toward home on that first afternoon, you're focused on the drive. You need to make a series of choices about which route you take, whether you need to turn left or right at the next light, when you need to signal for that turn, and so forth. Over the course of the next few weeks, as the route becomes more familiar to you, you become less aware of the decision-making process involved in your drive. One day, a month or two into your new job, you spend your drive home mulling over a tense conversation that you had with a coworker at the end of the day, and you're a bit surprised when you pull into your driveway. "Home *already*?" you ask yourself. The series of discrete actions that you need to take in order to get home from work aren't a matter of conscious decision making anymore; you drive home as if on autopilot. You've developed a habit.

We experience many of our daily activities in this way, performing them without much conscious deliberation. Once we've learned the basic routine, we don't think much about what we're doing as we brush our teeth or ride a bike or drive a car. Rituals, when enacted repeatedly over time, can take on this habitual character as well. Through some combination of imitation and formal education, a child who attends a school in which children recite the Pledge of Allegiance every morning learns the routine. Eventually, she recites the pledge with the ease of habit, uttering the words and inhabiting the postures without considering what needs to be said or done at each moment. Her repetition of the pledge, day after day, creates a habit. The child can now enact the ritual without much conscious thought or decision making along the way.

The standard model for studying habit—particularly in contemporary neuroscience—takes its inspiration from the nineteenth-century psychologist and philosopher William James.[12]

12. Several of the most prominent researchers of the neuroscience of habit, including Anthony Dickinson and Ann Graybiel, cite James as the starting point for their definition of habit. James's influence is particularly resonant with the account of "chunking" proposed by Graybiel. Graybiel's research suggests that habits are gradually built up through the repeated performance of complex multistep actions. "Chunked" representations of these actions are formed in the brain, where they are bundled and stored together. Once the chunked representation of a sequence of acts has been formed and stored, it can be triggered by a familiar cue or context. When

In his treatise on psychology, James writes that even "the most complex habits" are "nothing but *concatenated* discharges in the nerve-centers, due to the presence there of systems of reflex paths, so organized as to wake each other up successively—the impression produced by one muscular contraction serving as a stimulus to provoke the next until a final impression inhibits the process and closes the chain."[13] These neurological pathways, James suggests, link complex sequences of behavior composed of the smaller and simpler units of thought or action. Once formed, James argues, such a pathway "diminishes the conscious attention with which our acts are performed."[14] According to this "neuro-model," habits encode sequences of acts in ways that make them relatively automatic, inflexible, and unconscious. They become mechanical.

This way of characterizing habit more or less coheres with our ordinary use of the term, and it has framed neuroscientific research in ways that have proven productive. But this model of habit, while illuminating *some* aspects of how habits are formed

---

you get into your car in the parking lot at work, you trigger the sequence of acts by which you drive home from work. Because the entire sequence is stored as a unit, you are no longer making the discrete decisions that were involved the first few times that you drove home. The context and cue trigger the habit sequence. The next thing you know, you are pulling into your driveway without having given it much thought. Graybiel, "Habits, Rituals, and the Evaluative Brain," *Annual Review of Neuroscience* 31 (February 2008): 359–87. Dickinson's work tends to emphasize a dichotomy between goal-directed behavior and habit; behaviors are goal-directed in an early stage of habit learning but become automatic such that the behavior continues even when the goal or reward is removed (think: Pavlov). Beginning with this view of habit in mind, researchers design experiments that aim to get at that sort of behavior. This is not a problem, per se, unless we are unclear on what that research does, and does not, tell us about the various forms that habit and habituation might take. See Dickinson, "Actions and Habits: The Development of Behavioural Autonomy," *Philosophical Transactions of the Royal Society* 308.1135 (1985), https://doi.org/10.1098/rstb .1985.0010.

13. William James, *The Principles of Psychology*, vol. 1 (1890; New York: Dover, 1950), 108.

14. James, *Principles of Psychology*, 114.

and used, may lead us to miss much of what is worth considering under the banner of "habit." In particular, it obscures both the normativity and the flexibility of habits in use. Habits shape and are shaped by social norms. We also alter our habits, working to change them or adapt them to new circumstances. On these points, Aristotle's model of habit may serve us better.

Aristotle thinks of at least some of our habits less as rigid routines than as dispositions. These dispositions are *acquired*, learned through practice and habituation, and they are *goal-directed*. Driving a car, for instance, involves what Aristotle calls *technē*, a technical habit or craft, as well as a *telos*, a goal or end. In order to drive home from work, you need to have acquired the technical habits of doing so through education, practice, and repetition. These habits might include engaging the turn signal, accelerating at an appropriate rate, beginning to push the brake pedal at the right distance from the stoplight, and so forth. Notice that many of these habits involve making judgments—about how quickly you ought to accelerate, given the traffic, or when exactly you ought to hit the brakes, given how short the yellow lights are in a particular part of town. Far from overriding your ability to make judgments, the acquisition of the habits associated with driving a car requires that you become increasingly skilled at making them. When you drive your car home from work, you put these habits to use in the service of a goal or end: getting home. Given your goal, if, in the middle of the drive home, you notice something on the road in front of you, you'll swerve to avoid it. If you notice that there is traffic ahead, you may take another route. Your ability to think and respond to the novelty of the situation isn't incapacitated by your habit. Far from it. Your habits perfect your capacity to drive, which includes the ability to adjust your actions as needed in order to get where you're going. As neuroscientists Javier Bernacer and Jose Ignacio Murillo note in an article that argues for the relevance of Aristotle's model of habit for neuroscientific research, "driving is a conscious process overall: we decide to start the process, we consciously set the goal, and our driving is continuously available to conscious supervision. . . . [H]abits are at the service of goal directed behaviors."[15] In other words, people put their habits to use toward the ends that they believe are worth pursuing.

We deem some habits good and others bad, and the ends to which they are used may be worthy, or not. Let's say that the habits associated with driving a car are good ones to have, all things considered. Those habits can be put to use in driving into a crowd of protestors whose political stance one disagrees with, or they can be put to use in driving a wounded protestor to the hospital. One uses the habits toward a bad end (violently harming someone with whom one disagrees) and the other uses them toward a good end (assisting someone who is suffering). Likewise, a person may have developed the habits associated with the rituals of mourning in the Jewish tradition. These habits include, to recall an example explored elsewhere in the book, the recitation of the Mourner's Kaddish, the prayer recited after the death of close kin. According to the Jewish tradition, such habits are good ones for Jews to have. To put them to use in mourning a loved one is a way of giving that person or the relationship shared with them their due. This puts the habit to use toward a good end. But a person with the habits of mourning may also put them to use in order to impress or appease another, or to gain undue status in a group—bad ends.

For Aristotle, habits perfect our capacity to perform certain sequences of acts, to good or bad ends. *Virtues*, meanwhile, are acquired dispositions to think and act rightly and well, toward good ends. Like habits, virtues are developed through repeated performance or habituation into a practice. Aristotle writes that "virtues . . . we acquire, just as we acquire crafts [*technē*], by having first activated them. For we learn a craft by producing the same project that we must produce when we have learned it; we become builders, for instance, by building, and we become harpists by playing

15. Javier Bernacer and Jose Ignacio Murillo, "The Aristotelian Conception of Habit and Its Contribution to Human Neuroscience," *Frontiers in Human Neuroscience* 8.883 (2014), https://doi.org/10.3389/fnhum.2014.00883.

the harp. Similarly, then, we become just by doing just actions, temperate by doing temperate actions, brave by doing brave actions."[16] Habituation, on this view, can make certain sequences of thought and action more nearly spontaneous. But Aristotle cautions that virtues are not unreflective or mechanical, not least because a virtuous person has the practical wisdom needed to discern *how* to act in *which* contexts at *which* times—when to put which habit to use, and toward what ends. For Aristotle, the moral life involves the development of habits and dispositions that align a person's desires and their actions in pursuit of good or worthy ends.[17] It involves, in other words, the development of virtues.

Ritual, Virtue, and Ethical Formation

Saba Mahmood draws on Aristotle's model of habit and virtue to understand women's participation in the mosque movement in Cairo, Egypt. Mahmood describes women teaching classes, leading prayer meetings, dedicating themselves to daily prayer practices, and choosing to wear a hijab. She argues that such practices are not, or not only, expressive; they also shape and transform the women who undertake them into subjects with particular habits and dispositions. By focusing on how rituals and bodily practices shape subjects, Mahmood argues, her work "productively reverses the

16. Aristotle, *Nicomachean Ethics*, II.2.1103a.

17. Thanks to John Bowlin for his insight on this point. David Decosimo's *Ethics as a Work of Charity: Thomas Aquinas and Pagan Virtue* (Stanford: Stanford University Press, 2014), 72–105, further develops this insight through his engagement with Thomas Aquinas's transformation of Aristotle's account of habit. Decosimo notes that, for Aquinas, every habit is good or bad, in itself, apart from any end to which it may be put, "depend[ing] on its relation to the capacity it disposes." Apart from this, or in addition, habits may be put to good or bad ends, as when (to use Decosimo's example) a person puts their good habit of bike riding to use in running over stray cats (a bad end). Decosimo writes, "Habits, then, are creatures of potentiality that perfect for good or ill a capacity that is capable of being disposed in various ways" (75).

routing from interiority to exteriority."[18] This reversal means that "the *work* bodily practices perform in crafting a subject—rather than the *meanings* they signify—carry analytic weight."[19] Mahmood focuses on the practices and processes by which participants in the mosque movement try to cultivate the virtue of piety.

Piety, according to the participants in the mosque movement, is a "quality of being 'close to God,'" a quality that ought to permeate *all* of one's acts but that must be cultivated through specifically pious acts.[20] Note the broadly Aristotelian view that underlies the women's self-understanding—a virtuous disposition is cultivated through repeated acts of virtue. Just as one becomes just by performing just acts, a person becomes pious by performing pious acts.

Salat took on a central role in the women's understanding and cultivation of piety. Not only was the performance of *salat* one of the basic conditions of piety, but it was also understood to be the primary means of cultivating it. But the desire to perform *salat* did not come naturally. Mahmood conveys a conversation among a group of women in a mosque in downtown Cairo, the subject of which was the desire to pray. A woman asked a question about the Fajr prayer: "The young woman expressed the difficulty she encountered in performing the task of getting up for the morning prayer and asked the group what she should do about it." Mona, a woman in her mid-thirties and a local leader, asked her, "Do you mean to say that you are unable to get up for the morning prayer *habitually and consistently*?"[21] The young woman agreed. Mona then suggested that the young woman begin to conduct all of her daily activities with the intention of pleasing God, in order to cultivate piety and, then, the desire to perform the morning prayer.

18. Saba Mahmood, *Politics of Piety: The Islamic Revival and the Feminist Subject* (Princeton: Princeton University Press, 2005), 121.

19. Mahmood, *Politics of Piety*, 122.

20. Mahmood, *Politics of Piety*, 122–23.

21. Mahmood, *Politics of Piety*, 124 (emphasis in original).

Mona's reply, Mahmood notes, revealed her sense that the desire to pray—to perform that central act of piety—is not natural and often doesn't precede the habit of acting piously. Rather, it has to be cultivated through the repetition of pious acts; it is an object of moral pedagogy. "Desire in this model is not the *antecedent* to, or cause of, moral action, but *its product*."[22]

Mahmood describes Mona's teachings in terms of an Aristotelian conception of *habitus*, a set of dispositions, acquired through repeated practice, that coordinates bodily acts with mental states (including thoughts, emotions, and intentions).[23] Mahmood's Aristotelian conception of *habitus* differs somewhat from that of Pierre Bourdieu.[24] It's worth taking a detour through Bourdieu's slightly different way of talking about *habitus* in order to clarify the difference.

Bourdieu argues that the norms of a society tend to become encoded in people's embodied dispositions. These dispositions—collections of habits of thought, perception, and action—are what Bourdieu calls *habitus*. He writes:

> The structures constitutive of a particular type of environment . . . produce *habitus*, systems of durable transposable *dispositions*, structured structures predisposed to function as structuring structures, that is, as principles of the generation and structuring of practices and representations which can be objectively "regulated" and "regular" without in any way being the product of obedience to rules, objectively adapted to their

22. Mahmood, *Politics of Piety*, 126 (emphasis in original).

23. Mahmood, *Politics of Piety*, 136.

24. Mahmood briefly distinguishes between her use of the term *habitus* and Bourdieu's, noting that she "draws on a longer and richer history of this term, however, one that addresses the centrality of gestural capacities in certain traditions of moral cultivation and that is therefore analytically more useful for my purposes" (*Politics of Piety*, 136). She continues, a few pages later, "What I find problematic in [Bourdieu's] approach is its lack of attention to the pedagogical process by which a habitus is learned" (139).

goals without presupposing a conscious aiming at ends or an express mastery of the operations necessary to attain them and, being all this, collectively orchestrated without being the product of the orchestrating action of a conductor.[25]

A person's *habitus* is largely developed in early childhood, through imitation, discipline, and education. It then structures a person's perceptions, thoughts, and actions, reproducing the environment in which that person's *habitus* was formed in the first place. These processes are often unconscious and invisible to the people participating in them (that is, all of us); as Bourdieu writes, the development of *habitus* and its subsequent role in reproducing the conditions of its development are "orchestrated" without any conductor responsible for the orchestrating.

Bourdieu's interest in *habitus* is connected to his curiosity about how relationships of domination and subordination are reproduced, often without threat of violence and without the explicit intention of the people involved in those relationships. In his work on gender-based domination, for instance, Bourdieu argues that it is through the development and deployment of the gendered *habitus* that masculine domination is perpetuated. Bourdieu writes, "The work of [the] transformation of bodies, which is both sexually differentiated and sexually differentiating, and which is performed partly through the effects of mimetic suggestion, partly through explicit injunctions and partly through the whole symbolic construction of the view of the biological body . . . produces systematically differentiated and differentiating *habitus*."[26] Where gender relations are characterized by domination, this domination is written into the *habitus* of people of different genders. As Bourdieu writes:

These ways of bearing the body, which are very deeply associated with the moral restraint and the demureness that are

---

25. Pierre Bourdieu, *Outline of a Theory of Practice* (Cambridge: Cambridge University Press, 1977), 72.

26. Bourdieu, *Masculine Domination*, 55.

appropriate for women, continue to impose themselves unconsciously on women even when they cease to be imposed by
clothing (like the small, quick steps of some women wearing
trousers and flat heels). And the relaxed poses and postures,
such as leaning back on two legs of a chair or putting the feet
on a desk, which some men—especially those of high status—
sometimes allow themselves as a sign of power or, which
amounts to the same thing, of self-assurance, are literally un-
thinkable for women.[27]

The construction of the gendered body and the deployment of
gendered schemes of action and relation depend on imitation,
discipline, and the symbolic environments in which bodies and
embodied actions are caught up in the power relations among
people of different genders. Think of the phenomenon of man-
spreading, compared with the bodily postures traditionally considered to be "ladylike": legs together, crossed ankles, folded
hands in lap. As Iris Marion Young suggested, men expand to take
up space; women contract.[28]

Mahmood and Bourdieu share an interest in the role that rituals
and other bodily practices play in shaping subjects. Both recognize
that, through such practices, people come to have particular habits
and dispositions. But whereas Bourdieu is mainly concerned with
the unconscious processes by which the *habitus* takes shape and,
relatedly, how the *habitus* then unwittingly participates in the reproduction of norms, structures, and power relations, Mahmood
focuses on the self-conscious and intentional processes by which
people transform their habits and dispositions. And she argues
that the women in the mosque movement describe and engage
these processes in terms resonant with the Aristotelian conception. The women in the mosque movement view their desired

27. Bourdieu, *Masculine Domination*, 29.
28. Iris Marion Young, "Throwing Like a Girl: A Phenomenology of Feminine
Body Comportment, Motility, and Spatiality," *Human Studies* 3.2 (April 1980):
137–56.

habits and dispositions as the result of intentional practice in the service of ethical formation. Although the women themselves don't use the Aristotelian terms, it is this more self-conscious conception of *habitus* that is taken up in Islamic philosophy and that influences the women's understanding of what piety is and how a person becomes pious.

The participants in the mosque movement understand *salat* as "one among a continuum of practices that serve as the necessary means to the realization of the pious self, and that are regarded as the critical instruments in a teleological program of self-formation."[29] Through prayer and other daily practices, the women cultivate the habits and dispositions that accord with their desire to become pious. In other words, they engage in bodily practices to align their *first order desires* with their *second order volitions*. As Harry Frankfurt uses these terms, first order desires are people's ordinary, everyday desires—for instance, the desire to get out of bed to pray. Second order volitions are desires *about* first order desires and passions—such as the desire to be pious. Frankfurt writes, "Besides wanting and choosing and being moved *to do* this or that, men may also want to have (or not to have) certain desires and motives. They are capable of wanting to be different, in their preferences and purposes, from what they are."[30] This capacity for reflective self-evaluation is what makes second order volitions possible. "Someone has a desire of the second order either when he wants simply to have a certain desire or when he wants a certain desire to be his will."[31] A person can experience their second order volitions as in line with their first order desires, as in the case of a second order desire to be pious and a first order desire to pray, or as being at odds with them, as in a second order desire to be pious and a first order desire to sleep in during the usual prayer time.

29. Mahmood, *Politics of Piety*, 128.
30. Harry G. Frankfurt, *The Importance of What We Care About* (Cambridge: Cambridge University Press, 1998), 12.
31. Frankfurt, *The Importance of What We Care About*, 16.

Rituals play a role in training people's desires, including training them to accord with their second order desires, representing the sort of people they wish to be. The young woman who was struggling to perform the Fajr prayer had the second order volition to be a pious Muslim. She understood piety to involve the habitual and consistent performance of *salat*, including the dawn prayer that she struggled to perform. Mona's advice to her was to cultivate the first order desire to pray, the desire that would get her out of bed in the morning to enact the Fajr prayer, by cultivating the *habitus* of the pious Muslim—to become pious by performing ordinary acts of piety. If you want to be a pious Muslim, you must cultivate the *habitus*—the embodied desires, habits, and dispositions—of someone who is pious. And the way that you cultivate the *habitus* of a pious Muslim is by engaging in pious acts. Do the thing that you want to want to do, even though you don't find yourself wanting to do it *yet*. Dispositions are acquired through practice.

Second order volitions concerning the sort of people we want to be, and the sort of will we want to have, can direct the practices in which we engage as we attempt to cultivate first order desires (and habits and dispositions) that align with those second order volitions. But it is worth keeping in mind that second order volitions are no more "given" or self-evident than first order desires. They, too, are the product of particular pedagogies, whether conscious or unconscious, and they may require both reflection and discipline to interrogate and change. I may find that my second order volition to eat less sugar conflicts with my first order desire to order the chocolate cake; it might be worth asking *why* I want to eat less sugar and how this emerges from or intersects with prevailing norms about bodies and health that I may or may not actually endorse, as well as whether and how I might train my desires to accord with that volition if endorsed. Mahmood's account highlights the contingency of first order desires and the practices by which people work to cultivate and change them, but in so doing, she largely takes the women's second order volitions as given. In the context of the Islamic revival, the desire to be a pious Muslim has its own origins and assumptions, and those too might be sites of reflection, cultivation, or critique for those who find themselves with this desire. Certainly, it would be wrong to assume that this volition does not carry with it its own set of beliefs and attitudes, including beliefs about what piety is, to whom or to what it is owed, whether it is a good thing, and why someone might want to cultivate it, as well as what the various agents supporting or promoting that particular conception of piety have to gain or lose from its adoption. Second order volitions are *also* the product of particular pedagogies in this way; they emerge in distinct social and political contexts and often deserve our reflection.

Mahmood's interlocutors in *Politics of Piety*, including Mona and the young woman with whom she converses, arrive on the scene with the second order volition to be pious Muslim subjects already in place. They want to want to pray. This second order volition is related to a set of commitments and dispositions that the women already have—commitments regarding what it is to be a pious Muslim woman and about whether it is a good thing to be a pious Muslim woman, the disposition to act in order to bring it about so that they are. These are theological, ethical, and political commitments, with their own histories and attending debates. According to the women in the mosque movement, who have a second order desire to be pious but cannot always muster the desire to get out of bed to pray, the first order desire to pray is understood as the product rather than the antecedent to moral formation. But what of their second order volition—the desire to be pious?

While it is true that the repeated enactment of a ritual can be part of a process of ethical formation—cultivating habits and dispositions that a practitioner or an authority figure considers to be good ones to have—this process need not be unconscious or unreflective. The distinction between first order desires and second order volitions can help us see how the desire to become pious Muslim women is itself part of a theologically, ethically, and politically contested terrain over what a "pious Muslim" is or ought to be. Rituals can habituate people into particular dispositions, but the process of habituation ought to be understood in the context of people's second order volitions as well as *debates* about them. Only then can we see how the repetition that creates habits does not merely reproduce existing power relationships and social structures but also participates in the contestation over those relationships and structures and over the kinds of people that we ought to become.

Habituation and Freedom

Mahmood is interested in how the women participating in the mosque movement understand the relationship between their desires and their practices. As we have seen, she argues that they understand desire to be a product of moral pedagogy. It is through the repetition of socially prescribed activities that they work to cultivate a *habitus*. These activities include rituals like daily prayer, which are governed by a set of norms and standards that are not of participants' own choosing. In order to perform the rituals, the women submit to the norms and standards that govern them. This account of desires as the *product* of submission to norm-governed activities stands at odds with a model of subjectivity that distinguishes between "a person's 'true' desires and those that are socially prescribed."[32] Such a distinction, Mahmood insists, makes no sense when action in accordance with convention is understood to be the precondition for desire—indeed, the precondition for the emergence of the moral subject.

The women in the mosque movement act in accordance with a model of subjectivity that stands at odds with what Mahmood characterizes as a liberal conception of freedom. On such a conception, "an individual is considered free on the condition that she act autonomously: that her actions be the result of her own choice and free will, rather than of custom, tradition, transcen-

32. Mahmood, *Politics of Piety*, 149.

dental will, or social coercion."[33] Mahmood introduces the anxiety of liberal feminists and political theorists concerning whether the mosque participants, who sought to conform their will to the demands of a patriarchal tradition, could be said to be *free*. "For some scholars of gender," Mahmood writes, "women of the kind I worked with are often seen as depriving themselves of the ability to enact an ethics of freedom, one founded on their ability to distinguish their own (true) desires from (external) religious and cultural demands."[34] She continues, "How does one rethink the question of individual freedom in a context where the distinction between the subject's own desires and socially prescribed performances cannot be so easily presumed, and where submission to certain forms of external authority is a condition for the self to achieve its potentiality?"[35]

One implication of Mahmood's suggestion is that the desire for freedom is itself a product of a moral pedagogy. If *that's* the case, then, returning to the American context in which I've been considering civic ritual, we might hypothesize that it is only through participation in certain kinds of norm-governed activities that citizens come to desire the freedom deemed appropriate to democratic citizenship. But what *is* that freedom, if not the "liberal conception of freedom" that Mahmood criticizes?[36]

We are born into a world in which many of the norms in play and the ends being sought have been set by others, long before we arrive. We are shaped by these norms and disposed toward these

33. Mahmood, *Politics of Piety*, 148.

34. Mahmood, *Politics of Piety*, 148.

35. Mahmood, *Politics of Piety*, 149.

36. I still wonder whether it is possible for processes of habituation to extinguish the free will in the way that Mahmood suggests that the mosque movement participants aim to do. I've found Laidlaw's engagement with Mahmood instructive on this point. Among other things, he complicates her account of freedom, distinguishing in more detail than I do here among the many senses in which the participants in the mosque movement may or may not be said to be "free," including reflective freedom and various senses of political freedom. See Laidlaw, *The Subject of Virtue*, 138ff.

ends from the start. As we go along, we also engage in more intentional processes of ethical formation, performing acts in order to
cultivate habits and dispositions we have come to think are worth
having. You did not design the car that you drive or write the traffic
laws that govern how cars are to be used. But in acquiring the habits associated with driving a car and submitting to the rules and
norms that govern that practice, you gain skills and abilities that
you didn't have before. You're now able to do the thing that the
habits enable you to do. You can drive. We can think of this in
terms of positive liberty, understood as the capacity to achieve
certain ends. That capacity is made possible by your acquired habits. People's practical ability to put their habits to use toward their
ends, meanwhile, also depends on a degree of negative liberty—
freedom from undue encumbrances. You can't drive home from
work if there are police blockades along the road. In such a case,
your negative liberty—your freedom from certain forms of interference or domination—has been curtailed.[37] Notice that neither
of these ways of talking about freedom demands a distinction between a person's true desires and a set of social conventions, nor
does the desire for either sort of freedom presume a "true" self
with desires or choices unconstrained by norms and conventions.

37. We can further distinguish between freedom conceived as non-interference
and freedom conceived as non-domination. The former conceives freedom as the
absence of interference from others; a person is free to the extent to which she is
unimpeded in her actions, plans, and projects. (This is roughly what Isaiah Berlin
called negative liberty in "Two Concepts of Liberty," in *Four Essays on Liberty* [Lon-
don: Oxford University Press, 1969], 118–72.) The latter conceives freedom as security against domination. On this view, a person can be said to be free insofar as no
one *stands in a position* to interfere *arbitrarily* in their actions, plans, and projects.
(See Philip Pettit, *Republicanism: A Theory of Freedom and Government* [Oxford: Oxford University Press, 1997], and Quentin Skinner, *Liberty before Liberalism* [Cam-
bridge: Cambridge University Press, 1998], as well as, in relation to concerns about
religion, Jeffrey Stout, "Religion Unbound: Ideals and Powers from Cicero to King,"
2017 Gifford Lectures, https://www.giffordlectures.org/lectures/religion-unbound
-ideals-and-powers-cicero-king.)

In fact, norms and conventions are a precondition for the desire for and exercise of freedom, conceived in both of these ways.

According to the classical republican tradition that has influenced American civil religion, these positive and negative liberties are both important to the health of the republic.[38] The first is captured by the tradition's emphasis on the cultivation of civic virtue, and the latter by its emphasis on securing citizens against domination. Civic virtues are dispositions to think and act rightly and well, for the sake of the common good, and, like other virtues, they are acquired through practice. In a democratic republic, these might include habits of civic participation, of courage and hope, of tolerance and honesty, put to use toward the ends of justice and freedom, properly conceived. Such freedom involves, crucially for the republican tradition, security against domination understood as the condition of being at the mercy of another's arbitrary interference.[39] Consider an example. A woman who is an undocumented

38. See Gorski, *American Covenant*.

39. As Patchen Markell has argued, however, security against domination is not the only thing that we should be concerned about in a *democratic* account of freedom. We ought also to be concerned about people's participation in the processes by which their interests and ends are achieved. The struggle against domination is a struggle for control over setting one's own ends, whereas the struggle against usurpation is a struggle for involvement in the processes by which those ends are achieved. A robust conception of political freedom ought to have multiple facets, nondomination and involvement among them. There is, of course, a vast territory here; by no means do I wish to suggest that non-domination and involvement are sufficient or exhaustive for an account of political freedom. Related to Markell's notion that political freedom requires *participation* in bringing about one's ends is Sharon Krause's suggestion that one component of a plural conception of political freedom is "collective world-making, through which individuals can experience the transformative power of their own agency" (Krause, *Freedom beyond Sovereignty: Reconstructing Liberal Individualism* [Chicago: University of Chicago Press, 2015], 185). Although Markell and Krause come down differently with respect to political liberalism and the idea of the individual as the locus of freedom and agency, they share a sense that freedom requires this kind of political world-making *and* that such world-making activity can be formative for those who undertake it. See also Patchen Markell, "The Insufficiency of Non-Domination," *Political Theory* 36.1 (2008): 9–36. Furthermore,

immigrant to the United States finds work as a nanny, taking care of two children in a family's home. She is paid fairly and treated well by that family. Is she free? If freedom is taken to involve security against domination, then no, she is not. Although her employers treat her well, they are in a *position* to change their minds arbitrarily and with impunity. They could stop paying her, force her to work overtime without pay, or worse. Because of the power relations at work in their arrangement, and the lack of social, economic, and legal options for undocumented immigrants, she would have limited recourse against their unjust treatment. She remains dominated and therefore unfree insofar as her employers stand in a position to interfere arbitrarily with her and her projects—whether or not they choose to do so.

This may raise the question, once again, about the relationship between freedom and habituation. Acquiring a habit, or engaging in a process of ethical formation like that described by Mahmood, appears to involve submitting to a set of rules or norms that are not of one's own choosing. In many cases, it also involves submitting to another's authority—for example, the authority of God, clergy, or political leaders. When a person is habituated into a practice, they may acquire the habits of a submissive or subordinate subject, a person who submits habitually and consistently to the authority of another. Is *that* a kind of unfreedom? Are there persons, including divine persons, to whom one *rightly* owes deference or submission? Are there persons, including divine persons, religious or political authorities, parents or teachers, to whom one *rightly* owes piety?

A monk bows in prayer to an almighty God. A subject kneels before a king. A football player takes a knee during the national

---

given my dual interests here in civic virtue and non-domination, I'm intrigued by Melvin Rogers's suggestion that it is not the conception of freedom that best distinguishes the liberal and republican traditions but rather their compatibility (or not) with a robust conception of civic virtue ("Republican Confusion and Liberal Clarification," *Philosophy and Social Criticism* 34.7 [2008]: 799–824).

anthem. In each of these cases, the person who makes the gesture is not only inculcating the habit of undertaking the gesture itself. They are also cultivating—or, in taking a knee, resisting—the dispositions typically or normatively deemed appropriate to the one who makes such a gesture. In many social and political contexts, bowing, kneeling, and prostration are what Roy A. Rappaport calls "postures of subordination."[40] They are bodily postures or gestures that people with relatively low social status assume in the presence of those with relatively high social status, as when a human being bows before the divine sovereign or an ordinary subject bows before a powerful king.[41] Postures of subordination are connected to, and made meaningful in, particular relationships and contexts of power, domination, and subordination. They express and enact something about the relationship between the person making the gesture and the person, place, or thing toward which they direct their gesture. But these gestures can also habituate the people who enact them into the practice of doing so with the force of habit and cultivate the disposition of a subject who bows or kneels—which is, again, in many contexts, a submissive or deferential subject.[42]

In her influential work *Ritual Theory, Ritual Practice*, Catherine Bell argues that these postures and gestures are best understood

40. Roy A. Rappaport, *Ritual and Religion in the Making of Humanity* (Cambridge: Cambridge University Press, 1999), 142.

41. Rappaport, *Ritual and Religion in the Making of Humanity*, 142.

42. As Rappaport notes, the subordination that is expressed by postures of subordination could be easily communicated verbally, raising the question of why such ritualized gestures are made at all. Rappaport writes, "Since such messages are often transmitted by physical display rather than speech it is plausible to assume that the display indicates more, or other, than what the corresponding words would say, or indicates it more clearly. By kneeling or prostrating himself a man seems to be doing more than *stating* his subordination to an order. He is *actually subordinating himself* to that order" (*Ritual and Religion in the Making of Humanity*, 142). The ritualized acts of bowing, kneeling, and prostration are not only expressions of subordination; they are ways of enacting or performing subordination. I addressed the performative dimensions of rituals in chapter 3 and will leave it aside here.

as part of a process of *ritualization*. This is the process by which
people set some activities apart from other, more quotidian ones.
People ritualize activities by deploying certain strategies: repeat-
ing them, invoking tradition, embedding sacred symbols in them,
formalizing them. By deploying these strategies, Bell argues,
people not only ritualize their activities, distinguishing them from
others, but also produce "ritualized bodies," bodies with the habits, dispositions, and practical knowledge appropriate to their social environment or context. According to Bell:

> The molding of the body within a highly structured environ-
> ment does not simply express inner states. Rather it primarily
> acts to restructure bodies in the very doing of the acts them-
> selves. Hence, required kneeling does not merely *communicate*
> subordination to the kneeler. For all intents and purposes, kneel-
> ing produces a subordinated kneeler in and through the act it-
> self. . . . What we see in ritualization is not the mere display of
> subjective states or corporate values. Rather, we see an act of
> production—the production of a ritualized agent able to wield
> physically a scheme of subordination or insubordination.[43]

Ritualized activities, Bell argues, are habituating. Participation
in ritualized activities shapes the participant into a subject with
the habits and dispositions appropriate to the environment in
which she acts. Kneeling, for example, does not merely express the
kneeler's subordination. It produces a subordinate subject.

On Bell's account, much like Bourdieu's, participation in ritualized activities produces a ritualized body. Ritualized bodies, in turn,
tend to reproduce ritualized activities and environments. This is an
ongoing and repetitive process. As Bell writes: "Essential to ritualization is the circular production of a ritualized body which in turn
produces ritualized practices. Ritualization is embedded within the
dynamics of the body defined within a symbolically structured

---

43. Bell, *Ritual Theory, Ritual Practice*, 100.

environment."[44] In a context in which kneeling is understood as a posture of subordination (in what Bell refers to as the "symbolically structured environment"), the act of kneeling actually produces a subordinate body, one with the habits and dispositions of the subordinate subject. That subject is then able to perform the practices appropriate to her environment (in our example, the postures of subordination), thereby reproducing the context in which kneeling is a way of making oneself subordinate. Ritualization is, for Bell, an iterative process in which ritualized bodies perform ritualized acts that produce ritualized bodies, all within a ritualized and symbolically structured environment.

Ritualized bodies are invested with practical knowledge, the sort of know-how that is required to navigate ritualized environments and to reproduce them. This is akin to the Aristotelian insight that a virtuous disposition is not a matter of mechanical habit but of practiced skill and *phronēsis*, practical wisdom. Barbara Myerhoff gives us a great example of how this sort of practical knowledge can help people navigate situations that initially appear to be unruly or threatening to individual or social order. She describes a birthday party in a Jewish senior center that took an unexpected turn when the guest of honor, Jacob, died in the middle of the celebration. The attendees quickly shifted their ritual frame from birthday party to memorial service. Several of the men pulled out their yarmulkes and covered their heads. The rabbi spoke, and the group recited the Mourner's Kaddish. There were other "spontaneous expressions of traditional Jewish mourning customs" too: "Batya reached down and pulled out the hem of her dress, honoring the custom of rending one's garments on news of a death. Someone had draped her scarf over the mirror in the ladies' room, as tradition requires. Heschel poured his glass of tea into a saucer."[45] The attendees improvised a memorial service, turning a moment

44. Bell, *Ritual Theory, Ritual Practice*, 93.

45. Barbara G. Myerhoff, "A Death in Due Time: Construction of Self and Culture in Ritual Drama," in *Rite, Drama, Festival, Spectacle: Rehearsals toward a Theory*

of confusion and potential crisis into a familiar, if heartrending, ritualized environment. The attendees, themselves elderly Jews, were subjects with the habits, dispositions, and practical knowledge to conduct themselves in the right way at the moment of Jacob's death, reproducing a Jewish ritual frame and ritualized environment. They were not following a script, strictly speaking, nor were they enacting a mechanical habit; they were drawing on habits, dispositions, and practical knowledge to craft a ritually appropriate response to a novel situation.

The process that Bell describes as the production of the ritualized body is closely connected to Bourdieu's work on *habitus* and shares its emphasis on the unconscious or unknowing deployment of bodily habits. Bell suggests that when people enact rituals, even when they produce them in new situations or to new ends, they are engaged in a kind of illusion of their own freedom. She calls this "redemptive hegemony," the reproduction of ideology by people who believe themselves to be acting freely. I'm not so sure. Were the partygoers at the Jewish senior center reproducing ideology or improvising on a script? Maybe both, although I think that there are legitimate ways to talk about habituation and freedom that neither imagine these options to be at odds with one another nor imagine freedom to be illusory. Rituals contribute to the development of habits and dispositions. By repeatedly enacting a ritual, a person develops a set of embodied habits and dispositions appropriate to their social environment. Some of these habits and dispositions may be resistant to change. But rituals are also undertaken in the service of intentional processes of formation in which people work to cultivate new habits and dispositions, different from the ones they have, or at odds with dominant norms. They put their habits to use toward new ends, or work to change habits to achieve the ends they already have.

of Cultural Performance, ed. John J. MacAloon (Philadelphia: Institute for the Study of Human Issues, 1984), 149–78.

Ritual, Improvisation, and Refusal

When people enact rituals, over and over again, the routines may become habits, and practitioners may develop the virtues, habits, and dispositions of certain kinds of subjects. But practitioners do not become automatons. In fact, they may become able to *deploy* rituals in new and flexible ways, putting habits to use in pursuit of new ends. Habituation into a practice and its related dispositions can make improvisation and novel expression possible. By way of analogy, consider a poet who writes a new poem or a composer who writes a new piece of music. The poet is versed in the grammar of the language in which they write before they experiment with word and form. The composer understands the conventions of a musical tradition before they draft their score. And they know not only the rules of grammar or music but also the small rituals of usage and syntax that are already in use, the patterns of language or tones that mean different things or evoke different responses. Habituation into a set of normatively approved performances in some domain may be a precondition for creative or transformative action in that domain. Without the basic habits of an idiom—a language, a musical tradition, a set of verbal and gestural acts—such action is impossible. The positive freedom that is enabled by this habituation and mastery can be called "expressive freedom."[46]

To achieve this sort of freedom, a person needs to develop the sorts of habits that are involved in what Aristotle calls *technē*. As we have seen, these are technical habits, those that involve practiced learning of technical skills. To play the piano, or drive a car, or build a cabinet—or at least to do such things *well*—a person needs to develop a set of habits and then put those habits to use in doing the thing that they enable the person to do. But, as Aris-

---

46. In discussing "expressive freedom," I am following Robert Brandom's use of the term to characterize people's capacity to achieve linguistic novelty within the constraints of an idiom. Brandom, "Freedom and Constraint by Norms," *American Philosophical Quarterly* 16.3 (July 1979): 194–95.

totle suggests, the technical habits that these practices involve are rarely isolated from other habits and dispositions, including the use of practical wisdom to make judgments about when and how to put one's habits to use. These dispositions *are* reflective, and they are made possible by the expressive freedom that habituation into a practice enables.

Debates about the words and gestures that ought to be a part of the Pledge of Allegiance, or, to take an example of another civic ritual, the U.S. National Anthem, are partly about what virtues, habits, and dispositions the people weighing in on those conflicts think that political subjects ought to have and to cultivate. They are also about whether, and how, to exercise political freedom. From John Carlos and Tommie Smith's raised-fist salute during the national anthem on the medal stand at the Mexico City Olympics in 1968 to Colin Kaepernick's taking a knee during the national anthem at the start of NFL games in 2016, people's improvisation within or refusal of civic rituals is as much a part of these practices as the creation and implementation of them.

"The Star-Spangled Banner" was adopted as the U.S. National Anthem in 1931, and it has been sung at the beginning of NFL games since World War II. Just before the game begins, the players and the people in the crowd stand, men remove their helmets or hats, and many people place a hand over their heart. They face the U.S. flag and sing the national anthem. As a ritual in an American civil religion, the national anthem, like the pledge, can be understood as a political action that deploys powerful shared symbols to provoke a collective emotional experience and forge solidarity. To view civic ritual in these terms is Durkheim's legacy. But while the symbols involved in the national anthem *are* powerful—the flag as symbol of the nation-state, of course, but also the symbolic significance of the postures assumed—this analysis doesn't get at the formative work that the ritual does. Like the pledge, the national anthem is intended to bring about and enforce habits and dispositions of respect, deference, and patriotism.

FIGURE 4.1. NFL players Colin Kaepernick
and Eric Reid kneel during the U.S. National
Anthem at Bank of America Stadium in
Charlotte, North Carolina, September 18, 2016.
(Jeff Siner/Charlotte Observer/Tribune News
Service via Getty Images)

In 2016, and in connection with nationwide protests against anti-
Black violence, NFL players Colin Kaepernick and Eric Reid began to
kneel during the national anthem. Reflecting on their protest, Reid
later wrote that "we chose to kneel because it's a respectful gesture.
I remember thinking our posture was like a flag flown at half-mast
to mark a tragedy."[47] In protest and mourning, Kaepernick's and

47. Eric Reid, "Why Colin Kaepernick and I Decided to Take a Knee," *New York
Times*, September 25, 2017, https://www.nytimes.com/2017/09/25/opinion/colin
-kaepernick-football-protests.html.

Reid's bodies became flags flown at half-mast. Kneeling, often a posture of subordination, became in their protest a gesture of both sorrow and defiance, of bodies that would not stand tall in pious patriotism in the midst of tragedy.[48] Clearly, there is symbolic significance to this posture, and the act of refusal can be understood in these symbolic or expressive terms. Kaepernick, Reid, and others who later joined their protest refused to enact the postures that symbolize deference, enacting instead a posture associated with mourning. But we can also understand their protest in light of the expressive freedom made possible by habituation into a practice. Kaepernick and Reid knew their way around the ritual. Hundreds, maybe thousands, of times they had stood for the anthem in the usual and prescribed way. They had acquired the habits put to use in the ritual, and they could continue to do so, probably with the ease of second nature. Instead, they took on another posture to provoke reflection on the habits, virtues, and ends that Americans ought to have. Should people display and cultivate piety toward a country marred by racism and police violence? And if, as Kaepernick and Reid insisted, protest was itself a patriotic act, then what forms ought patriotism and piety to take?

Theirs was an act of expressive freedom within a ritual frame. It was also a polarizing act. Trump weighed in on the matter, stating that players who wouldn't stand for the anthem should be

---

48. Reflecting on continuities between the raised fist of the Black Power movement and the raised hands ("Hands up, don't shoot!") of the Black Lives Matter movement, Lindsay Reckson considers how a gesture of sorrow or surrender can become, through its public and participatory repetition, a gesture of defiance: "To throw one's hands up in the stadium, in the street, and (perhaps most powerfully) for the camera is to convert that gesture of surrender into something else: a shared performance that makes visible the deeply historical and split-second choreographies of power in which bodies deemed criminally other—deemed threatening, which is to say deemed black—become the objects of state violence. 'Hands up' cites and reroutes these choreographies, a physical disruption not unlike playing dead in solidarity with the dead, a form of protest to which it is closely aligned." Reckson, "Hands Up," *Avid*, December 11, 2014, http://avidly.lareviewofbooks.org/2014/12/11/hands-up/.

fired. And indeed, when Kaepernick became a free agent in 2017, he remained unsigned and filed a lawsuit against NFL team owners for colluding to keep him out of the league on account of his political views.

Rituals draw on the precedents of a shared practice to stake a claim about the people, goods, and values that the ritual ought to engage. When people enact rituals, they make judgments (sometimes unconsciously, other times highly self-consciously) about whether and how their enactment ought to follow these precedents. When other NFL players followed Kaepernick's and Reid's example—along with high school and college athletes across the country—they were taking up Kaepernick's and Reid's precedent and their inauguration of a new routine. Those who participated in the protest certainly expressed various things—sorrow at the unjust deaths of Black Americans, anger at the persistence of white supremacy, and solidarity with Kaepernick and Reid, for example—and also resisted their own habituation into the practice of standing for the singing of the anthem. Whether or not participation in the protest was enough to cultivate new habits and dispositions is debatable—probably not on its own—but for many protestors, this ritual innovation and protest made the national anthem and the dispositions expressed, enacted, and cultivated in it matters of self-conscious reflection.

In other cases, people have created and implemented brand-new rituals to encourage or cultivate habits and dispositions in opposition to the dominant norms of a broader society. "Lift Every Voice and Sing," sometimes referred to as the Black national anthem, was written in 1900 by James Weldon Johnson and John Rosamond Johnson. It was quickly adopted for widespread use in Black civic life and ceremonial events. In the first half of the twentieth century, in the American South, Black students in racially segregated schools often began their school day not, or not only, with the Pledge of Allegiance but with "Lift Every Voice and Sing." As Imani Perry notes, "Guided group singing of 'Lift Every Voice and Sing' was a means of socializing black children. . . .

The immanence of daily singing developed into an intimately held knowledge. Not simply of history but also resilience and resistance. It, along with a host of complementary ritual practices, created young people who were able to recast and ultimately transform this nation and world."[49]

As part of what Perry calls "black formalism"—a set of rituals with "embedded norms, codes of conduct, and routine, dignified ways of doing and being"—"Lift Every Voice and Sing" shaped the dispositions of those who sang it.[50] Perry continues: "For schoolchildren the song stood as an invocation, setting the terms as to how one ought to approach the school day. At graduations and at the conclusion of meetings of professional organizations it also could serve as a benediction. That Black formal culture often took on a liturgical structure makes sense given how central church was to Black life. But it also indicates that there was a ritual devotion to the art of discipline and achievement in the face of Jim Crow."[51] The singing of the hymn was both performative (an invocation) and formative (a means of cultivating virtues). As a ritual of Black civic life, the singing of "Lift Every Voice and Sing" was part of a process by which Black Americans cultivated habits and dispositions necessary for "resilience and resistance."

Such rituals are adopted, adapted, and resisted in order to cultivate the habits and dispositions that the people adopting, adapting, and resisting them think are good to have. These habits and dispositions, then, can be put to use in pursuit of ends that may be good or bad. In a political context, these ends may be just and democratic, or not. Conflict over civic rituals is often about this. The rituals that constituted Black formalism challenged the notion of citizenship and difference-effacing unity imagined by, for instance, Bellamy as he wrote the Pledge of Allegiance.

49. Imani Perry, *May We Forever Stand: A History of the Black National Anthem* (Chapel Hill: University of North Carolina Press, 2018), 84.

50. Perry, *May We Forever Stand*, 7.

51. Perry, *May We Forever Stand*, 87.

Through these rituals, Black Americans worked to cultivate habits and virtues needed to resist racial domination and to uplift Black citizens in the context of a Jim Crow America that would refuse to do either.[52]

Such rituals can pose a challenge to unjust and dominating political structures. They do so by taking up the questions raised early in this chapter and answering them in ways counter to dominant, and dominating, political norms: What kind of people will civic rituals constitute? What virtues, habits, and dispositions ought the citizens of a democratic society to have? And how will these things—a *demos* and the various people it comprises—be formed and sustained? These are political questions. The contexts in which they are asked are rarely just or democratic to begin with; answers to them are likely to benefit some and not others. Rituals have surely contributed to the formation and perpetuation of those unjust and undemocratic arrangements. But the solution is not necessarily to do away with rituals altogether. It is, rather, to engage in the power analysis that considers who gains or loses power in a particular ritual, whose power is legitimate, which habits and dispositions allow ordinary political subjects to work in concert to bring about just and democratic ends. Rituals can form virtuous citizens as well as vicious ones; the habits that they foster can be habits of acquiescence or engagement. They can inculcate the dispositions of quietists who go along with the way things are, or of democratic actors who exercise freedom in the struggle for justice.

---

52. In July 2020, in response to nationwide protests against anti-Black violence, the NFL appeared to recognize that it had been on the wrong side of history in its condemnation and blackballing of Colin Kaepernick for kneeling during the national anthem. The league's response? It announced that "Lift Every Voice and Sing" would be performed before its season-opener games in the fall. This was, I suspect, a cynical response, for as a Black civic ritual, the hymn has a long history of being co-opted by white institutions interested in performing inclusion.

5

Expressing Beliefs, Passions, and Solidarity

I WAS a senior in college when the United States invaded Iraq in 2003. During the early weeks and months after the invasion, I took part in a weekly candlelight vigil in the town square. Some of the participants were college students like I was; others were older college-town hippies, active members of the military from the nearby naval base, veterans, and local clergy. Among the participants were members of multiple religious traditions and none. As the sun set, we gathered to light candles and to stand together in silence.[1]

We participants did not have a complex script to follow; we gathered, lit our candles, stood together for a while, and then disbanded. It was a simple routine and open to all who opposed the war. Nevertheless, the vigil involved a repeatable, and repeated, sequence of acts, carried out in accordance with norms and in the service of things that the participants cared about. We lit candles, symbolic in many religious traditions of the divine light or spark. (In fact, the candles that we used were the very same ones used in

---

1. As I was finalizing the manuscript for this book, I learned that the vigil has continued to take place every Friday at 5:00 p.m. up to the present: Halina Bennet, "Let's Try Love: Brunswick Group Fights for Peace," *Bowdoin Orient*, November 12, 2021.

many candlelight church services—small white votives surrounded by a little ring of paper to catch the drips; I remember picking them up for the vigil one week from the local Unitarian Universalist church.) With our candles burning, we stood in silence, solemn and formal. In following the routine of countless other vigils, we joined the significance of our act to those others—from the Christmas Eve vigils in churches around the world to the very local and then relatively recent vigil held on my college campus at dusk on September 11, 2001. Those precedents provided context and weight to our gathering. We repeated our candlelight vigil every week, at the same time and in the same place.

The vigil was a response to an unjust war, sold to the American public through jingoism and deceit. We objected to the war, to the injustice and the lies. We mourned the loss of human life; we rejected the nationalist narratives that rationalized and even celebrated the death of innocents. We hated the war, and so we gathered to light candles and stand in silence.

But what kind of response is *that*? A vigil rarely ever changes the events to which it responds. It is a kind of witness or watchful waiting, often in sorrow, in solidarity, and, sometimes, in hope. I suspect it is the type of political act that tempts analysts to distinguish between prefigurative (read: expressive) and strategic (read: effective) politics and between rituals and ordinary action. But these distinctions do not hold. A vigil *is* expressive, and it also *does* things. We need a way of talking about what it is and does—both as a political act and as a ritual—that better captures what and how rituals can express.

In the previous chapter, I argued that people's repeated enactment of a ritual can give rise to habits and dispositions, while also cultivating the reflective and expressive resources to challenge and change them. I introduced the idea of expressive freedom, the idea that habituation into, and mastery of, a social practice can enable people to do something novel within the practice. I argued that expressive freedom can be turned to democratic ends in the pursuit of political freedom. Building on these ideas, in this chapter, I focus on *expression* itself: how rituals express beliefs, passions, and solidarity, and why this matters for their political use and power.

———

The idea that rituals are *expressive* has its critics in the study of religion. Talal Asad's influential essay on the genealogy of the concept of "ritual" exemplifies this scrutiny and skepticism.[2] Asad sets out to show how the concept of ritual has changed over time, with what he characterizes as the modern concept of ritual as expressive replacing an earlier concept of ritual as disciplinary. By characterizing "ritual" as expressive, Asad suggests, modern scholars of religion have lost a medieval and early modern insight that rituals are part of a process of moral and spiritual discipline—ways of cultivating virtues, habits, and dispositions. The *Rule* of Saint Benedict, for example, governed the lives of those in the medieval monastic order, prescribing monks' daily schedules and practices in order to facilitate the formation of Christian virtues. Asad argues that "in this conception, there could be no radical disjunction between outward behavior and inner motive, between social rituals and individual sentiments, between activities that are expressive and those that are technical."[3] He suggests that when "ritual" came to be conceptualized as a separate category of behavior— symbolic or expressive, rather than technical or effective—this understanding of rituals as formative activities was forgotten. Asad seeks to revive what he views as the earlier understanding of the concept of ritual, according to which "apt performance involves not symbols to be interpreted but abilities to be acquired according to rules that are sanctioned by those in authority: it presupposes no obscure meanings, but rather the formation of physical

2. Talal Asad, *Genealogies of Religion: Discipline and Reasons of Power in Christianity and Islam* (Baltimore: Johns Hopkins University Press, 1993), 55–79.

3. Asad, *Genealogies*, 63.

and linguistic skills."[4] He argues that it is a mistake to assume that rituals symbolize or express beliefs; in the cases that most interest Asad, they seem instead to inculcate abilities and skills in accordance with scripts, rules, and authorities.

The genealogical claim that a medieval and premodern conception of ritual as disciplinary was replaced by a modern conception of ritual as expressive seems, at the very least, too simple. As examples throughout this book have suggested, there is no shortage of modern scholars and practitioners of ritual who think of, and experience, ritual as formative; likewise, classical, medieval, and early modern texts suggest that what various rituals expressed mattered to the people instituting and participating in them.[5]

As I argue in this chapter, people *do* express things in and through their participation in rituals. How they do so can vary widely, and can involve speech acts, symbolic actions, normative postures and gestures, and interaction with sacred objects. How could people *not* express things in rituals? Rituals are laden with conventions, symbols, and norms. Implicitly or explicitly, they endorse, enact, and even transform those conventions, symbols, and norms. Rituals are not *only* expressive—as we've seen, they can be formative and performative too—but they can and do involve expression, and understanding *what* people express in rituals

4. Asad, *Genealogies*, 62. Even within the twentieth-century anthropological archive, however, Asad finds an alternative view in Marcel Mauss's conception of *habitus*, which emphasizes the embodied and learned nature of practical reason. This idea is also central to Bourdieu's practice theory (which, as we've seen, influences Bell's work on ritualization), although Asad does not discuss Bourdieu except to note that Bourdieu fails to cite Mauss's use of the term *habitus*.

5. Jeffrey Stout pointed out to me in correspondence that even Asad's own example of the *Rule* of Saint Benedict is more complicated than he lets on, since Benedictine practice involved reading scripture, particularly the Psalms, during the Hours. Two influential Benedictine monks, Gregory and Halmo, stressed the need for exegesis and interpretation of the nonliteral passages of scripture, of which there are many, suggesting that the *meaning* of the words read or recited mattered to them.

and *how* is part of understanding their political significance and their democratic possibilities.

In the case of the candlelight vigil, among the things that the members of that loosely organized group expressed were the belief that the invasion of Iraq was unjust, anger about the injustice, grief at the resort to violence, mourning for the war's victims, solidarity with those affected, and hope that the war would end. Only some of these things are beliefs, such as the belief that the invasion was unjust. Others, such as hope that the war would end, are propositional attitudes distinct from belief. Still others, such as anger about the injustice and grief at the resort to violence, are passions. Some of these things, in turn, presuppose beliefs, commitments, valuations, and other sorts of attitude. There is a vast territory here. Insofar as debates about what rituals do have focused on belief, they have overlooked many of these politically significant forms of expression: anger at injustice, grief for loss and harm, solidarity with the victims of state-sanctioned violence.

The ways that people express beliefs, commitments, attitudes, passions, and other things in rituals are also multiple: some rituals involve the linguistic expression of propositional attitudes, while others involve the non-linguistic expression of attitudes or passions. Rituals can be intentionally or unintentionally expressive, and what people express can be explicit or implicit in the activity. Most importantly, when rituals express things, they do so not in a way that reveals the practitioner's otherwise private state of mind but in a way that is public and that distributes goods—in this case, obligations and entitlements, including obligations and entitlements to be held accountable, or to hold someone else accountable, for a belief or other attitude. Ritual, as Robin Wall Kimmerer writes, "focuses attention so that attention becomes intention. If you stand together and profess a thing before your community, *it holds you accountable.*"[6] Let's see how.

---

6. Robin Wall Kimmerer, *Braiding Sweetgrass: Indigenous Wisdom, Scientific Knowledge and the Teachings of Plants* (Minneapolis: Milkweed Editions, 2013), 249 (emphasis added).

What *Is* Expression?

Before coming to an account of what and how rituals express, I want to outline a social practical approach to expression more broadly—to specify, that is, what is *done* in acts of expression. To say that someone expresses something is to say that they have communicated something. But communication can take place intentionally or unintentionally, and what is communicated can be explicit or implicit in the act of expressing. Often, when we say that a person expresses something in her speech or action, we mean that she is *intentionally* communicating a belief, attitude, or emotion to some other person. When I say to you, "The Iraq war was unjust," I am expressing my commitment to the truth of that claim. My expression is both intentional as an act of communication and explicit in the content that I am communicating. I intend to express my belief to you, and I am making that belief explicit.

An expressive utterance—one that, say, expresses a preference or a belief—is an act in normative social space. It changes people's obligations and entitlements. When I tell you that the Iraq war was unjust, I am communicating my belief about the war and thereby entitling you to attribute that belief to me. I am also assigning myself responsibility for that belief. For this reason, expression belongs in the realm of performatives, utterances that bring about a change in the social world. As I have discussed, things like promising and apologizing are classic examples of performatives; by uttering the words "I promise" or "I'm sorry," a person does the work of promising or apologizing.

As performatives, expressive utterances bring about a change in the social world. When I tell you about my views on the Iraq war, I am not merely reporting on something that is independent of the utterance. I am also *doing* something that has its own social effects: I am undertaking an act of expression. This runs counter to our ordinary way of thinking about "expression," which is more like what Richard Moran calls "the sense of expression as indication," as in, an indication of what the speaker believes or feels. On this view, a person successfully expresses something when the thing expressed reveals or represents what she believes or feels. The outward expression is a sign of the internal mental state. An alternative to this view, Moran suggests, is "the sense of expression as a *social relational act* addressed to another person."[7] In the first sense—expression as indication—expression is taken to be a verbal sign of a person's interior beliefs or feelings. In the second sense—expression as a social relational act—expression is taken to be a move within the context of a relationship that changes one or another person's normative statuses, such as what they are obligated to do, what they are entitled to believe, what they can expect of one another, and what they can be held responsible for. In this case, a person successfully expresses something when an audience recognizes her as having done so. It is this second sense that interests me here.

The shift that Moran describes is from the question of what is *revealed* by the expression to the question of what is *done* in the act of expression. But what is it that an act of expression does, if not reveal the speaker's mind or intentions? Paradigmatically, an act of expression gives the hearer or witness *entitlement* to attribute the belief or attitude that was expressed to the speaker and to hold her responsible for it. When I tell you that the Iraq war was unjust, you can now attribute that belief to me and hold me accountable when I fail to act in accordance with my expressed belief. If I don't show up for the vigil, or I avoid eye contact and mutter some excuse when you ask me to sign on to a statement publicly condemning the war, you have good reason to ask why I'm not acting in accord with my expressed belief.

This gets to the role of sincerity in expression. On the indicative account of expression, the speaker's sincerity is treated as a guarantee that what she expresses is a genuine representation of her beliefs and attitudes. But sincerity does not play the role of guarantor in the social relational account of expression. Instead, the

7. Richard Moran, *The Exchange of Words: Speech, Testimony, and Intersubjectivity* (Oxford: Oxford University Press, 2018), 108 (emphasis added).

speaker's sincerity gives the hearer a sense of what the speaker is assuming responsibility for in her expression. The analogy with promising is helpful here. When a speaker promises something, and the hearer or witness recognizes that the speaker has promised something, then a promise has been made—even if it turns out that the speaker did not have the intention to do the thing that she promised to do.[8] The same is true of expression. A speaker may express something—a belief or an emotion, for instance—and be recognized by an audience as having expressed something without this meaning or guaranteeing that the audience now knows the speaker's mind or intentions. As Moran puts it, "An utterance may in fact fail to be sincere and yet still be the performance of the act in question: an act of telling or promising."[9] I am still undertaking an act of promising even if I don't intend to make good on my promise, and others are still entitled to hold me accountable for having made (and broken) my promise. Likewise, I am still undertaking an act of expression even if I am not sincerely committed to the content of my expression, and others are still entitled to attribute to me the commitment thus expressed. In fact, both speaker and hearer can *know* that the speaker does not believe the thing that she expresses and it can still have the relevant function as an act of expression.

Characterizing expression as a social relational act, we can begin to see how recognition, responsibility, and authority come into play in what appears to be a rather simple utterance. If a speaker expresses something to an audience and the audience refuses to recognize the speaker's act as an *expression,* then the act of expression is infelicitous. If the audience recognizes the act *as* expression but fails to bring about the relevant changes in normative status (attributing the belief, holding the speaker responsible for it, and so forth), then, too, it has been infelicitous. This can happen when the power relations between speaker and audience are unjustly

8. Moran, *The Exchange of Words,* 108.
9. Moran, *The Exchange of Words,* 1.

asymmetrical. As Fricker argues, one important category of epistemic injustice is testimonial injustice, when a speaker's testimony
is not believed because the speaker is denied credibility. The denial
of credibility is often systematic, as in situations of gender and
racial domination.[10] In certain instances, the testimony of women
and people of color is less likely to be taken seriously than that of
white men. Prejudice and bias on the part of the audience can limit
their ability to recognize a speech act as the type of speech act that
it was intended to be and to take on the normative statuses that a
speech act of that type is supposed to create or enable. Along similar lines, Kukla argues that, for women in particular, emotional
speech acts are often interpreted as "mere *expressions* of emotion,"
including grief and anger, "incapable of bearing cognitive content
that is accountable to external facts about how things are" rather
than as rational responses to such facts about people's situations
and experiences.[11] In such cases, the expression of grief or anger
is taken up (and dismissed) as the *wrong* kind of act, as an irrational display of emotion rather than as an apt response to and attitude toward injustice.

Rituals, of course, are not straightforwardly linguistic. Even
when they do involve language, it is rarely the sort of sincere and
self-aware speech that characterizes the paradigmatic cases of expression. Nevertheless, there are three aspects of this account of
expression that are worth carrying forward into our consideration
of the political significance of ritual. The first is the idea that expression is not indicative but social relational. The second is the role of
sincerity *not* as access to the speaker's mind or intention but as an
assumption of responsibility—accountability—for what has been
expressed. And the third is the sense that expressive acts, like other
performatives, change people's normative social statuses insofar as
they are *recognized* and taken up by others. Each of these three features helps make sense of what ordinary acts of expression do, as

10. Fricker, *Epistemic Injustice*, 21.
11. Kukla, "Performative Force," 451.

well as how enactments of rituals *express*—and what such expression has to do with recognition, power, and justice.

Expressing Beliefs

Although skepticism about the expression of *belief* seems to be at the center of the concern about the conception of ritual as expressive, some rituals *do* appear to express beliefs. In Judaism, a centerpiece of morning and evening services is the recitation of the *sh'ma*: "Sh'ma Yisrael! Adonai eloheinu, Adonai echad! / Hear O' Israel! The Lord our God, the Lord is One!" This statement, from Deuteronomy 6:4, expresses and affirms belief in the unity and singularity of God. Through a set of linguistic and bodily actions, the recitation of the *sh'ma* expresses belief and related attitudes (about the importance of that belief, its role in constituting the community, and so forth).[12] In Islam, the recitation of the *shahada*—"There is no God but God, and Muhammad is the messenger of God"— involves bearing witness, or testifying, to a central tenet of the tradition. It expresses a belief, often in the presence of others.

In Christianity, a ritual expression of belief may take the form of a creed. "Creed" comes from the Latin *credo*, meaning, quite literally, "I believe." A creed is a codified statement of beliefs that are normative within a religious community. The creed is recited in the context of a liturgy, understood as a socially recognized, routinized, norm-governed sequence of acts—that is, a kind of ritual. A Roman Catholic, for example, might recite the Apostles' Creed at the beginning of praying the rosary or in the context of a baptismal ceremony; each of these rituals includes the creed as

12. Surrounded by a series of additional blessings that are read silently, the first line of the *sh'ma* is typically recited out loud and in unison, when enacted as part of the liturgy; depending on the community, people may close or cover their eyes while reciting it. According to the tradition, Jews are also obligated to recite the prayer at bedtime and upon waking in the morning, as well as when death is imminent, including in cases of martyrdom, thereby reaffirming their belief *and* ritualizing death itself.

well as other verbal and gestural acts. A further example is the
Nicene Creed. This statement of Christian belief dates to the fourth
century, when it was written by the Council of Nicea (325 CE),
with additions by the Council of Constantinople (381 CE), to
clarify the tenets of the emerging Christian church in the wake of
the Arian controversy.[13] The writing of the creed and its adoption
into the liturgy were intended to establish what was or would become orthodox Christian doctrine—what was, in other words, to
be normative for the Christian community. Today, it is the most
widely accepted authoritative statement of the Christian faith,
although it is not uncontested (more on this in a moment). Here
is the Nicene Creed, in a translation used in the Roman Catholic
liturgy in English:

> I believe in one God,
> the Father, the Almighty,
> Maker of all that is, seen and unseen.

> I believe in one Lord, Jesus Christ,
> the only Son of God,
> eternally begotten of the Father,
> God from God, Light from Light,
> true God from true God,
> begotten, not made, consubstantial
> of one Being with the Father.

> Through him all things were made.
> For us men and for our salvation
> he came down from heaven,
> and by the Holy Spirit was incarnate of the Virgin Mary,
> and became man.

13. The Arian controversy was a fourth-century theological dispute between
Arius and Athanasius of Alexandria (and their followers) concerning the relationship
between God the Father and God the Son and, relatedly, the divinity of Christ.

For our sake he was crucified under Pontius Pilate;
he suffered death and was buried.
On the third day he rose again
in accordance with the Scriptures;
he ascended into heaven
and is seated at the right hand of the Father.

He will come again in glory to judge the living and
    the dead,
and his kingdom will have no end.

I believe in the Holy Spirit, the Lord, the giver of life,
who proceeds from the Father and the Son.

With the Father and the Son he is worshipped and
    glorified.

He has spoken through the Prophets.

I believe in one holy catholic and apostolic Church.

I acknowledge one baptism for the forgiveness of sins.

I look for the resurrection of the dead,
and the life of the world to come. Amen.

The Nicene Creed codifies a set of claims about the nature of
God and about salvation history. It also lays out the speaker's
attitudes or stances toward those claims: believing in them, acknowledging them, hoping for them to come about. One way to
understand the recitation of the Nicene Creed, then, is as a performative that expresses a set of attitudes toward the content and
claims that are contained within it or presupposed by it. In reciting the words, the speaker assumes responsibility for that content and those claims.

In ordinary speech, if I say to you, "I believe in God the Father,"
you may take me to be expressing my trust in God, an attitude that
makes sense only if I also believe that God the Father exists. In my
statement to you, I assume responsibility for that claim. But what

about creedal recitation? If I make a similar statement in the context of reciting a creed, do I mean what I say? Do I assume some kind of responsibility? I think so! I will return to this question in a moment, but for now, it is worth noting, at a minimum, that the people who write creeds, incorporate them into liturgies, and argue over them take the content of those creeds seriously as among the things that participants in the liturgy ought to be responsible for.

Now, a complication of this idea about responsibility-taking is that one way that people try to shape children into responsible subjects is by inculcating commitments in them that those children have not chosen to undertake as a result of independent reasoning. As a child is learning to recite the Nicene Creed, for example, she is likely to learn to speak the words without fully understanding their theological significance. She is habituated into the practice of reciting the creed and participating in the liturgy, with one intended result being the development of the right sorts of attitudes toward the content of the creed, including belief that the salvation history laid out in the creed is true. The creed has a pedagogical function, teaching the tenets of a tradition at the same time that it forms the commitment to those tenets. Responsibility follows. A child who commits herself to the Nicene Creed at her first communion might become accountable in the eyes of her community or church officials for living in accord with the creed even if she does not understand the content well enough to be said to believe it. (One reason why some Protestant denominations instituted adult baptism is the sense that a person ought to be able to understand and believe what they are publicly committing themselves to and, thus, being held responsible for.) [14]

14. James K. A. Smith adds another dimension to this when he argues that critics of infant baptism miss that baptism is not about the expression of beliefs so much as it is about the formation and affirmation of kinship in Christ. I would argue that it is *both*, although it is not the infant (obviously) whose expression of beliefs matters to the formation of kinship in such a case. See Smith, *Imagining the Kingdom: How Worship Works* (Grand Rapids, MI: Baker Academic, 2013), 115ff.

A second complication is that people often disagree about what, exactly, is or should be expressed in and through any particular ritual. What people believe they are taking responsibility *for* in reciting a creed is likely to differ. Rituals are polyvalent, even as those who hold power in the communities in which various rituals are enacted may try to set or settle their meanings. Conflict over the wording of the Nicene Creed suggests that its content and claims matter to the people who have been involved in crafting, instituting, and reciting it. It is not enough to get the sound of the words right, and to recite them together; people also care that the beliefs and attitudes expressed in those words are the right ones to express. For example, the addition of the phrase "and the Son" (known as the "filioque") in the article on the procession of the Holy Spirit, adopted by many Latin-speaking churches in the sixth century and incorporated into liturgical practice in Rome in 1014, was not—and still is not—accepted by the Eastern Orthodox Church. In fact, the adoption of the filioque contributed to the schism between the Eastern Orthodox and Roman Catholic churches in 1054. Other Christian denominations (such as the Society of Friends and the Unitarian Universalists) reject the creedal formulation altogether.

To my mind, however, these two complications don't detract from the idea that rituals can be expressive or that expression involves responsibility-taking. In fact, I think they underscore these ideas. That's because, in the kinds of cases just described, people care enough about the rituals and their content to try to shape young people who will take responsibility for them, and to argue over what they *ought* to mean and what ought to follow from them.

Moreover, when a person recites the *sh'ma*, the *shahada*, or the Nicene Creed, whether or not she takes herself to be expressing a belief or attitude, she signals her commitment to a community or group. Back in the discussion of hailing and interpellation, I noted that the beginning of the *sh'ma* names the community for whom the content of the prayer is normative, calling them to attention: "*Hear*

O' Israel!" Likewise, when the Nicene Creed takes the plural form, as it sometimes does in Christian liturgies ("*We* believe . . ." as opposed to "I believe . . ."), its expression of shared identity and group membership is made explicit, signaling that "we" are the people who are bound together by the belief (hope, doubt, assertion, and so forth) that these claims are true. The "*We* believe . . ." that is implicit in the recitation of the creed in liturgical settings, and occasionally explicit in its plural form, establishes the boundaries around a community of shared belief. Those who refuse to recite the creed, or who recite it in an altered form, raise questions about who is to be included in and excluded from that community.

The Pledge of Allegiance is not *exactly* a creed, insofar as it does not take the explicit form of "I believe . . . ," but its recitation does express a set of beliefs and attitudes. So, while the pledge does not state, as the Nicene Creed does, "I believe in one God, the Father, the Almighty," it does refer to a nation that stands "under God," presupposing belief in the existence of such a God. As a child raised in a theologically skeptical household, I worried about the "under God" part of the pledge (worries about the rest of it would come later). Every day as a public school student I was expected to stand, face the U.S. flag hanging in my homeroom class, place my hand over my heart, and recite the pledge along with the voice over the loudspeaker and the chorus of voices of the children in my classroom. Sometime around fourth grade, I began to substitute "under goodness" for "under God"—an awkwardly Platonic formulation but one that seemed to my ten-year-old self like a better expression of what I was committed to. It seems to me now that I implicitly recognized that reciting the Pledge of Allegiance meant assuming responsibility for a set of propositions, at least some of which I was not committed to. And so I would not say all of the prescribed words.

Recitation of the Pledge of Allegiance involves an implicit expression of shared identity and group membership. Children stand together and say the same words, each one's expression of allegiance to flag and republic matched by the others' such that their expressed beliefs, commitments, and attitudes and their collective act constitute a shared identity. This is one reason why a child's refusal to stand and recite the Pledge of Allegiance makes the news every now and then. A child refuses to stand; her teacher forces her to stand; her parents object to the teacher's disciplinary action; administrators and lawyers get involved; the media reports on the conflict and the pundits weigh in.[15] At issue in these incidents and reactions to them is the question: How do the members of a group think about and react to a person who refuses to express her belief in the (supposedly) shared commitments of that group? That question connects back to the boundary work that rituals do by demonstrating one of the ways that people's anxieties about group boundaries and the policing of those boundaries show up in and motivate rituals.

The expression of beliefs is important enough to many people's understanding of liturgical prayer, creedal recitation, pledging, and undertaking an oath that they often argue over their content and truth value. We have seen already that the disagreement over

15. Recent incidents have challenged state laws that require students to stand (in possible violation of students' First Amendment right to free speech and Fourteenth Amendment right to equal protection under the law). At the time of writing, a case challenging a Texas law that requires public school students to stand and recite the Pledge of Allegiance (unless their parents sign a waiver) is making its way through the courts. See Emma Platoff, "Attorney General Ken Paxton Defends Texas Law Requiring Students to Stand for Pledge of Allegiance," *Texas Tribune*, September 28, 2018, https://www.texastribune.org/2018/09/25/ken-paxton-texas-law-student-stand-pledge-allegiance-/; Alex Horton, "A Black Student Refused to Recite the Pledge of Allegiance—Challenging Texas Law Requiring It," *Washington Post*, September 26, 2018. Other recent cases have involved teachers coercing or punishing students who refuse to recite the pledge. See, for example, Lindsay Bever, "This Child Sat for the Pledge—So His Teacher 'Violently' Snatched Him from His Chair, Student Says," *Washington Post*, September 15, 2017, https://www.washingtonpost.com/news/education/wp/2017/09/15/this-child-sat-for-the-pledge-so-his-teacher-violently-snatched-him-from-his-chair-he-says/?utm_term=.9ceb48c8d0dc; Mitchell Byars, "Colorado Teacher Pleads Guilty to Child Abuse after Forcing Student to Stand for Pledge of Allegiance," *Denver Post*, September 1, 2018.

the addition of the filioque to the Nicene Creed contributed to the schism between the Roman Catholic and Eastern Orthodox churches. That disagreement remains, and other disagreements over the Nicene Creed have joined it in the intervening centuries. Consider, for instance, Christian feminists' and womanists' calls to reinterpret, resignify, or even reject scriptures and liturgies that contain androcentric and masculinist metaphors for God. Such metaphors are centered on or emerge from men's perspectives, encoding the beliefs, norms, and valuations that are typically associated with masculinity and maleness in a patriarchal society. Christian scriptures and liturgies often refer to God as father, king, and lord. Christian feminist and womanist theologians have argued that these metaphors cast God as both a (patriarchal) male and a dominator.[16] The patriarchal father, king, and lord all have and exercise power over others in ways that are arbitrary and unaccountable. To cast God in these terms is to imagine God's power as arbitrary and unaccountable, too—and, hence, as unjust and dominating. Feminist and womanist theologians have argued that when God is conceived or represented in androcentric and masculinist terms by the members of a patriarchal tradition, that conception or representation both mischaracterizes God and licenses bad social, political, and theological commitments. As Rosemary Radford Ruether writes, "We need to find a new language that cannot be as easily coopted by the systems of domination."[17]

16. The relationship among gender, God-talk, and Christian theology was an important site of feminist theological work in the 1980s and 1990s. See, for instance, Rosemary Radford Ruether, *Sexism and God-Talk: Toward a Feminist Theology* (Boston: Beacon Press, 1993); Delores Williams, *Sisters in the Wilderness: The Challenge of Womanist God-Talk* (Maryknoll, NY: Orbis Books, 1993); and Rebecca Chopp, *The Power to Speak: Feminism, Language, God* (Eugene, OR: Wipf and Stock, 1991). Jewish feminists have made similar criticisms of Jewish texts and liturgies; see, e.g., Judith Plaskow, *Standing Again at Sinai: Judaism from a Feminist Perspective* (New York: HarperCollins, 1991); and Rachel Adler, *Engendering Judaism: An Inclusive Theology and Ethics* (Boston: Beacon Press, 1998).

17. Ruether, *Sexism and God-Talk*, 66.

Feminist and womanist theologians, therefore, have worked to resignify, replace, and reject androcentric metaphors for God. This work emerges from their concerns about what beliefs and other propositional attitudes people express when they use such language and what other beliefs (as well as norms, practices, and social arrangements) are licensed by them.

Feminist and womanist criticism and constructive work has extended to creedal formulations and confessions. The Nicene Creed, for instance, depicts God as "Father" and as "almighty," and refers to Jesus and the Holy Spirit as "Lord." Some English translations have introduced gendered language that is not present in the original Greek: the pronoun "he" for the Holy Spirit, for example, and the phrase "for us men" and "and became man" in the description of Jesus's salvific mission and incarnation. These latter concerns can be, and sometimes have been, addressed through the adoption of alternative translations. The former concerns are more difficult to address. Some feminist and womanist theologians have argued for the reinterpretation and resignification of the Nicene Creed; by changing people's understanding of the words being used, they aim to change what is expressed and licensed by those words. As Janet Martin Soskice writes, "Given the universal and egalitarian nature of the Christian faith, [critics] say, we can no longer say the creedal 'for us men and for our salvation' or 'almighty and most merciful Father.' This language must go."[18] Soskice's strategy is to recognize that the meaning of symbols and metaphors can shift and multiply and to mine the tradition for alternative meanings for patriarchal symbols. In *Gender and the Nicene Creed*, to take another example, Elizabeth Rankin Geitz offers a feminist reading of Christian scripture and an egalitarian account of God's power in order to recontextualize and resignify the language of

18. Janet Martin Soskice, *The Kindness of God: Metaphor, Gender, and Religious Language* (Oxford: Oxford University Press, 2007). See also the excellent forum on "divine fatherhood," convened and edited by Juliane Hammer and Vincent Lloyd, https://tif.ssrc.org/category/exchanges/divine-fatherhood/.

the Nicene Creed.[19] Others have argued for the introduction of new and additional words—such as feminine metaphors for God—or, more radically, for the abandonment of such liturgies all together.

The point here is that creeds, among other sorts of rituals, can express beliefs and attitudes. This is among the reasons that people institute and adopt them; it is also among the reasons that people contest and reject them. That debates about the beliefs and attitudes being expressed and licensed by various formulations of the Nicene Creed are among the things that have caused fissures within the Christian church suggests that it matters enormously to many of the people involved what people express when they recite the creed.

Let's return, then, to the question I posed earlier: When I express a belief or attitude in the context of reciting a creed, am I *really* assuming responsibility for it? As I said before, I suspect that the answer is yes. But my answer to that question depends, again, on my sense that expression is not *indicative*—in the sense of unveiling a state of mind that's otherwise private and obscure—but *social relational*. When I express something to you—a belief or an attitude, for example—you are entitled to attribute that belief or attitude to me and to hold me accountable for it. It is a social act, in the context of the relationship between us as speaker and hearer, that changes the obligations and entitlements that we hold relative to one another.

Nothing about this picture of responsibility and accountability changes in the context of ritual. When I express something in the context of enacting a ritual—in, say, reciting a creed—others who witness my enactment are now entitled to attribute the thing expressed to me and to hold me accountable for it. Of course, a femi-

---

19. See, Elizabeth Rankin Geitz, *Gender and the Nicene Creed* (Harrisburg, PA: Morehouse Publishing, 1995); also Piet Naude, "Can Our Creeds Speak a Gendered Truth? A Feminist Reading of the Nicene Creed and the Belhar Confession," *Scriptura* 86 (2004): 201–9.

nist may recite the Nicene Creed, in its traditional form, in the context of a Sunday morning church service, without being committed to the belief that "God is the Father." Nevertheless, her act is a social relational one, in which she may be taken to have assumed responsibility for what she expressed. Knowing her feminist commitments, a friend may ask, "How can you *say* that?" Or, "Do you *really* believe that?" And she might respond, "Well, not in the plain sense." Or, "No, I don't believe it, but I recite the creed for these other reasons."[20] In reciting the creed, she assumes responsibility for the beliefs and attitudes expressed, such that others can ask, "Why did you do that?" and she owes them a response.[21] If I stand and recite the Pledge of Allegiance, or sing the national anthem, in the wake of Kaepernick's and Reid's protest, my friends and comrades can ask me why I did that, or what I meant by it. I have assumed responsibility, and they can hold me accountable.

This complicates any straightforward distinction between ritual speech and action, on the one hand, and ordinary speech and action, on the other, along the lines of sincerity or authenticity. Adam Seligman and colleagues pose such a distinction when they argue that ritual and sincerity are two different modes of acting in the world. Ritual creates a "subjective world" that is

---

20. There is also the possibility that she hasn't given much thought to the meaning of the words or the beliefs expressed therein. The responsibility can be *retrospective*—that is, the friend's question prompts her to give a backward-looking account of what she might have meant, even if she didn't previously think about her meaning, beliefs, and responsibility in those terms. If we're stuck thinking about expression in the indicative sense, it is hard to see how this works. It sounds like the feminist ritualist is being disingenuous in giving an account of what she's assuming responsibility for after the fact. But if we're thinking about expression in the social relational sense, it is possible to see how the content and meaning of her expression take shape in the speech act and others' uptake of it.

21. Elizabeth Anscombe makes the pertinence of this question—"Why did you do that?"—central to her account of what makes an act intentional. See Anscombe, *Intention* (Oxford: Blackwell, 1957).

shared by all of those who participate in the ritual order. Sincerity, by contrast, aims at shoring up an "as is" world, one that reflects the authentic beliefs and feelings of individuals.[22] Ritual speech and sincere speech, ritual action and sincere action—these stand in tension, according to Seligman and his coauthors, with "sincere" objections to the ritual order interrupting and fragmenting the shared subjunctive world that ritual creates. The implication is that people's beliefs and attitudes about the subjunctive world created in ritual belong to some other mode of being. According to this view, when people make claims about what ought to be believed or done, they have moved out of the ritual order and into the sincere one.

This is relevant to the discussion of the politics of ritual for the following reason: if rituals create a "subjunctive world" that's shared by participants and undermined by contestation, then rituals only enter into a politics in a vaguely communitarian way—deploying shared symbols and forging solidarity. While rituals can certainly do those things, I've argued that they can be—and often are—sites of disagreement and dissent as well. Are feminist and womanist criticisms of the Nicene Creed "sincere," with those criticisms undermining the shared identity and world that the ritual creates? The relationship that I've charted between rituals and their enactments is more complex, more dialectical and diachronic than that. In this and other cases, people don't seek to undermine ritual full-stop; rather, they affirm some features of the ritual and challenge others, staking a claim about how to carry on in the spirit of the best precedents. They contest aspects of the subjective world that a particular ritual or ritual order creates, ask who benefits from the enactment of that world, and insist on alternatives that do justice to the world that *they* believe ought to be.

By thinking of sincerity *not* in terms of "authenticity" but in terms of what people assume responsibility for, we can make better sense of conflicts over rituals. And because social relational acts

22. Seligman et al., *Ritual and Its Consequences*, 4.

of assuming responsibility, and holding accountable, are among the most important acts undertaken by democratic actors, we can begin to see how rituals, thus understood, express beliefs, attitudes, and other things in ways that matter to our politics. Taking this account of expression, and of ritual, with us, let's turn now to the passions—and their much-debated role in politics.

Expressing Passions

Rituals can and do express things. Some rituals express beliefs and other propositional attitudes. Other rituals don't express beliefs but do express other kinds of things, including non-propositional attitudes and emotions. These can include the passions, such as wonder, fear, shame, grief, and anger. The passions are strong emotional states that are responsive to the world and that motivate or mobilize people's actions in it.[23] They are responsive to the world in the sense that they are provoked by events and experiences that reach beyond the boundaries of people's own subjectivities; they motivate or mobilize people's actions in the world by orienting them toward the world in a particular way. Wonder, for example, is an affective response to being confronted with the limits of one's understanding of the world, and it draws one toward the unknown, to try to think about it, even to understand and come to know it. Anger, to take another example, is an affective response to perceived injustice, a sense that something or someone has been wronged, and it involves the desire for restitution or recompense for that injustice. That desire may motivate the person who is experiencing anger to express her anger at the injustice, to try to hold the wrongdoer to account, or to right the wrong that has been done.

While some characterize anger and other vehement passions as irrational emotional states that need to be contained and corrected

---

23. A full account of the passions is beyond my scope here. I have benefited enormously from Philip Fisher's account in *The Vehement Passions* (Princeton: Princeton University Press, 2002).

by dispassionate reason, many others have argued for the importance of the passions in ethical and political life.[24] Anger, on Aristotle's view, is a passionate response to a violation of justice. Aristotle argues that "the person who is angry at the right things and
toward the right people, and also in the right way, at the right time,
and for the right length of time, is praised."[25] Anger can be a *virtuous* response to wrongdoing and a spur to political action to address it. It is also, on Aristotle's view, a golden mean. It stands between the bad temperedness of the tyrant and the in-irascibility of
the complacent. For these reasons, Aristotle argues, anger is a kind
of spiritedness that is essential to the practice and preservation of
freedom.[26] Because of their salience in contemporary protest and

24. Albert O. Hirschman's *The Passions and the Interests: Political Arguments for
Capitalism before Its Triumph* (Princeton: Princeton University Press, 1977) is a wonderful intellectual history of how rationality, and particularly a kind of rational self-
interest, came to occupy a position of supremacy over the passions in political and
economic thinking in the seventeenth and eighteenth centuries. More recently, political theorists and scholars of social movements have increasingly considered, and
lauded, the role of emotions and passions in democratic politics. Among this burgeoning literature see, for instance, Jeff Goodwin, James M. Jasper, and Francesca
Polletta, eds., *Passionate Politics: Emotions and Social Movements* (Chicago: University
of Chicago Press, 2001); Deborah B. Gould, *Moving Politics: Emotion and ACT UP's
Fight against AIDS* (Chicago: University of Chicago Press, 2009); Cheryl Hall, *The
Trouble with Passion: Political Theory beyond the Reign of Religion* (New York: Routledge, 2005); and Sharon Krause, *Civil Passions: Moral Sentiment and Democratic
Deliberation* (Princeton: Princeton University Press, 2008).

25. Aristotle, *Nicomachean Ethics*, IV.5.1125b.

26. Twentieth-century liberationist thought, particularly from women of color
feminists, has stressed the importance of anger in politics—both as an apt response
to injustice and as a source of motivation and endurance in the struggle to overcome
it. See, for instance, Audre Lorde, "The Uses of Anger: Women Responding to Racism," in *Sister Outsider* (New York: Crossing Press, 2007), 124–33; and, in response
to the anti-racism protests in summer 2020, Candace Jordan, "In Defense of Anger
in Anti-Racist Protest," June 15, 2020, https://berkleycenter.georgetown.edu
/responses/in-defense-of-anger-in-anti-racist-protest. On anger (and grief) in the
democratic organizing of the Industrial Areas Foundation, see Stout, *Blessed Are the
Organized*, esp. 53–69. I discuss Aristotle's view of anger, and the role it plays in Jeffrey

social movements, and the attention given to them in political theory, I focus here on anger and grief, although a passion such as wonder may be equally suited to a treatment of the politics of ritual (and, particularly, to a politics properly attuned to the world or universe beyond the human).

Passions appear when the boundary of the self or the group is threatened or impinged upon. Anger flares when we are slighted or unjustly treated by others. Grief erupts when we lose those people and things that we love. Wonder emerges when we hit up against the limits of our knowledge, even our very *capacity* for knowledge. In each case, the passion responds to a boundary that's threatened or traversed. Given this connection between the passions and boundaries, it is no surprise that rituals often express passions, since rituals are involved in the work of creating, maintaining, and traversing the boundaries of people and groups.

Ritual expressions of grief are most familiar from burial rites and mourning rituals. Grief is a passion that erupts in response to loss. We might distinguish among three ways in which people *express* grief. One would be straightforward and explicit linguistic expressions of grief. A friend asks a mourner how she is doing in the face of her loss, and the mourner utters the words that try to capture and communicate her grief and loss. A second would be *ritual* expressions of grief, the religious and cultural practices in which people participate upon the death of a loved one and in the days, weeks, and months to follow: funerals and memorial services, burials, and other rites of mourning. A third would be non-linguistic and non-ritual expressions of grief. It may be tempting to call these "natural" or "spontaneous" expressions of grief, but even these are likely to be learned and norm-governed responses to loss. Just think about the difference among weeping, wailing,

---

Stout's work on democratic practice, in a talk titled "Anger in Democracy" (Conference in Honor of Jeffrey L. Stout, Princeton University, September 8, 2018). Cf. Martha C. Nussbaum, *Anger and Forgiveness: Resentment, Generosity, Justice* (Oxford: Oxford University Press, 2016).

and ululating. Each of these expresses grief; each would be appropriate and even expected of a mourner in one context or community and utterly unexpected or inappropriate in another. We might think of these second and third categories, ritual and nonritual expressions of grief, in terms of those social practices that involve routinized sequences of acts and those that don't.

Each of these is capable of communicating, intentionally or unintentionally, explicitly or implicitly, the mourner's grief to others. In the first case, the mourner expresses her grief in the context of a speech act, the purpose of which is straightforwardly and explicitly communicative. Recall Moran's claim that expression involves the speaker's assumption of responsibility for what's expressed: "When the person expresses herself . . . she doesn't simply provide a window onto her state of mind, but also 'owns up' to the attitude in question, acknowledges it, and assumes a certain kind of responsibility for it, and for the hearer's knowledge of it."[27] Part of what *this* sense of expression entails is the intention to communicate and the assumption of responsibility for what is communicated. It is an intentional act of communication. The third case is quite different. The mourner's grief is communicated in the action and her performance of it, regardless of her *intention* to communicate that grief. If there are witnesses, they may be entitled to attribute grief to her, based on her action. But the presence of witnesses is irrelevant; her act is not performative or social relational in that sense.

For the present task of thinking through the politics of ritual, however, it is the second case that is most important. This case stands somewhere between the other two. The mourner participates in rituals that are both expressive and performative. They *express* her grief in ways that are norm-governed and social relational. They also *enact* her grief, in the sense that they simply *are* ways of grieving. To participate in mourning rituals is to undertake the work of mourning.

27. Moran, *The Exchange of Words*, 86.

Mourning rituals and burial rites express grief through routinized sequences of words, gestures, postures, and other bodily acts. They are the conventional bodily enactment of the passion, grief, for the members of a particular community or tradition, and they are taken by the members of that community or tradition to express grief at the loss of someone who matters to them.

Like many traditions, Judaism prescribes a series of actions for mourners that give shape and expression to the experience of grief. These actions begin immediately after the death of a loved one and continue, at gradually diminishing degrees of intensity, for a full year. These include the weeklong period of "sitting shiva," when mourners stay home to receive visitors who offer their condolences. While sitting shiva, mourners traditionally sit on low benches or stools to symbolize the discomfort of their grief. They do not wear makeup or leather, they do not shave, and their mirrors are draped with fabric. Upon returning home from the burial, the mourners light a candle that burns for the entire seven days. (Mourners continue to light a candle every year on the *yahrzeit*, or anniversary of the death.) For as long as a year, depending on the mourner's relationship to the deceased, they recite the Mourner's Kaddish daily. At the one-year anniversary of the death, the mourners return to the cemetery to recite the Mourner's Kaddish and to unveil the tombstone.

Jewish mourning rituals express grief and constitute ways of grieving. They express grief by giving public voice and form to moods, states, and attitudes. They communicate. But they also just *are* the normative ways of grieving in a Jewish community. I mean to avoid, on the one hand, the suggestion that what is "really real" lies somewhere within the mourner (the "actual" grief) and, on the other hand, the claim that the action in which the mourner engages bears no relation to her attitudes. Each of these claims errs in bifurcating her supposedly private attitudes and her public actions. Ritual expressions of grief are ways of grieving, even as they are shaped by routines, norms, and conventions. They are both communicative and performative, expressing grief and doing the work of grieving.

Mourning rituals can also create and distribute normative statuses. Someone who is denied burial rites or public mourning is, in essence, denied standing in their community. This can be an injustice of the kind discussed in chapter 2, stemming from the absence or denial of a ritual and the goods distributed therein. It is a failure both to recognize a person's rightful status and to render unto them the goods that are their due. Something like this was at issue when Michael Brown was killed in Ferguson, Missouri, and the police left his body lying in the street for hours. The obvious and central injustice in this case was his death at the hands of the police. But an additional injustice stemmed from the state's treatment of Brown's body in the hours following his death. By denying his family and friends the right to treat his body in the normatively approved ways, the state attempted to deny him the status accorded to members of the community and to deny his loved ones their status as mourners.[28] Judith Butler has powerfully raised the issue of "grievability" as a central question of contemporary politics: "An ungrievable life is one that cannot be mourned because it has never lived, that is, it has never counted as a life at all. . . . The differential distribution of public grieving is a political issue of enormous significance."[29] Mourning rituals can appear in protests as a way of expressing grief and demanding its recognition.[30]

28. As mentioned in the introduction, in the early days of the Covid-19 crisis in the United States, one protest of President Trump's inaction and failures of leadership involved a procession of cars that drove to a Trump golf course near Philadelphia and dumped mock body bags at the entrance. Here, the treatment of the body bags—the "bodies" unidentified in nondescript bags, unceremoniously dropped at the gate to the golf course—mimicked the absence of collective mourning rituals during this time of social distancing. It also signaled the disregard that the president's policies and pandemic response showed to the lives of ordinary people. Similar protests took place at other Trump properties in the following weeks.

29. Judith Butler, *Frames of War: When Is Life Grievable?* (New York: Verso, 2009), 38.

30. There is an extensive, and growing, literature on the politics of mourning. Particularly influential for my thinking on ritual, politics, and mourning have been Butler, *Frames of War*, and *Precarious Life: The Powers of Mourning and Violence* (New York: Verso, 2004); Honig, *Antigone, Interrupted*; and Pool, *Political Mourning*.

When the AIDS organization ACT UP held its first political funeral in Washington, D.C., in 1992, demonstrators literally brought the victims of the AIDS epidemic into public view, carrying the ashes of dead friends and family members through the streets of the capital to the White House. A leaflet announcing the action read: "Bring your grief and rage about AIDS to a political funeral in Washington, D.C."[31] These political funerals were rituals; they were funeral processions and mourning rites in which people grieved and called for others to recognize and respond appropriately to their grief and anger. As Deborah Gould writes, "These funerals transformed the staggering personal losses into a political as well as a personal tragedy, into an injustice that should motivate lesbian and gay indignation, fury, and direct-action activism."[32] They mobilized people's grief in loss and anger at injustice to demand better health care and access to life-saving drugs for those still living with AIDS. In this sense, the political funerals did what Heather Pool describes as "us[ing] the deaths of everyday people to demand changes in the conditions of future *life*."[33] One way that people do this is by performing rituals that enact, and demand that others recognize, the normative status of the dead and of those who grieve them.

Something similar has taken place in Black Lives Matter protests, beginning in the mid-2010s and continuing to the present. The movement's slogan—"Black lives matter!"—asserts what is denied by police violence that disproportionately impacts Black people. The movement's political actions—which include die-ins and mourning rituals—collectively embody and express grief at Black deaths, a passion that stands at odds with that expressed by

---

31. Gould, *Moving Politics*, 230.

32. Gould, *Moving Politics*, 233.

33. Pool, *Political Mourning*, 22 (emphasis in original). Pool's work has been especially helpful to me in thinking about what's *political* about political mourning, although her account does not discuss rituals and their particular use and power in political mourning.

police violence, judicial failings, and white indifference. The state left Michael Brown's body lying in the street for hours. Black Lives Matter protestors took to those streets to assert that Black lives matter and Black deaths would be mourned. Political mourning of this kind, as Pool argues, can lead people to redraw the boundaries of inclusion in a political community and to take responsibility for the conditions under which their fellow citizens live. Black Lives Matter, she writes, "is a democratic movement calling us to revisit the contours of American identity and our responsibility toward one another."[34]

Several protests put the connection between the Black Lives Matter movement and the ritual expression of grief front and center. One protest against police violence and systemic racism, discussed in the introduction, took place in the wake of a Grand Jury's decision not to indict the police officer responsible for the death of Eric Garner. Jewish protestors gathered on a street in the Upper West Side of Manhattan and recited the Mourner's Kaddish. Following the recitation of the prayer, the protestors said the names of more than twenty Black men who had recently been killed by the police and then the words, "I am responsible." This spoken affirmation of responsibility made explicit what in the ritual was implicit: that in taking on the obligation to say Kaddish for Eric Garner, the participants made themselves responsible to him and responsible for grieving him.

In this act, protestors drew on an existing set of songs, prayers, and rituals to express their grief at Garner's death. This grief was closely connected to another passion—anger. Black Lives Matter protests express grief at loss *and* anger at the injustice of that loss. They also express the desire that something be done to address the injustice. The expression of grief and anger in and through ritual is one way of responding to, and against, norms about whose lives

34. Pool, *Political Mourning*, 128.

matter that are embedded in laws, institutions, and political processes.[35]

Expressing Solidarity

Émile Durkheim, and the tradition of social theory that follows from him, emphasizes the role of rituals in creating and maintaining solidarity. Durkheim argues that rituals are powerful symbolic actions, which forge a collective out of disparate individuals. He writes, "It is by uttering the same cry, pronouncing the same word, or performing the same gesture in regard to some object that [individuals] become and feel themselves to be in unison." When

35. Joseph R. Winters's *Hope Draped in Black* recommends an ethos of "melancholic hope," often displayed and enacted in the Black literary and aesthetic tradition, which involves dwelling in and with loss, and refusing the narrative of racial progress that weaves the suffering of Black people into a story of overcoming and reconciliation, à la American exceptionalism. Winters hints at the idea that there might be ongoing practices and mourning rituals that can help cultivate and sustain such an ethos, even as he cautions against mourning rituals that seek to foreclose the losses that have been sustained. I take my work here to be contiguous with his suggestion and caution. Winters, *Hope Draped in Black: Race, Melancholy, and the Agony of Progress* (Durham: Duke University Press, 2016).

Ritual expressions of grief can also call for the recognition of the value or dignity of non-human lives, of the more-than-human. Motivated by grief and anger, radical eco-activists protest to draw attention to the value of more-than-human lives and to express their grief and anger at the disregard for and destruction of those lives. This, too, should also be understood as a kind of political mourning. As Sarah M. Pike notes in *For the Wild*, eco-activists' "protests work as ritual practices to express loss at the same time that they constitute the meaning of that loss" (194). Tree-sits and hunger strikes, Pike argues, are ritual acts of protest. They respond to human disregard for the lives of trees, other plants, and non-human animals, in part by treating those lives as grievable. They express grief and anger, and call for recognition of those passions by demanding changes to the economic and political structures that treat the more-than-human inhabitants of our world as disposable. In "Indigenous Rituals Remake the Larger-than-Human Community" (in *Reassembling Democracy*, ed. Harvey et al., 69–85), Graham Harvey makes a similar claim about Indigenous rituals that enact, and demand recognition of, the personhood of more-than-human beings.

people enact a ritual together, they are joined in a collective experience around shared symbols and sacred things. This experience fosters feelings of unity, of belonging. It "set[s] the collectivity in motion."[36] As I suggested earlier, it is this view of ritual that is most often used to explain the significance of *civic* rituals such as the Pledge of Allegiance. In the last chapter, I insisted on civic rituals' formative function as well and argued that protests of such rituals are, in part, about the habits, dispositions, virtues, and ends that citizens ought to have. Here, with rituals' relationship to solidarity in mind, I want to consider how rituals might *enact* something like solidarity, not necessarily or only by deploying shared symbols but by distributing obligations and entitlements.

Solidarity—at least, in many of the term's most significance usages—is not only about *feelings* of unity and belonging. It is also about relating to and acting with others in ways that recognize interdependence and responsibility for the common good. Around the same time that Durkheim was theorizing social cohesion, "solidarity" also emerged as a central concept of Catholic social teaching, connected to the idea of the common good. In the papal encyclical *Rerum Novarum* (1891) and continuing through the twentieth century, papal teaching recognized human beings' social and economic interdependence and urged the cultivation of relationships, practices, and institutions for the benefit of all.[37] The concept became central, too, in the international labor movement. Invoked now in the idea of the "solidarity economies"—a term that encompasses a variety of cooperative, worker-owned, and other alternative economic models within and alongside capitalist economic formations—the idea of solidarity centers interdependence and interconnection among a diverse people.[38]

36. Durkheim, *The Elementary Forms of Religious Life*, 258.

37. Pope Leo XIII, *Rerum Novarum*, http://www.vatican.va/content/leo-xiii/en/encyclicals/documents/hf_l-xiii_enc_15051891_rerum-novarum.html.

38. See Leah Hunt-Hendrix's history of the ideal of solidarity from the nineteenth century to the present ("The Ethics of Solidarity: Republican, Marxist, and Anarchist Interpretations" [PhD diss., Princeton University, 2014]). Thanks to my colleague Craig Borowiak for introducing me to the literature on solidarity economies, and for

Rituals can foster solidarity not only in the sense that they can generate *feelings* of unity but also in the sense that they can express and enact these relationships of interdependence. To see how this is so, let's return to the social relational account of expression with which this chapter began. When someone makes a promise to someone else, they create new statuses of obligation and entitlement. Other things being equal, the one who makes the promise is obligated to do the thing that they promised; the one to whom the promise is made is entitled to expect that the promise will be fulfilled. Likewise, a ritual can express solidarity in a way that issues obligations and entitlements. When someone expresses solidarity with another person or group, they are expressing their commitment to stand with them. They create new obligations and entitlements. They communicate that they can be counted on to act in certain ways and that others are entitled to expect them to act in those ways and to hold them accountable if they do not. A ritual that expresses solidarity authorizes an obligation, for the one, and an expectation, from the other, that the expresser will do what they say they are going to do.

To be in solidarity with a person or group is to stand with them in front of, or in the face of, someone or something else. As with grief, the expression of solidarity in rituals is both communicative and performative. It is not only a matter of signaling, "I stand in solidarity with this person or group," but also a way of *being* in solidarity with them. Rituals that express solidarity often involve actually standing (or sitting) with or in the place of the person or group with whom one takes oneself to be in solidarity, putting one's body on the line for the sake of that person or group and one's relationship with them.[39]

---

his own work mapping solidarity economies in the United States. See http:// cborowiak.haverford.edu/solidarityeconomy/.

39. Nichole M. Flores draws on Catholic social thought and Latine theology to distinguish among four dimensions of solidarity: intellectual, practical, consumptive, and aesthetic. As I understand it, the solidarity that is expressed and embodied in rituals has both practical and aesthetic qualities: it involves collective embodied action—this is the "*standing* with" of solidarity—as well as "uniting around signs

Let's look at an example: the rituals enacted in Tahrir Square in Cairo, Egypt, during the pro-democracy protests in 2011. On a series of Fridays in late January and February, tens of thousands of Muslims gathered in Tahrir Square for Juma prayers. They were surrounded by Coptic Christians and secularists who used their bodies as shields to protect those praying. On the following Sundays, Christians held Mass in the square, protected by Muslims. Ali Aslam describes the scene:

> These prayers were remarkable at many levels. Not only did the scale of the prayers rival only the Hajj or annual pilgrimage to Mecca in numbers and visual impact, but also these prayers were unique in how inclusive and pluralistic they were. Egyptians had few points of reference to comprehend the presence of non-Muslims participating in the prayers and Muslims participating in a Coptic Mass for Martyrs of the Revolution the previous Sunday. Nor did they have experience with men and women standing, in some cases, next to one another, shoulder to shoulder in prayer rather than in segregated areas . . . Coptic Christians and secularists stood forming a human barrier around Muslim worshippers, securing the safety of those participating in the *Salat-al-Juma* on the Friday of Rage and the Friday of Departure. Muslims in the Square performed the same task during Christian services on the following Sunday mornings.[40]

These ritual acts, Aslam argues, were crucial in generating the conditions necessary for the growth of the pro-democracy movement. Through them, Muslims, Christians, and secularists "were generating trust by enacting trust."[41] Their rituals, in other words, en-

[and symbols] that promote justice or injustice." See Flores, *The Aesthetics of Solidarity: Our Lady of Guadalupe and American Democracy* (Washington, DC: Georgetown University Press, 2021), 141.

40. Ali Aslam, "Salat-al-Juma: Organizing the Public in Tahrir Square," *Social Movement Studies* 16.3 (2017): 302.

41. Aslam, "Salat-al-Juma," 304.

acted and embodied trust and solidarity among diverse citizens, which then made it possible for others to take on the risk of joining the movement.[42]

Because the expression of solidarity involves undertaking a commitment and a willingness to be held responsible for that commitment, the protestors in Tahrir Square earned the trust of others, who were witnesses to these ritual acts and who then became democratic actors themselves. As a result of interreligious and sectarian rituals, performed in public, other Egyptians from diverse religious traditions took up the call to political action. Though Aslam does not use the term, we might see in his analysis of these rituals a prefigurative politics at work, one in which rituals enact and embody the solidarity of the democratic community that these political actors hope for, while also creating the conditions for others to join in solidarity and democratic action.

In *Ritualized Faith*, Terence Cuneo suggests that the rites of repentance in the liturgies of the Eastern Orthodox Church express solidarity with "the least of these." He writes that "the activity of repenting is another way by which the people express solidarity with those for whom they pray. It is another way to acknowledge our common condition."[43] Cuneo describes, for instance, the opening petitions (the Great Litany) of the Liturgy of St. John Chrysostom, which begins:

DEACON: In peace, let us pray to the Lord.
PEOPLE: Lord have mercy [*and so after each petition*].
DEACON: For the peace from above and for the salvation of
    our souls, let us pray to the Lord.

---

42. Aslam draws on Michael Suk-Young Chwe's notion of "rational rituals" to describe how rituals generate trust. Chwe takes a game-theoretical approach, suggesting that rituals coordinate action and communicate what is "common knowledge" to others. See Chwe, *Rational Ritual: Culture, Coordination, and Common Knowledge* (Princeton: Princeton University Press, 2001).

43. Terence Cuneo, *Ritualized Faith: Essays on the Philosophy of Liturgy* (Oxford: Oxford University Press, 2016), 36.

For the peace of the whole world, for the welfare of the holy
churches of God, and for the union of all, let us pray to the
Lord.

For this holy house and for those who enter with faith,
reverence and the awe of God, let us pray to the Lord.

For our Metropolitan, for our Bishop, for the honorable
Priesthood, the Diaconate in Christ; for all the clergy and
people, let us pray to the Lord.

For the President of our country, for all civil authorities, let us
pray to the Lord.

For this city, for every city and country, and for the faithful
dwelling in them, let us pray to the Lord.

For travelers by land, by sea, and by air; for the sick and the
suffering; for captives and their safety and salvation, let us
pray to the Lord.

For our deliverance from all affliction, wrath, danger, and
constraint, let us pray to the Lord.[44]

Cuneo points out how the Great Litany moves outward from the
congregation to the city, to the country, and to all those who are
suffering. After each line, the people repeat their petition, "Lord
have mercy," seeking God's mercy for themselves ("this holy house
and . . . those who enter") as well as for religious and civil authorities, for travelers, for the sick and suffering, and for captives. He
notes that the "our" in the last line ("For our deliverance") might
refer to those offering the prayer or to all of those who have been
named in it. If the latter interpretation is right, Cuneo suggests,
"the Great Litany itself would be a vivid case of the *people expressing union or solidarity* with those for whom they pray."[45] Cuneo
argues that the expression of solidarity—a way of standing with
"the mourners, the meek, and the distressed"—lies at the heart of
participation in the liturgy.[46]

44. Quoted in Cuneo, *Ritualized Faith*, 26.
45. Cuneo, *Ritualized Faith*, 27 (emphasis added).
46. Cuneo, *Ritualized Faith*, 32.

Cuneo's suggestion is intriguing. But his formulation may run the risk of conflating solidarity with the oppressed with compassion for the suffering. It evokes a *feeling* of unity but not (necessarily) a commitment or new set of obligations and entitlements. Because solidarity is relational, and involves both one's commitment to stand with others and others' entitlement to hold one responsible for that expressed commitment, it goes beyond compassion in undermining the one-sided and dominating relational structure in which those who are oppressed or suffering are denied the means to hold others accountable.

Beyond these two examples are countless other rituals that are worth considering as expressions of solidarity: an iftar that brought hundreds of Palestinians together, seated along a table the length of a street, in an East Jerusalem neighborhood where Palestinian families faced imminent eviction; a neighborhood walk, modeled on the Roman Catholic devotional practice the Stations of the Cross, in which diverse residents walked to a series of sites of recent gun violence, stopping at each to pray together; a proposed campus-wide act of foot-washing as a counterprotest against a protest staged by the virulently anti-LGBTQI Westboro Baptist Church at a small liberal arts college.[47] Notably, the foot-washing ritual didn't quite happen; Jonathon Kahn writes beautifully about the idea, which he and his students planned and proposed when

47. At the time of writing, I have not come across any scholarship on the iftars in Sheikh Jarrah in spring 2021, but there are several news reports. See, for instance, Suman Priya Mendonca, "What Is Sheikh Jarrah Turmoil? Iftar Turns Violent, 15 Arrested in Jerusalem," *International Business Times*, May 7, 2021, https://www .ibtimes.sg/what-sheikh-jarrah-turmoil-iftar-turns-violent-15-arrested-jerusalem -video-57316; I wrote about the Good Friday Stations of the Cross in the Germantown neighborhood in Philadelphia in "Toward an Ethics of Social Practice," in *Everyday Ethics: Moral Theology and the Practices of Ordinary Life*, ed. Michael Lamb and Brian A. Williams (Washington, DC: Georgetown University Press, 2019); Jonathon Kahn, "When the Westboro Baptist Church Came to Vassar College: A Quixotic Story of Foot Washing, Activist Pedagogy, and the Secular Liberal Arts," *Soundings: An Interdisciplinary Journal* 103.1 (2020): 1–34.

Westboro Baptist Church announced their intention to protest at the gates of Vassar College. Vassar's administration made clear that this strange counterprotest would not happen. For Kahn, however, what would have been powerful about the ritual stems from what made it strange to the administrators: its bodily and affective nature. Rather than responding to Westboro Baptist Church with speeches and verbal affirmations of love and tolerance, the foot-washing would have countered Westboro Baptist Church's presence with a ritual act that embodied new intimacies and solidarities among diverse participants.

What makes these rituals interesting as political actions is not the degree of publicity or participation. Some took place in private institutions and others on public streets; some involved dozens and others thousands of people. Some groups were more diverse than others, and along different lines. But in each case, participants enacted (or, in the case of the foot-washing, proposed to enact) these rituals as collective actions that expressed solidarity with others, in the face of oppression, threat, or harm. In each case, the people who participated in the ritual both *expressed* that solidarity and *enacted* it, by sitting or standing together, protecting others, or casting their lot together, while also making themselves responsible to one another.

Rituals can issue and alter people's normative statuses, changing, for instance, what people owe to one another and what they can expect from one another. Expressions of belief, passion, or stances such as solidarity in rituals are not *merely* verbal signs of internal mental states. Neither are they meaningless formulae. They are, or can be, ways for people to communicate who or what they stand for and with. Such acts of communication are embedded in relationships, including relationships of accountability. Just as promises can create obligations and entitlements, so too rituals of solidarity. If I make a promise to you, you can expect me to fulfill my promise and you may hold me accountable if I don't keep my promise. If I express my solidarity with you, you can expect me to stand and act with you and you may hold me accountable if I don't show up. Because rituals are shared and norm-governed, they are activities that others can acknowledge, recognize, and respond to.

This claim runs against criticisms of the idea that rituals can communicate beliefs or other attitudes or that they can be the sort of thing for which we take responsibility. The idea that rituals are meaningless, or more pointedly, Asad's claim that they are not texts to be decoded but scripts to be followed, undercounts the performative and recognitive aspects of what rituals do.[48] If rituals are meaningless, or if they are mere scripts to be followed, why do people bother arguing about them or changing them? The fact that people do these things suggests that it matters what is expressed and done in rituals. Nor is this a uniquely modern phenomenon. The content and form of rituals were not static and taken for granted—a settled script—in premodern communities and then suddenly up for debate in modernity. It has always been the case that people have argued over rituals when their content and form no longer appeared fitting to the circumstances and commitments with which people found themselves.

Conclusion

This chapter opened with a candlelight vigil, and it has considered some of the sorts of things that rituals such as vigils can express—things that include beliefs and other propositional attitudes, but also non-propositional attitudes. Rituals can express passions, such as grief and anger, and stances, such as solidarity. When they do so, they can be calls for recognition and they can create lines of accountability.

I want to close the chapter with a quite different example: the Unite the Right rally in Charlottesville, Virginia, on August 11 and 12, 2017. Unite the Right was a white supremacist gathering to protest against the removal of a statue of Robert E. Lee and to

48. See, for instance, Frits Staal, "The Meaninglessness of Ritual," *Numen* 26 (1979): 2–22; Asad, *Genealogies*, 62.

galvanize the far right. Participants included self-identified members of various alt-right, neo-Confederate, neo-Nazi, and white nationalist organizations. On the evening of Friday, August 11, in anticipation of a larger rally to be held the following morning, a group of white supremacists participated in a torchlit march through the campus of the University of Virginia. The participants were primarily white men, although a handful of white women also marched. Many of them carried tiki torches; some also bore symbols and insignia of white supremacist and antisemitic organizations and movements. As they walked toward the statue of Thomas Jefferson at the center of UVA's campus, they chanted slogans that included "White lives matter!" "You will not replace us!" and "Jews will not replace us!"

In the words, gestures, and symbols of the rally, the participants expressed beliefs, passions, and solidarity. Their chants expressed a belief, for instance, in the white replacement conspiracy theory, the theory that liberal elites are plotting to replace white people demographically and as holders of cultural and political power. They also expressed grievance and anger at their sense that they are being wronged, usurped. This, in turn, is connected to their desire for retribution against those who they believe would usurp them. Their desire for retribution lends the menacing tone to the slogan, "You [/"Jews"] will not replace us!" In chanting this slogan, they expressed solidarity with other aggrieved and angry white men and a clear delineation of group boundaries ("you/Jews" are not "us"). We might think of this solidarity, as Nichole Flores suggests, as the "negative solidarity" of a group "united around a hateful cause."[49]

As Nick Crossley notes, "each society has its own habitual stock of 'protest rituals,'" normative ways of publicly expressing political dissent.[50] The candlelight vigil and the torchlit march are two of

---

49. Flores, *Aesthetics of Solidarity*, 137.
50. Nick Crossley, "Ritual, Body Technique, and (Inter)subjectivity," in *Thinking through Rituals: Philosophical Perspectives*, ed. Kevin Schilbrack (New York: Routledge, 2004), 47.

ours. In a Facebook post immediately after the rally, Charlottes-ville mayor Michael Signer wrote, "When I think of candlelight, I want to think of prayer vigils. Today, in 2017, we are instead see-ing a cowardly parade of hatred, bigotry, racism, and intolerance march."[51] Within the stock of protest rituals, the contrast between the candlelight vigil and the torchlit march is stark. Whereas the candlelight vigil may call to mind the Christmas Eve candlelight service, awaiting the celebration of the birth of the one who, ac-cording to the Christian tradition, bears the promise of a peace that is not-yet, the torchlit march calls to mind KKK rallies, in which violent white supremacists bear torches and burn crosses to terrorize and instill fear. Both are rituals, routines, governed by the norms of a group. Both express a politics. The flame that sym-bolizes divine light can also express destructive rage.

At a counterprotest on the following day, an interreligious and interracial group of clergy, trained in nonviolent resistance, stood in a line with arms linked. Standing like that, arm-in-arm, their bodies were interconnected, their postures expressing their inter-dependence and solidarity. Many of them wore robes, stoles, and other markers of their religious offices, connecting their counter-protest to the symbols of the religious traditions and positions they inhabited. They joined their voices, singing, among other songs, "This Little Light of Mine," reasserting for themselves and others the sacred symbolism of the candle as opposed to the vio-lent rage expressed by the bearers of the previous night's torches.[52] Across religious traditions, across race and gender and age, the clergy members stood together, in front of white supremacists

51. Quoted in Matt Pierce, "Chanting 'Blood and Soil,' White Nationalists with Torches March at University of Virginia," *Los Angeles Times*, August 11, 2017, http://www.latimes.com/nation/la-na-white-virginia-rally-20170811-story.html.

52. For an account of the multiple roles that clergy played over the course of the weekend, see Jack Jenkins's article: "Meet the Clergy Who Stared Down White Supremacists in Charlottesville," August 16, 2017, https://archive.thinkprogress.org/clergy-in-charlottesville-e95752415c3e/.

who yelled at them and sought to harm them, and they expressed, in song, symbol, and gesture, the politics that they sought. Like the candlelight vigil, this clergy-led counterprotest drew on a stock of protest rituals to express, not least, the belief that a more just and democratic society is worth fighting for, and the hope that it may yet be achieved.

Conclusion

THE RITUALS OF OUR POLITICS

THIS BOOK has been about the ordinary and extraordinary ways that people coordinate their activities, in accordance with shared norms and conventions, to create, maintain, and transform themselves and their societies. In and through rituals, people mark boundaries, distribute goods and ills, shape habits and dispositions, and express commitments and attitudes. They create, sustain, and transform their communities, not least the systems of meaning and power of those communities. Rituals are, I've argued, political.

When people argue about the rituals that they have on hand, when they adapt them and innovate upon them, and even when they reject them or create new ones in their stead, they often do so in response to disagreements and debates about the people and communities that existing rituals create, maintain, or express commitment to. Who are the "we" invoked or enacted by the ritual? What do "we" care about? What kind of people, with what kinds of dispositions and what kinds of relationships and communities, ought "we" to be? At these moments of contestation, adaptation, and innovation, the politics of ritual becomes obvious. An ordination ceremony is political when women enact it to claim authority that they have not been granted by patriarchal governing bodies. The Eucharist is political when it takes place across a nation-state border that is maintained through xenophobic policies and policing. The Mourner's Kaddish is political when it is recited on a city street in grief and anger in response to another police killing of a Black American.

But these rituals are no less political when they are more ordinarily enacted. What I mean is this: an ordination ceremony *always* distributes authority to some and not to others. What is typically taken for granted about who is eligible to participate, and who is recognized in and through the ritual as having been authorized, by whom, to do what, has political significance. The Eucharist *always* enacts a community—the body of Christ—with different boundaries than those of the penultimate communities of this finite world in which we live, while also distributing power, authority, and status differentially among people occupying various roles: priests and laity, men and women, Christians and non-Christians. The Mourner's Kaddish *always* answers the questions: Who is to be mourned? Whose lives matter to "us"? And who counts as the "us" here? In answering such questions, rituals create, sustain, and transform communities.

Of course, the fact that rituals are political in this sense does not tell us much about their *democratic* possibilities. Elites can institute rituals to project and secure their power. Groups can enact rituals to mark their boundaries and maintain their social arrangements, whether or not those boundaries and arrangements are just. This kind of boundary work always excludes some people, even as it includes and incorporates others. When rituals distribute goods and ills, they can do so in ways that are good or bad, just or unjust, for the various members of those groups. When they shape subjects, the resulting habits and dispositions may be virtuous or vicious, and may encourage democratic action or curtail it. When rituals express commitments or attitudes, these can be commitments and attitudes fueled by hatred and resentment as easily as by political friendship, reciprocity, and trust.

The rituals of democratic life—those that create, sustain, and transform properly democratic communities—will be those that

contest unjust power relations and political structures, acknowledge and distribute authority and accountability, and encourage
and cultivate democratic virtues and habits of participation. To
find such rituals, we need not limit ourselves to the obvious, to
civic rituals such as the Pledge of Allegiance or to ritual-like activities such as voting. Indeed, as *democratic* rituals, those activities
may leave us wanting. They are instituted and regulated by elites;
they tend to focus on the nation-state as the site of political authority; they enact a political community whose boundaries are
worth contesting. What if we look, instead, to the multiplicity of
rituals in which people act together to contest existing systems of
meaning and power and to transform them? Such democratic rituals include many of what, following Rev. Bill Wylie Kellerman,
may be called "liturgical direct actions," rituals with deep roots in
religious communities, enacted in public and participatory ways
to counter state power.[1] Such rituals are unlikely to be shared by
all citizens but may nevertheless help form civic virtue and enact
democratic possibilities. A community iftar on the eve of Palestinian evictions, a Catholic Mass at the U.S.-Mexico border, a shiva
on a New York City street: each of these actions protests domination and unjust exclusion by redrawing the boundaries of a community, recognizing the rightful status of those typically excluded
from that community and expressing solidarity with them. In
each, religious subjects habituated into a practice—a ritual and
the habits and dispositions that usually attend it—innovate within
it in the service of just and democratic ends.

1. Bill Wylie Kellerman, *Seasons of Faith and Conscience: Explorations in Liturgical
Direct Action* (Eugene, OR: Wipf & Stock, 1991). Along these lines, C. Melissa Snarr's
work on the living wage movement highlights the role of religious rituals and what
she calls "liturgical activism" in creating collective identity among activists, lowering
the perceived barriers to political participation for those familiar with the rituals, and
negotiating the boundaries of what is considered to be sacred and profane. See Snarr,
All You That Labor: Religion and Ethics in the Living Wage Movement (New York: New
York University Press, 2011), 122–39.

When Jewish activists recited the Mourner's Kaddish for Eric Garner, they took an ordinary ritual and enacted it on the streets of the city. In its usual setting, the Mourner's Kaddish is a ritual expression of grief. Habituation into the practice of reciting the Mourner's Kaddish involves learning the words of the prayer, along with its gestures and postures, and the contexts in which it is appropriate to recite it. For most observant Jews, habituation into the practice of reciting the Mourner's Kaddish takes the form of imitation and education as a child. Much of this is rote learning. Seeing and hearing adults recite the prayer week after week in synagogue services, a child learns the words, the gestures and postures, the context, the norms that attend the prayer and its recitation whether or not that child thinks or understands much about them. Rote learning is often the first part of the process of forming a ritualized body, one that is capable of reproducing the ritual in the right ways at the right times.

But, as I've argued, habituation into a practice—even when it involves rote learning—rarely results in mechanical habit. It needn't only reproduce more of the same. The protestors who recited the Mourner's Kaddish to mark the death of Eric Garner and to protest the lack of accountability for police officers responsible for that death and others expressed their grief at Garner's death, anger at the injustice, and solidarity with Garner and other victims of police violence, their families, and their communities. Their expressive act was made possible, and meaningful, by their habituation into the practice of reciting the Mourner's Kaddish. They could recite the words, adopt the postures, engage the norms that attend it. But they recited the prayer for a person who was not Jewish and thus, according to the tradition, for whom they had no *obligation* to recite the prayer. And they recited the prayer in public, on the street, in the context of a protest. Those contextual changes matter to their prayer's meaning and its possible effects. Their enactment of the prayer was *not* mere rote. It was made possible by habituation into a practice but involved the sort of reflection and innovation that emerge from that habituation.

Habituation was the precondition for expressive freedom, then directed toward democratic ends in the struggle for justice.

By reciting the Kaddish in this new context, protestors drew on the precedents of the practice and their habituation into normative ways of enacting it. Their spoken affirmation of responsibility made explicit what in the ritual was implicit: that in taking on the obligation to say Kaddish for Eric Garner, the participants made themselves responsible to him and responsible for grieving him. They staked claims about whose lives mattered, whose lives were grievable, and who deserved to be recognized as a member of the community. In the act itself, and in the politics it prefigured, it redistributed the goods of social and political life and redrew boundaries of obligation and concern.

———

There is, these days, a yearning for rituals, for routines that are shared and significant. You can see it in the chants and rallies of right-wing populists, and in the public liturgies of progressive faith-based social movements. You can see it in the return of Reform Jewish synagogues to the celebration of traditional liturgies and minor holidays that had been cast aside in the early twentieth century, and in a project like Nuns and Nones that brings "spiritual but not religious" millennials together with Roman Catholic women religious for gatherings and religious practice. You can see it in the massive turnout for the public viewings and funerals of George Floyd and Rep. John Lewis, and in the innovations of rituals to mourn the victims of Covid-19. You can see it in ways small and large, in religious traditions and in political life. This yearning for rituals follows from decades of the increasing privatization and individuation of American public life—the defunding of public institutions and spaces, the community-destroying mobility of workers demanded by a neoliberal economy, the diminishment and collapse of associational life. Formal membership in religious institutions has fallen dramatically over the past several decades, as has membership in old-school civic organizations such as the Rotary Club and the Freemasons. Even fraternities and sororities are—reasonably—under increased scrutiny and pressure.

This desire for ritual and for the range of relationships that sustain (and are sustained by) rituals can take the form of nostalgia for a past that is imagined to be characterized by close-knit communities and solidarity, by a sense of shared purpose and values. Nostalgia typically makes for bad politics; rituals can thrive in clearly defined groups, even as those groups have been rightly criticized for hoarding power and resources and excluding people unjustly. This particular nostalgia also depends on people imagining that there was a time and place when communities weren't so beset by conflicts and contestation, when folks agreed about what the rituals were, about how the community should be defined, about who deserved what goods and who should be recognized as having what status, and about what kinds of people they wanted to become.

I doubt there's ever been such a time and place, on any scale or for any duration. Moreover, there are communities worth tending through rituals, and communities that are rotten at the core. Rituals can support authoritarian regimes, distribute power unequally, produce subjects at odds with democratic ideals. But they need not. And the loss of ritual, including the rejection of ritual by those on the political left who worry about its alignment with traditionalism and authoritarianism, has only supported the further privatization and individualization of social and political life. If it is the case that associational life and its attending rituals have declined, then it is also the case that we have fewer and less effective means for caring for or contesting those things that have been taken and treated as sacred in our communities. Our attention to what Bonnie Honig has called "public things" becomes inadequate; left untended, those things begin to disappear.[2]

---

2. On this idea of "public things," see Bonnie Honig, *Public Things: Democracy in Disrepair* (New York: Fordham University Press, 2017), esp. 1–12.

Turning away from ritual is, as Mary Douglas noted in her criticism of the student protests of the 1960s and 1970s, a good way to *fail* at social and structural change. Writing about the anti-ritualism that characterized religious reform and progressive politics at that moment, she insisted that "instead of anti-ritualism it would be more practical to experiment with more flexible institutional forms and to seek to develop their ritual expression."[3] Instead of abandoning ritual, reformers and radicals would do well to see how rituals can shape different sorts of selves and societies. In our own moment of political upheaval and unraveling, Douglas's charge is worth taking up.

This book's account of rituals—as frequent sites of contestation, and as always-already implicated in politics of one or another sort—aims to temper anti-ritualism and to tap into the yearning for rituals while resisting the tendency to nostalgia. Rituals involve some of the central processes of politics—processes by which people allocate goods, recognize statuses, grant authority, and hold accountable. At the same time, they shape the habits and dispositions of the people who participate in these processes, shaping political actors of one sort or another. And because rituals are value-intensifying, they can help sustain public things, the places, objects, and institutions that are held in common by the members of a public, taken and treated as shared and special— even as sacred. They are ways of valuing those things, together. It is through collective actions and activities that people tend to the goods of their common life—and expand access to those goods— even as they go on arguing about them.[4]

What is worth yearning for—in religious communities, in democratic movements, in all of the many places where people

3. Douglas, *Natural Symbols*, 159.
4. This may sound a bit like Durkheim's contention that a religion involves a group of people coalescing around shared beliefs and practices concerning sacred things. According to Durkheim, it is through rituals that people tend to their public things, their sacred objects and shared ideals.

spend their lives—are rituals that create and sustain groups that are coalitional and intersectional, rituals that are capable of doing the sorts of things that this book has argued that rituals can do: distributing goods justly, recognizing legitimate authority, shaping decent and courageous people. This requires not nostalgia but imagination and flexibility—to recognize and riff on precedent, to innovate within existing forms, to create and care for new ones as we enact the democratic politics we desire and reclaim the power and political significance of rituals to make a world anew.

ACKNOWLEDGMENTS

I BEGIN with gratitude to the teachers who first helped me pose the questions about religion, politics, and ritual that I take up in these pages, especially Elizabeth Pritchard, Amy Hollywood, Ron Thiemann, and Jeff Stout. I am indebted to each of them for teaching me their ways of asking and answering these questions. I am indebted, too, to my wonderful students, with whom I have continued thinking through them and who answer with innovations of their own.

I wrote the first draft of this book during a sabbatical with support from the Provost's Office at Haverford College. I'm grateful to the College for its support for faculty research and writing. Special thanks are due to Anna-Alexandra Fodde-Reguer and Elana Wolff for their help with this project and much else, and to Hannah Kolzer and Nina McKay for their research assistance. Over the past several years, I have presented and workshopped parts of the book at Bowdoin College, Brown University, Haverford College, Jewish Theological Seminary, Templeton Honors College at Eastern University, LaSalle University, and the Danforth Center for Religion and Politics at Washington University. I am grateful to audiences and participants on each of those occasions for their attention and insights.

Fred Appel shepherded the book through the publication process, and it has been a pleasure to work with him again. Thanks, too, to Jenn Backer, James Collier, Virginia Ling, and Jenny Wolkowicki for editorial and production assistance. Three anonymous readers for Princeton University Press provided thoughtful and generous feedback that challenged me to clarify the stakes of the project and the resources of ritual theory for thinking about contemporary politics. Kali Handelman read a draft of the manuscript and offered helpful advice about how to revise.

Friends and colleagues have sent articles, posed questions, read chapters, and made suggestions that have enriched the book in countless ways. I'm so grateful for their encouragement and advice. Many thanks to John Bowlin, Christopher DiBona, Nyle Fort, Pika Ghosh, Guangtian Ha, Amy Hollywood, Chumie Juni, Ken Koltun-Fromm, Naomi Koltun-Fromm, Brett Krutzsch, Laura Levitt, Tal Lewis, Paige McGinley, Anne McGuire, Lou Ruprecht, David Harrington Watt, terrance wiley, and Joe Winters for these contributions and more. My thinking and writing about rituals, borders, and boundaries are indebted to conversations in a yearlong faculty seminar on that topic with Craig Borowiak, Imke Brust, Paulina Ochoa Espejo, Elena Guzman, Lindsay Reckson, and Bethel Saler. Alda Balthrop-Lewis, Fannie Bialek, Sarah Stewart-Kroeker, Shira Billet, and Emily Dumler-Winckler read some very early chapters, and some very late ones, and insisted throughout that the project was still worth pursuing. Their encouragement, in this and in much else, has been a gift. Joel Schlosser and Jeff Stout read a complete draft and helped me see what the book could become and what it would take to get there. Nick Wolterstorff's generous reading of the manuscript helped me sharpen the argument in the final stages of revision. Laura Been, Lou Charkoudian, Katy Corbin, Lindsay Reckson, and Erin Schoneveld provided pep talks, commiseration, and solidarity. I couldn't have written this thing without the community we've created together.

There aren't adequate words for the gratitude due to my family—to my parents, who taught me some things about how to innovate within ritual, and to my children, who give me hope that the communities we yearn for may one day be. To my husband, Ethan, whom I'm so lucky to walk alongside. Big hugs and root beer floats for all.

Finally, this book emerges from beautiful gatherings, in person and, through a couple terrible years, online, with Fannie Bialek, Josh Dubler, Daniel May, Steve Bush, and Alda Balthrop-Lewis. We walked in the woods, penned manifestos, broke bread together, and shared the delights and trials of writing. This book would have been impossible, and the process much less joyful, without them. It is dedicated to them, in love and gratitude.

BIBLIOGRAPHY

Adler, Rachel. *Engendering Judaism: An Inclusive Theology and Ethics.* Boston: Beacon Press, 1998.

Agger, Inger. "Calming the Mind: Healing after Mass Atrocity in Cambodia." *Intercultural Psychiatry* 52.4 (August 2015): 543–60.

Allen, Danielle S. *Talking to Strangers: Anxieties of Citizenship since Brown v. Board of Education.* Chicago: University of Chicago Press, 2004.

Althusser, Louis. "Ideology and Ideological State Apparatuses: Notes towards an Investigation." In *Lenin and Philosophy and Other Essays.* Trans. Ben Brewster. London: New Left Books, 1971.

Anscombe, G.E.M. *Intention.* Oxford: Blackwell, 1957.

Aristotle. *Nicomachean Ethics.* Trans. Terence Irwin. 2nd ed. Indianapolis: Hackett, 1999.

Asad, Talal. *Genealogies of Religion: Discipline and Reasons of Power in Christianity and Islam.* Baltimore: Johns Hopkins University Press, 1993.

Aslam, Ali. "Salat-al-Juma: Organizing the Public in Tahrir Square." *Social Movement Studies* 16.3 (2017): 297–308.

Austin, J. L. *How to Do Things with Words.* 2nd ed. Cambridge, MA: Harvard University Press, 1975.

Bell, Catherine M. "'The Chinese Believe in Spirits': Belief and Believing in the Study of Religion." In *Radical Interpretation of Religion,* ed. Nancy K. Frankenberry, 100–116. Cambridge: Cambridge University Press, 2002.

———. "Performance." In *Critical Terms for Religious Studies,* ed. Mark Taylor, 205–24. Chicago: University of Chicago Press, 1998.

———. *Ritual: Perspectives and Dimensions.* Oxford: Oxford University Press, 1997.

———. *Ritual Theory, Ritual Practice.* Oxford: Oxford University Press, 1992.

Bellah, Robert N. *The Broken Covenant: American Civil Religion in a Time of Trial.* Chicago: Chicago University Press, 1992.

———. "Civil Religion in America." In *Beyond Belief: Essays on Religion in a Post-Traditional World,* 168–89. New York: Harper & Row, 1970.

Bellamy, Francis. "The Story of the Pledge of Allegiance to the Flag." *University of Rochester Library Bulletin* 8.2 (Winter 1953). https://rbscp.lib.rochester.edu/3418.

Bennet, Halina. "Let's Try Love: Brunswick Group Fights for Peace." *Bowdoin Orient*, November 12, 2021.

Berlin, Isaiah. "Two Concepts of Liberty." In *Four Essays on Liberty*, 118–72. London: Oxford University Press, 1969.

Bernacer, Javier, and Jose Ignacio Murillo. "The Aristotelian Conception of Habit and Its Contribution to Human Neuroscience." *Frontiers in Human Neuroscience* 8.883 (2014). https://doi.org/10.3389/fnhum.2014.00883.

Bever, Lindsay. "This Child Sat for the Pledge—So His Teacher 'Violently' Snatched Him from His Chair, Student Says." *Washington Post*, September 15, 2017. https://www.washingtonpost.com/news/education/wp/2017/09/15/this-child-sat-for-the-pledge-so-his-teacher-violently-snatched-him-from-his-chair-he-says/?utm_term=.9ceb48c8d0dc.

Book of Common Prayer. New York: Oxford University Press, 1928.

Bourdieu, Pierre. *Language and Symbolic Power*. Ed. John B. Thompson. Trans. Gino Raymond and Matthew Adamson. Cambridge, MA: Harvard University Press, 1991.

———. *Masculine Domination*. Trans. Richard Nice. Stanford: Stanford University Press, 2001.

———. *Outline of a Theory of Practice*. Cambridge: Cambridge University Press, 1977.

Braithwaite, John. "Repentance Rituals and Restorative Justice." *Journal of Political Philosophy* 8.1 (2000): 115–31.

Brandom, Robert. "Freedom and Constraint by Norms." *American Philosophical Quarterly* 16.3 (July 1979): 187–96.

———. *Reason in Philosophy: Animating Ideas*. Cambridge, MA: Harvard University Press, 2009.

Breines, Wini. *The Great Refusal: Community and Organization in the New Left: 1962–1968*. New York: Praeger, 1982.

Bretherton, Luke. *Christ and the Common Life: Political Theology and the Case for Democracy*. Grand Rapids, MI: Eerdmans, 2019.

———. "Politics in the Service of Society: My Response to My Interlocutors." *Studies in Christian Ethics* 33.2 (2020): 262–70.

Brown, Karen McCarthy. *Mama Lola: A Vodou Priestess in Brooklyn*. Berkeley: University of California Press, 2001.

Brown, Wendy. *Walled States, Waning Sovereignty*. New York: Zone Books, 2010.

Bush, Stephen S. *Visions of Religion: Experience, Meaning, and Power*. Oxford: Oxford University Press, 2015.

Butler, Judith. *Excitable Speech: A Politics of the Performative*. New York: Routledge, 1997.

————. *Frames of War: When Is Life Grievable?* New York: Verso, 2009.

————. *Notes Toward a Performative Theory of Assembly.* Cambridge, MA: Harvard University Press, 2015.

————. *Precarious Life: The Powers of Mourning and Violence.* New York: Verso, 2004.

Byars, Mitchell. "Colorado Teacher Pleads Guilty to Child Abuse after Forcing Student to Stand for Pledge of Allegiance." *Denver Post,* September 1, 2018.

Carrasco, David. *City of Sacrifice: The Aztec Empire and the Role of Violence in Civilization.* Boston: Beacon Press, 1999.

Cass, Julia. "Philadelphia's Woman Priest Talks about Her Defiance." *Philadelphia Inquirer,* August 4, 1974, 1-D.

Castor, N. Fadeke. *Spiritual Citizenship: Transnational Pathways from Black Power to Ifá in Trinidad.* Durham: Duke University Press, 2017.

Chopp, Rebecca. *The Power to Speak: Feminism, Language, God.* Eugene, OR: Wipf and Stock, 1991.

Chwe, Michael Suk-Young. *Rational Ritual: Culture, Coordination, and Common Knowledge.* Princeton: Princeton University Press, 2001.

Craig, David. "Debating Desire: Civil Rights, Ritual Protest, and the Shifting Boundaries of Public Reason." *Journal of the Society of Christian Ethics* 27.1 (Spring/ Summer 2007): 157–82.

Cressler, Matthew J. *Authentically Black and Truly Catholic: The Rise of Black Catholicism in the Great Migration.* New York: New York University Press, 2017.

————. "Vatican II, Black Power, and the Emergence of Black Catholic Liturgies." *U.S. Catholic Historian* 32.4 (Fall 2014): 99–119.

Crossley, Nick. "Ritual, Body Technique, and (Inter)Subjectivity." In *Thinking through Rituals,* ed. Schilbrack, 31–51.

Cuneo, Terence. *Ritualized Faith: Essays on the Philosophy of Liturgy.* Oxford: Oxford University Press, 2016.

Dandelion, Pink. *The Liturgies of Quakerism.* New York: Routledge, 2005.

Davis, G. Scott. *Believing and Acting: The Pragmatic Turn in Comparative Religion and Ethics.* Oxford: Oxford University Press, 2012.

Decosimo, David. *Ethics as a Work of Charity: Thomas Aquinas and Pagan Virtue.* Stanford: Stanford University Press, 2014.

Dickinson, Anthony. "Actions and Habits: The Development of Behavioural Autonomy." *Philosophical Transactions of the Royal Society* 308.1135 (1985). https://doi .org/10.1098/rstb.1985.0010.

Douglas, Mary. "Deciphering a Meal." *Daedalus* 101.1 (Winter 1972): 61–81.

————. *Natural Symbols: Explorations in Cosmology.* 1970. London: Routledge, 1996.

————. *Purity and Danger: An Analysis of Concept of Pollution and Taboo.* London: Routledge, 2002.

Durkheim, Emile. *The Elementary Forms of Religious Life.* Trans. Carol Cosman. Ed. Mark Cladis. Oxford: Oxford University Press, 2001.

Ellis, Richard J. *To the Flag: The Unlikely History of the Pledge of Allegiance.* Lawrence: University Press of Kansas, 2005.

Farneth, Molly. "For These Progressive Jews, Prayer Is Part of the Protest." *Religion & Politics*, September 10, 2019. https://religionandpolitics.org/2019/09/10/for -these-progressive-jews-prayer-is-part-of-the-protest/.

———. *Hegel's Social Ethics: Religion, Conflict, and Rituals of Reconciliation.* Princeton: Princeton University Press, 2017.

———. "Toward an Ethics of Social Practice." In *Everyday Ethics: Moral Theology and the Practices of Ordinary Life*, ed. Michael Lamb and Brian A. Williams. Washington, DC: Georgetown University Press, 2019.

Fassin, Didier. "Policing Borders, Producing Boundaries: The Governmentality of Immigration in Dark Times." *Annual Review of Anthropology* 40 (2011): 213–26.

Fingarette, Herbert. *Confucius: The Secular as Sacred.* Long Grove, IL: Waveland Press, 1972.

Fisher, Philip. *The Vehement Passions.* Princeton: Princeton University Press, 2002.

Flores, Nichole M. *The Aesthetics of Solidarity: Our Lady of Guadalupe and American Democracy.* Washington, DC: Georgetown University Press, 2021.

Fort, Nyle. "Refusing to Give Death the Last Word." *Boston Globe*, June 4, 2020. https:// www.bostonglobe.com/2020/06/04/opinion/refusing-give-death-last-word/.

Frankfurt, Harry G. *The Importance of What We Care About.* Cambridge: Cambridge University Press, 1998.

Fraser, Nancy. "From Redistribution to Recognition? Dilemmas of Justice in a 'Post-socialist' Age." *New Left Review* 212 (July/August 1995): 68–93.

Freeman, Jo. "The Tyranny of Structurelessness." *Berkeley Journal of Sociology* 17 (1972–73): 151–64.

Fricker, Miranda. *Epistemic Injustice: Power and the Ethics of Knowing.* Oxford: Oxford University Press, 2007.

Gan, Julia. "The Study of Lived Religion through Different Interpretations: An Ethnography on Perceptions of Singaporean Malay-Muslims' Islamic Prayer Ritual Practice." Undergraduate thesis, Haverford College, 2020.

Geitz, Elizabeth Rankin. *Gender and the Nicene Creed.* Harrisburg, PA: Morehouse Publishing, 1995.

Goodwin, Jeff, James M. Jasper, and Francesca Polletta, eds. *Passionate Politics: Emotions and Social Movements.* Chicago: University of Chicago Press, 2001.

Gorski, Philip S. *American Babylon: Christianity and Democracy Before and After Trump.* London: Routledge, 2020.

———. *American Covenant: A History of Civil Religion from the Puritans to the Present.* Princeton: Princeton University Press, 2017.

Gould, Deborah B. *Moving Politics: Emotion and ACT UP's Fight against AIDS.* Chicago: University of Chicago Press, 2009.

Graybiel, Ann. "Habits, Rituals, and the Evaluative Brain." *Annual Review of Neuroscience* 31 (February 2008): 359–87.

Grimes, Ronald L. *The Craft of Ritual Studies*. Oxford: Oxford University Press, 2014.

———. "Improvising Ritual." In *Reassembling Democracy*, ed. Harvey et al., 17–36.

Hall, Cheryl. *The Trouble with Passion: Political Theory beyond the Reign of Reason*. New York: Routledge, 2005.

Hall, David A., ed. *Lived Religion in America: Toward a History of Practice*. Princeton: Princeton University Press, 1997.

Harris, Ian. "Rethinking Cambodian Political Discourse on Territory: Genealogy of the Buddhist Ritual Boundary (*sīmā*)." *Journal of Southeast Asian Studies* 41.2 (June 2010): 215–39.

Harvey, Graham. "Indigenous Rituals Remake the Larger-than-Human Community." In *Reassembling Democracy*, ed. Harvey et al., 69–85.

Harvey, Graham, Michael Houseman, Sarah Pike, and Jone Salomonsen, eds. *Reassembling Democracy: Ritual as Cultural Resource*. London: Bloomsbury, 2021.

Haslanger, Sally. "What Is a Social Practice?" *Royal Institute of Philosophy Supplement* 82 (July 2018): 231–47.

Hirschman, Albert O. *The Passions and the Interests: Political Arguments for Capitalism before Its Triumph*. Princeton: Princeton University Press, 1977.

Holloway, Karla F. C. *Passed On: African American Mourning Stories*. Durham: Duke University Press, 2002.

Hollywood, Amy. "Performativity, Citationality, Ritualization." *History of Religions* 42.2 (2002): 93–115.

Hondagneu-Sotelo, Pierrette, et al. "'There's a Spirit That Transcends the Border': Faith, Ritual, and Postnational Protest at the U.S.-Mexico Border." *Sociological Perspectives* 47.2 (2004): 133–59.

Honig, Bonnie. *Antigone, Interrupted*. Cambridge: Cambridge University Press, 2013.

———. *Public Things: Democracy in Disrepair*. New York: Fordham University Press, 2017.

Horton, Alex. "A Black Student Refused to Recite the Pledge of Allegiance—Challenging Texas Law Requiring It." *Washington Post*, September 26, 2018.

Hunt-Hendrix, Leah. "The Ethics of Solidarity: Republican, Marxist, and Anarchist Interpretations." PhD diss., Princeton University, 2014.

James, William. *The Principles of Psychology*. Vol. 1. 1890. New York: Dover, 1950.

———. *The Varieties of Religious Experience: A Study in Human Nature*. New York: Modern Library, 2002.

Jay, Nancy. *Throughout Your Generations Forever: Sacrifice, Religion, and Paternity*. Chicago: University of Chicago Press, 1994.

Jenkins, Jack. "Meet the Clergy Who Stared Down White Supremacists in Charlottesville." August 16, 2017. https://archive.thinkprogress.org/clergy-in-charlottesville-e95752415c3e/.

Jordan, Candace. "In Defense of Anger in Anti-Racist Protest." June 15, 2020. https://berkleycenter.georgetown.edu/responses/in-defense-of-anger-in-anti-racist-protest.

Kahn, Jonathon. "When the Westboro Baptist Church Came to Vassar College: A Quixotic Story of Foot Washing, Activist Pedagogy, and the Secular Liberal Arts." *Soundings: An Interdisciplinary Journal* 103.1 (2020): 1–34.

Kellerman, Bill Wylie. *Seasons of Faith and Conscience: Explorations in Liturgical Direct Action*. Eugene, OR: Wipf & Stock, 1991.

Kent, Alexandra. "Peace, Power and Pagodas in Present-Day Cambodia." *Contemporary Buddhism* 9.1 (2008): 77–97.

Kertzer, David. *Ritual, Politics, and Power*. New Haven: Yale University Press, 1988.

Kimmerer, Robin Wall. *Braiding Sweetgrass: Indigenous Wisdom, Scientific Knowledge, and the Teachings of Plants*. Minneapolis: Milkweed Editions, 2013.

Krause, Sharon. *Civil Passions: Moral Sentiment and Democratic Deliberation*. Princeton: Princeton University Press, 2008.

———. *Freedom beyond Sovereignty: Reconstructing Liberal Individualism*. Chicago: University of Chicago Press, 2015.

Kukla, Rebecca. "Performative Force, Convention, and Discursive Injustice." *Hypatia* 29.2 (2014): 440–57.

Kukla, Rebecca, and Mark Lance. *Yo! and Lo!: The Pragmatic Topography of the Space of Reasons*. Cambridge, MA: Harvard University Press, 2009.

Laidlaw, James. *The Subject of Virtue: An Anthropology of Ethics and Freedom*. Cambridge: Cambridge University Press, 2014.

Lofton, Kathryn. *Consuming Religion*. Chicago: University of Chicago Press, 2017.

Lorde, Audre. "The Uses of Anger: Women Responding to Racism." In *Sister Outsider*, 124–33. New York: Crossing Press, 2007.

MacAloon, John J., ed. *Rite, Drama, Festival, Spectacle: Rehearsals toward a Theory of Cultural Performance*. Philadelphia: Institute for the Study of Human Issues, 1984.

MacIntyre, Alasdair. *After Virtue*. 3rd ed. Notre Dame: University of Notre Dame Press, 2007.

Mahmood, Saba. *Politics of Piety: The Islamic Revival and the Feminist Subject*. Princeton: Princeton University Press, 2005.

Manne, Kate. *Down Girl: The Logic of Misogyny*. Oxford: Oxford University Press, 2018.

Markell, Patchen. "The Insufficiency of Non-Domination." *Political Theory* 36.1 (2008): 9–36.

Martel, James R. *The Misinterpellated Subject*. Durham: Duke University Press, 2017.

Maruna, Shadd. "Reentry as a Rite of Passage." *Punishment and Society* 13.1 (2011): 3–28.

Mauss, Marcel. "Techniques of the Body." *Economy and Society* 2.1 (1973): 70–88.

McClymond, Kathryn T. *Rituals Gone Wrong: What We Can Learn from Ritual Disruption*. Oxford: Oxford University Press, 2016.

McWhorter, Ladelle. "Rites of Passing: Foucault, Power, and Same-Sex Commitment Ceremonies." In *Thinking through Rituals*, ed. Schilbrack, 71–96.

Mendonca, Suman Priya. "What Is Sheikh Jarrah Turmoil? Iftar Turns Violent, 15 Arrested in Jerusalem." *International Business Times*, May 7, 2021. https://www.ibtimes.sg/what-sheikh-jarrah-turmoil-iftar-turns-violent-15-arrested-jerusalem-video-57316.

Moran, Richard. *The Exchange of Words: Speech, Testimony, and Intersubjectivity*. Oxford: Oxford University Press, 2018.

Muir, Edward. *Ritual in Early Modern Europe*. 2nd ed. Cambridge: Cambridge University Press, 2005.

Myerhoff, Barbara G. "A Death in Due Time: Construction of Self and Culture in Ritual Drama." In *Rite, Drama, Festival, Spectacle*, ed. MacAloon, 149–78.

Naiden, F. S. *Ancient Supplication*. Oxford: Oxford University Press, 2006.

Naude, Piet. "Can Our Creeds Speak a Gendered Truth? A Feminist Reading of the Nicene Creed and the Belhar Confession." *Scriptura* 86 (2004): 201–9.

Noonan, John T., Jr. *A Church That Can and Cannot Change: The Development of Catholic Moral Teaching*. South Bend, IN: University of Notre Dame Press, 2005.

Nussbaum, Martha C. *Anger and Forgiveness: Resentment, Generosity, Justice*. Oxford: Oxford University Press, 2016.

Ochs, Vanessa L. *Inventing Jewish Ritual*. Philadelphia: Jewish Publication Society, 2007.

O'Dell, Darlene. *The Story of the Philadelphia Eleven*. New York: Seabury Books, 2014.

Partridge, Cameron. "Toward an 'Irregular' Embrace: The Philadelphia Ordinations and Transforming Ideas of the Human." In *Looking Forward, Looking Backward: Forty Years of Women's Ordination*, ed. Fredrica Harris Thompsett, 131–41. New York: Morehouse Publishing, 2014.

Perry, Imani. *May We Forever Stand: A History of the Black National Anthem*. Chapel Hill: University of North Carolina Press, 2018.

Pettit, Philip. *Republicanism: A Theory of Freedom and Government*. Oxford: Oxford University Press, 1997.

Pierce, Matt. "Chanting 'Blood and Soil,' White Nationalists with Torches March at University of Virginia." *Los Angeles Times*, August 11, 2017. http://www.latimes.com/nation/la-na-white-virginia-rally-20170811-story.html.

Pike, Sarah M. *For the Wild: Ritual and Commitment in Radical Eco-Activism*. Oakland: University of California Press, 2017.

Pike, Sarah M., Jone Salomonsen, and Paul-François Tremlett, eds. *Ritual and Democracy: Protests, Public and Performances*. Bristol, CT: Equinox, 2020.

Plaskow, Judith. *Standing Again at Sinai: Judaism from a Feminist Perspective*. New York: HarperCollins, 1991.

Platoff, Emma. "Attorney General Ken Paxton Defends Texas Law Requiring Students to Stand for Pledge of Allegiance." *Texas Tribune*, September 28, 2018. https://www.texastribune.org/2018/09/25/ken-paxton-texas-law-student-stand-pledge-allegiance-/.

Polletta, Francesca. *Freedom Is an Endless Meeting: Democracy in American Social Movements*. Chicago: University of Chicago Press, 2002.

Pool, Heather. *Political Mourning: Identity and Responsibility in the Wake of Tragedy*. Philadelphia: Temple University Press, 2021.

Pope Leo XIII. *Rerum Novarum*. http://www.vatican.va/content/leo-xiii/en/encyclicals/documents/hf_l-xiii_enc_15051891_rerum-novarum.html.

Rappaport, Roy A. *Ritual and Religion in the Making of Humanity*. Cambridge: Cambridge University Press, 1999.

Reckson, Lindsay V. "Hands Up." *Avid*, December 11, 2014. http://avidly.lareviewofbooks.org/2014/12/11/hands-up/.

Reid, Eric. "Why Colin Kaepernick and I Decided to Take a Knee." *New York Times*, September 25, 2017. http://www.nytimes.com/2017/09/25/opinion/colin-kaepernick-football-protests.html.

Rogers, Melvin. "Republican Confusion and Liberal Clarification." *Philosophy and Social Criticism* 34.7 (2008): 799–824.

Rotary International. "Join Rotary." https://www.rotary.org/en/get-involved/join.

Ruether, Rosemary Radford. *Sexism and God-Talk: Toward a Feminist Theology*. Boston: Beacon Press, 1993.

Saxby, Troy R. *Pauli Murray: A Personal and Political Life*. Chapel Hill: University of North Carolina Press, 2020.

Schilbrack, Kevin, ed. *Thinking through Rituals: Philosophical Perspectives*. New York: Routledge, 2004.

Schmidt, Leigh Eric. *Consumer Rites: The Buying and Selling of American Holidays*. Princeton: Princeton University Press, 1997.

Seipel, Brooke. "Trump: Dems Want Illegal Immigrants to 'Infest Our Country.'" *The Hill*, June 19, 2018. https://thehill.com/homenews/administration/392977-trump-dems-want-illegal-immigrants-to-infest-our-country.

Seligman, Adam B., et al. *Ritual and Its Consequences: An Essay on the Limits of Sincerity*. Oxford: Oxford University Press, 2008.

Skinner, Quentin. *Liberty before Liberalism*. Cambridge: Cambridge University Press, 1998.

Smith, James K. A. *Imagining the Kingdom: How Worship Works*. Grand Rapids, MI: Baker Academic, 2013.

Snarr, C. Melissa. *All You That Labor: Religion and Ethics in the Living Wage Movement*. New York: New York University Press, 2011.

Sojourners. "The Inn without Borders/La Posada sin Fronteras." Video. https://sojo.net/media/inn-without-borders-la-posada-sin-fronteras#.

Soskice, Janet Martin. *The Kindness of God: Metaphor, Gender, and Religious Language.* Oxford: Oxford University Press, 2007.

Staal, Frits. "The Meaninglessness of Ritual." *Numen* 26 (1979): 2–22.

Stalnaker, Aaron. *Mastery, Dependence, and the Ethics of Authority.* Oxford: Oxford University Press, 2020.

Stauffer, Aaron, ed. "Round Table Discussion: Organizing, Protests, and Religious Practices." *Political Theology,* March 18, 2021.

Stout, Jeffrey. *Blessed Are the Organized: Grassroots Democracy in America.* Princeton: Princeton University Press, 2010.

———. "Religion Unbound: Ideals and Powers from Cicero to King." 2017 Gifford Lectures. Video. https://www.giffordlectures.org/lectures/religion-unbound -ideals-and-powers-cicero-king.

Taylor, Mark C., ed. *Critical Terms for Religious Studies.* Chicago: University of Chicago Press, 1998.

Turner, Victor. *The Ritual Process: Structure and Anti-Structure.* Ithaca: Cornell University Press, 1969.

Tweed, Thomas A. *Crossing and Dwelling: A Theory of Religion.* Cambridge, MA: Harvard University Press, 2006.

U.S. Citizenship and Immigration Services. "Naturalization Oath of Allegiance to the United States of America." https://www.uscis.gov/us-citizenship/naturalization -test/naturalization-oath-allegiance-united-states-america.

van Gennep, Arnold. *Rites of Passage.* 7th ed. Chicago: University of Chicago Press, 1975.

Vesely-Flad, Rima L. *Racial Purity and Dangerous Bodies: Moral Pollution, Black Lives, and the Struggle for Justice.* Minneapolis: Fortress Press, 2017.

Wallace, Andrew. "11 Women Are Ordained." *Philadelphia Inquirer,* July 30, 1974, 1-A.

Wallis, Jim. "National Day of Mourning and Lament." National Council of Churches, June 1, 2020. https://nationalcouncilofchurches.us/a-national-day-of-mourning -and-lament/.

West, Betsy, and Julie Cohen, dir. *My Name Is Pauli Murray.* Amazon Studios, 2021.

Williams, Delores. *Sisters in the Wilderness: The Challenge of Womanist God-Talk.* Maryknoll, NY: Orbis Books, 1993.

Winters, Joseph R. *Hope Draped in Black: Race, Melancholy, and the Agony of Progress.* Durham: Duke University Press, 2016.

———. "Nothing Matters: Black Death, Repetition, and an Ethics of Anguish." *American Religions* 2.1 (2020): 1–4.

Wolterstorff, Nicholas. *Acting Liturgically: Philosophical Reflections on Religious Practice.* Oxford: Oxford University Press, 2018.

———. *Art Rethought: The Social Practices of Art.* Oxford: Oxford University Press, 2015.

———. *The God We Worship: An Exploration of Liturgical Theology.* Grand Rapids, MI: Eerdmans, 2015.

Wuthnow, Robert. *What Happens When We Practice Religion? Textures of Devotion in Everyday Life.* Princeton: Princeton University Press, 2020.

Young, Iris Marion. "Throwing Like a Girl: A Phenomenology of Feminine Body Comportment, Motility, and Spatiality." *Human Studies* 3.2 (April 1980): 137–56.

INDEX

A NOTE ON THE TYPE

This book has been composed in Arno, an Old-style serif typeface in the classic Venetian tradition, designed by Robert Slimbach at Adobe.